EXPRESSIONIST TEXTS

EXPRESSIONIST TEXTS

by

Oskar Kokoschka, August Stramm,
Georg Kaiser, Gottfried Benn, Ernst Toller,
Walter Hasenclever, Lothar Schreyer

Edited by Mel Gordon

PAJ Publications
New York

TO THE LATE WOLF YOUNIN
WHO ONCE PERFORMED IN A GERMAN EXPRESSIONIST FILM
AND HIS WIFE SYLVIA

Library of Congress Cataloging in Publication Data
Expressionist Texts
Sphinx and Strawman, Sancta Susanna, From Morn to Midnight, Ithaka, The Son, The Transfiguration, Crucifixion
Library of Congress Catalog Card No.: 86-63185
ISBN: 1-55554-012-0 (cloth)
ISBN: 1-55554-013-9 (paper)

ACKNOWLEDGEMENTS:
Oskar Kokoschka's *Sphinx and Strawman* appeared in *Voices of German Expressionism*, edited by Victor H. Meisel. Copyright © 1970 by Prentice-Hall, Inc. Reprinted by permission of the publisher.
Gottfried Benn's *Ithaka* appeared in *Gottfried Benn* by J. M. Ritchie. Copyright © 1972 by Oswald Wolff Publishers. Reprinted by permission of the publisher.

Printed in the United States of America

Publication of this book has been made possible in part by grants received from the National Endowment for the Arts, Washington, D.C., a federal agency, and the New York State Council on the Arts.

Contents

Expressionist Texts

Mel Gordon

The grimaces and shrieks of German Expressionism still rattle in our heads. From the blank-faced and kohl-eyed models of Schiaparelli to the latest music video styles of Heavy Metal, punk, and New Wave, the Expressionism of Central Europe's teens and twenties has resurfaced as a basic vocabulary for contemporary performance genres, especially those outside the tiny terrain of Broadway and university theatre. It is as if Caligari's somnambulant has reached across continents and decades to touch us again.

This anthology of dramatic texts includes works by famous and less well-known German Expressionist playwrights. In their time, these plays were staged in significant presentations. Rather than gather the "best" of Expressionist drama as seen in hindsight by American and German literary critics, I have collected texts that show the development and range of Expressionist performance. In a sense they are the "best" but from the eyes of the Expressionist theatre practitioners themselves. Both the choice of plays and my introductory writings are part of a plan to rejoin Expressionist dramatic literature to an understanding of its theatrical milieu.

Historically, Expressionism changed the rules by which dramas could be written, encoded, staged, and enjoyed. For the first time, the author's primary visions and thoughts, or ego, radiated beyond the playscript, through the performers' characterizations, onto the minds of the spectator. The play structures and the objective filters of the past were swept away; the Expressionist theatre revealed twisted but purer realities beyond the bourgeois façades of social piety and the rationally-bound conscious life. Because it dealt directly and forcefully with the artist's own crushed psyche and his ambiguous relation to a corrupt society, Expressionist drama—although it had a seductive appeal to writers internationally—only found its real audience in the morally-shattered young generation of Weimar Germany.

In the English-speaking world, theatrical Expressionism failed. Neither the German Expressionist playwrights nor the performance styles they inspired found much commercial interest among Broadway or West End producers. Even Eugene O'Neill's and Elmer Rice's Expressionist-influenced plays were rarely performed in a true Expressionist manner. Among the performing arts, the American popular cinema alone understood Expressionism's emotional impact and hidden humor. The celebrated sub-genres of Hollywood: the horror movie, the psychological crime thriller, and the science fantasy can trace much of their roots in the Expressionist ethos—and in fact preserved its forms and tenets for future generations. The delight American spectators still find in filmic characterizations of Peter Lorre and Bela Lugosi is not so much that their curious acting styles seem to come from Central Europe as from another world, the world of scenic Expressionism.

Despite the fact that Expressionist plays were published and widely read beginning in 1912, only a few were physically enacted before 1917. In part this was due to the First World War, with many of the Expressionists and theatre practitioners at the fronts, and the high degree of military censorship that prevailed. Yet, one notices a kind of reluctance by the Expressionists to actually stage their works. Although they praised the theatre as their greatest potential medium, a utopic space where "Man explodes in front of Man," Expressionists like Walther von Hollander were clearly worried that the too quick realization of Expressionist productions, especially in the acting, could prove to be a very costly failing. And in a way, their fears of imperfection were not unjustified.

From its beginnings in 1910 to its demise as a movement in Germany some fifteen years later, literary Expressionism promulgated the existence of a higher order of humanity, of a certain kind of individual who was neither merchant nor "blond beast," of an intellectual who could act, of the New Man. Like the movement itself, the Expressionists' conception of this ideal type underwent numerous and extreme transformations. At first he was described as a Nietzschean Nay-Sayer, the slayer of fathers and teachers, the destroyer of all bourgeois traditions (i.e., the students in Gottfried Benn's *Ithaka* [1914]). Later, during the war, the New Man appeared as an apostle of peace; he became an activist Christian, one who was capable of great feats of leadership and self-sacrifice, a lover of Mankind (i.e., Antigone in Walter Hasenclever's *Antigone* [1917]). In the last phase of Expressionism, or its "Black Period," the New Man was revealed as an Übermensch/Gandhian *manqué*, the individual with all the conventional attributes of the enlightened hero except the powers of social or political potency (i.e., Jimmy Cobbett in Ernst Toller's *The Machine-Wreckers*

[1922]).

Particularly in the second stage of Expressionism, the followers of Expressionism propagated the philosophy of the worth of Man—of *all* men. Essentially, they thought, Man was good, born good. Only a restrictive society and a denatured consciousness were preventing Man from searching and feeling the true, inner ecstatic reality of life. Instead, society's institutions—the family, the government, the military, the business and land-owning classes—were pushing Mankind into cycles of materialism and misery. There was only one solution, the Expressionists felt: revolution—not necessarily the substitution of one government for another, but rather a revolution of the spirit. If Man could learn to trust his emotions, then he would love all men, would experience "new love," and therefore would be in touch with the laws of the universe.

What united all of these conceits was the New Man's unique awareness of Mankind's—as well as his own—place in the universe and his ability to act upon it. No books of philosophy or psychology could instruct the New Man in this cosmic understanding; instead, he would have to seek it directly. Sometimes this could be accomplished through the exploration of his unconscious in dream, hypnotic, trance, or drug-induced states. Occasionally in physical states of pure action where the brain's censor would not function adequately, the New Man could discover that ecstatic, ineffable condition of "absolute Rapture." Like the medieval mystics, the Expressionists believed that only the possessed individual was capable of transcending his daily existence to make contact with the *Seele*, or soul. (In such a primordial state, one's entire being is expressed outside space and time; the possessed's muscles and joints may be twisted and contorted, sounds akin to animal barks or single syllables may be produced in his throat. According to the Expressionists, a man in that condition was experiencing the Cosmos.)

THEORY AND ROOTS OF EXPRESSIONIST ACTING

For the Expressionists, the new, untested Expressionist actor was not just a symbol or the physical rendering of the New Man: his abilities to transform himself from one soul-state to another, to emote the broadest range of feelings, to express the ecstasy of the playwright, and to guide the audience made him the New Man incarnate. The failure of Expressionist performance, they thought, would doom Expressionism as an artistic movement and philosophy.

Most of the important Expressionist statements on acting were prescriptive, coming months and years before the heyday of the Expressionist theatre. To a large degree, these articles, often in a manifesto or declamatory style, were authored by Expressionist playwrights and theoreticians and not by the to-be Expressionist directors or theatre workers themselves.

First and best-known of these statements, "Epilogue to the Actor," was written by the Expressionist playwright Paul Kornfeld in May 1916 as an afterword to his play *The Seduction* (1913), a year and a half before it was produced at the *Schauspielhaus* in Frankfurt by Gustav Hartung on December 8, 1917. As did other playwrights, Kornfeld worried that the nascent Expressionist actors would misunderstand or prove inadequate to the task of presenting his play. In "Epilogue to the Actor" Kornfeld exhorted the Expressionist actor not to behave

> as though the thoughts and words he has to express have only arisen in him at the very moment in which he recites them. If he has to die on the stage, let him not pay a visit to the hospital beforehand in order to learn how to die; . . . Let him dare to stretch his arms out wide and with a sense of soaring speak as he has never spoken in life; let him not be an imitator or seek his models alien to the actor. In short, let him not be ashamed of the fact that he is acting.

Only this sort of non-reality imitating actor could embody the single, pristine, emotional essence of the new drama, Kornfeld claimed. Through careful selection and avoidance of complex Naturalism, the new actor could be the necessary "representative of thought, feeling, or Fate." Despite the heavy Expressionist rhetoric, Kornfeld's model for the Expressionist actor was operatic—"The dying singer [who] still gives forth a high C"—and in some ways did not significantly differ from the conception of the Reinhardt or pantomimic actor.

Writing in the *Neue Rundschau* (1917/1), Walther von Hollander defined the essence of the yet-unseen Expressionist acting as the search for the final removal of all corporal disguises—clothing, skin—in order to uncover the actor's own *Seele*. Unlike the performer from the Neo-Romantic theatre,* who merely copied the established symbolic positions to signify his inner, soul-like feelings, the Expressionist actor would have to exhibit, through physical unmasking and submission, his own internal—cosmic—anxieties. Only then, after the actor had fully mined his deepest emotions, Hollander maintained, could his soul explode from the clutches of his body, gushing through his veins until his entire being became a physicalization of the *Seele*. Naturally, Hollander was not unaware of the difficulties in training for and in ultimately achieving such a state on the stage. But, he felt, the fate of Expressionism would rest upon its realization in the theatre: "If this form of acting does not develop of its own accord, then it will have to be consciously created."

There were also those who were more clearly optimistic, presuming that true Expressionism in acting was inevitable. Some believed that the correct recitation of Expressionist dialogue and Expressionist acting would follow naturally from the production of intense emotions—and vice-versa. In the *Neue Schaubühne* (1919/1), Friedrich Sebrecht affirmed that there was an intrinsic link between the actor's internal feelings and his physical actions, so that an actor could not feel—and therefore not express with his voice—a "concealed long-ing pain" without spasmodically convulsing his shoulders while speaking; he could not experience vocally and viscerally a deep melancholia without first forcing his vacuous, "chaotic and eternity-filled" eyes to bulge.

Some writers hoped that Expressionist acting, while expressing extreme emo-tions and demonstrating the inner, psychic transformations of the New Man, would also make concrete the entire human condition in a simplified fashion. Using Edschmid's dictum, "The sick man is not merely the cripple who suffers; he becomes sickness itself," they wanted the creation of absolute external states in the Expressionist acting and performance. But, for the most part, the Expres-sionist theoreticians were concocting theatrical manifestos in a vacuum.

Then in 1917 and in early 1918, a handful of Expressionist performances were mounted in Frankfurt, Dresden, Munich and Düsseldorf. Their reception was by no means a uniformly welcomed one. But, by the next year, as if they had come out of nowhere, Expressionist productions began to be viewed throughout Germany and to dominate the entire theatrical scene—particularly in Berlin.

Basically, the German Expressionist theatre can be divided into two distinct periods: 1) a stylistically pure early stage from 1917-1921 that culminated in the unusually vigorous 1919-1920 season in Berlin, and 2) a later period from 1921 to 1924, in which Expressionism having outlived its public novelty in the popular commercial theatre, combined with other avant-garde trends like Purism (Yvan Goll), the Bauhaus (Lothar Schreyer), Constructivism (Karl-Heinz Martin), and the New Objectivity (Leopold Jessner) along with various modern dance and operatic movements in Central Europe.

At the earliest stage, Expressionist directors and actors were most strongly af-fected by the proto-Expressionist (Strindberg, Wedekind, Kokoschka, Alfred Döblin, and Carl Sternheim) and Expressionist dramas themselves. The ma-jority of these texts provided detailed, almost operatic instructions as to the performers' movement and voice: "inside, breathing heavily, laboriously raises his head, later moves to a hand, then both hands, raising himself slowly, sing-ing, withdrawing into a trance," "seeking each other's eyes—swing arms—gradually all rising—bursting out in a joint cry," "suddenly weak in one arm," etc. Even the speaking parts were relatively clear and simplistic; the telegraphic or lyric dialogue frequently was keyed to unchanging stereotyped characters. Still, it was evident to the Expressionists that even the most descrip-tive stage directions and simple characterizations could not furnish the essential creative basis for their performances. Other stimuli were needed.

Like the graphic Expressionists, the theatrical Expressionists were attracted to the crafts of the German Middle Ages and Renaissance. Both the German Passion Play's repeated use of exaggerated character-gestures and grotesque comic poses of the medieval traveling-troupes (i.e., the six conventional distorted hand-gestures of Hans Sachs) were known and discussed by the Expressionists. In his "Development of the Actor's Art" (Munich, 1923), Hans Knudsen saw parallel uses of *mise-en-scène* in the Berlin premiere of Hasenclever's *Antigone* (1920) directed by Martin and in the spectacle productions of the seventeenth-century Jesuit theatre with their mass scenes and "celebratory tensions." In both performances, huge and pathetic gestures of heroism were brought to the foreground as ceremonial choruses and oversized scenic effects moved across the backstage.

Despite their symbolic role of bourgeois fathers to the Expressionists' rebel/sons the Neo-Romantics greatly affected the modes of Expressionist acting. With the notable exception of Kokoschka and the *Sturmbühne*, most of the theatrical Expressionists were as likely to be active in the German theatre itself than with the Expressionist movement before 1915; many of them were schooled at Reinhardt's studios, the most prestigious in Germany. For example, Fritz Kortner, one of the two most celebrated Expressionist actors, trained as a choral leader in Reinhardt's production of *Oedipus Rex* (1912). There he was taught not only a particular choral voice and diction but also the appropriate statuesque gestures that were meant to project across gigantic staging areas. As Kortner was later to discover, the very same movements when applied to a much smaller stage and auditorium were to have a completely different effect on the spectator and the speaker.

However, in no other field of performance does one find a strong, if relatively unexplored, similarity with Expressionist acting than in the Middle-European dance and cabaret of the 1910s. Not only did the German and Swiss dancers and choreographers influence the early theatrical Expressionists in the areas of movement-philosophy and technique, they were also largely responsible for the evolution of a new critical understanding and journalistic analysis that explained the performer's craft in terms of self-motivation and private expression.

Before the outbreak of the First World War, two distinct dance styles evolved from the revolt against classicism in Central Europe. The first was an off-shoot of the imitative Greek, individually expressive, and earth-bound style of Isadora Duncan. "Skirt dancers," somewhat in the manner of Loie Fuller, like the three Wiesenthal sisters (Bertha, Elsa, and Grete), adapted Duncan's free-style technique to great success around 1910. Also, at this time, the Swiss composer, Émile Jacques-Dalcroze began to teach his concept of *eurhythmics* at Hellerau, outside Dresden. Essentially, *eurhythmics* was an intricate music-based system of precise movement training and practice that taught the performers to translate "into attitude and gestures all the aesthetic emotions provoked by sound rhythms." Through the establishment of small studios elsewhere in Germany and through his own austerely rhythmic and classically styled opera productions beginning in 1913, Dalcroze and his methods became known throughout Europe. German theatre practitioners and directors, like the Goethean theosophist Rudolf Steiner—starting with his 1912 Mystery Plays in Munich—and Gottfried Hass-Berkow in Dresden utilized their own theatrical versions of *eurhythmics*.

Later, the theatrical Expressionists would compress and join these two ways of moving and working—the lyrical, unrestrained, emotive flow of Duncanism with the musically symbolic, muscular posturings of Dalcroze—to form an abrupt series of gesture-combinations that were begun in one kind of tempo and intensity and completed in another. These movement-hybrids were executed from one style to the next without any transitional gestures. Frequently, the movements were initiated in a monumental, intense, laboriously slow, Dalcroze-like tempo and then suddenly exploded into a string of disjointed, separate, staccato emotional-gestures that resembled the projection of minute flashes of Duncan's counterparts.

A third modern force in the pre-war Central European dance was that of the Hungarian-born Rudolf von Laban. According to Laban, all human movement could be divided into centrifugal movements, radiating from the center (i.e., in the arms: "scattering") or peripheral movements, inward from the extremities (i.e., "scooping"). To distinguish it from the more static *eurhythmics*, Laban called his system *eukinetics*. Like Dalcroze, he developed movement-choirs to realize his theories, but Laban's dancers performed in a music-less, plastic environment. Using only the beat of a tambourine for punctuation, the Laban Group shifted from one pure movement—sometimes expressing a single emotion like Joy, Wrath, Thoughtfulness, etc.—to another. The exercises were repeated until each dancer felt the "universal celebratory state" of motion. Laban was most interested in exploring the range and shape of human movement through his alteration of extremely emotional and expressive actions in the performer. Although his work was exhibited as early as 1910 in Munich, it was not until three or four years later that Laban's importance became recognized. By 1914, the year he moved to Switzerland—as did Dalcroze and Steiner—Laban had already pioneered the expressive study of the formal relationships between the performer's movements, his costume, and the shape and color of the stage and its decor.

Laban's most famous German pupil, Mary Wigman, developed an even more dynamic and personal style. Based on part on *eukinetics*, but with a greater emphasis on emotional intensity and freedom, Wigman's performance involved the spasmatic shift from complete tension to its complete retardation—of "thrust and pull-out." More concerned with primitive expressiveness and the grotesque (i.e., masking) than with pure scientific research of human motion, Wigman was closer to the central body of theatrical Expressionism. Still, her performances, although viewed quite early—1913 in Munich—probably had little effect on the Expressionist's work until late 1920 when she opened a dance studio in Dresden. In fact, Wigman's influence on theatrical performance, still largely undocumented, was likely greater outside Germany than in it during the middle and late twenties.

Another non-theatrical source of inspiration for the Expressionists were the

German solo and cabaret dancers of the time. Some, like the hypnotic dream-dancer from Munich, Madeleine, performed pure *Seele*-states. Madeleine's hypnotic performances were confirmed by medical authorities and impressed theatre and dance critics alike. Writing in the early 1910s for *Der Tag*, Alfred Kerr described how Madeleine was transformed from a state of catalepsy to hysteria at the sound of a musical note. Kerr was especially excited by the changes in her tonal manner of speaking/singing and in her eye-focus. Valeska Gert, the young grotesque-dancer who performed in Kokoschka's *Job* (1917), was also a favorite of the Expressionists. In a certain way, she was considered more of a contortionist than a dancer. Later, her way of negating the normative beauty of dance and her uniquely demonic persona propelled her into the stardom of Berlin cabaret.

But among the cabaret performers, none excited the theatrical Expressionists more — nor served as a more common acting model — than Frank Wedekind (1864-1918), the author of the proto-Expressionist, sexually/emotionally sprung Lulu plays. His style of acting in Munich before the war was praised by the Expressionists, the Dadas, and even by the anti-Expressionist playwright Bertolt Brecht. Hugo Ball, later to found the Dada movement in Zurich, described Wedekind's acting as "gruesome as *hara-kiri*," "flagellant," and "hypnotic" (*Phöbus*, No. 3, Munich, 1914). According to Ball, Wedekind destroyed the societal structure between the inner and outer impulses. He ripped and mutilated himself while remaining as naive "as a pony." Reportedly, there were convulsions throughout his body, in his brain, his throat, his legs. Ball compared Wedekind's deformed physicality on stage to a grotesque woodcut. In Max Krell's anthology, *German Theatre of the Present* (Munich, 1923), Kasimir Edschmid recalled Wedekind's animal-like, tortured presence as the greatest acting experience that he ever witnessed. It is also noteworthy that the other most lauded Expressionist actor — along with Fritz Kortner — Werner Krauss, worked with Wedekind before entering the Expressionist stage.

Possibly the most coherent and detailed analysis of the philosophical/technical aspects of theatrical Expressionism was published in a book that appeared long after the Expressionists' apogee, Felix Emmel's *The Ecstatic Theatre* (Prien, 1924). In his chapter on Expressionst, or ecstatic, acting, Emmel differentiated and described two kinds of actors: 1) the actor of nerves — as exemplified by the Neo-Romantic actor, AlbertBassermann, and 2) the actor of blood — as exemplified by Friedrich Kayssler, also a Neo-Romantic actor. Although both performers essentially came out of the same Reinhardt tradition, they worked and acted from theoretically opposed points of view. Bassermann generally created his stage-characters from the study of other men. His final presentation would be based on a combination of many individual characteristics that he observed in scores of people. His character-performances revealed a finely-drawn, psychological mosaic of many types that were bound together after much practice until his nerves were automatically capable of reproducing the illusion of a new, single character. Kayssler, on the contrary, always played himself. He allowed his changing stage personas to grow from the character-emotions rooted in his "soul," or from the flood and unity of his "blood." His acting rhythms and character motivations always came directly from his own internal experiences and essence.

Emmel saw these two popular ways of establishing characters as modern theatrical developments of two basic ancient or medieval traditions of transcendence. The first, nerve-acting, had its roots in the primitive impulse toward imitation and masking; in the carnival, mummings, and fairground booth of the Middle Ages and Renaissance. Looking at the variegated, many-formed externals of life, the ancient nerve-actor, according to Emmel, sought to capture their ever-changing nature in acting-styles that demonstrated Man's constant physical transformations and in the wearing of the masks that signified new personages. On the other hand, always seeking transformation from within, the blood-actor and his roots were closely bound up with the ancient shamans and German mystics. Instead of linking his ecstatic feelings or "extraordinary states of being" with divine or religious communion, the blood-actor became entwined in the Expressionist playwright's text. Working from that in peformance, he could allow "the tremendous ecstasies to soar from his soul," often—Emmel quoted from Kayssler's acting notes to make his point—in a conscious/subconscious/unconscious dream-state. Not surprisingly, Emmel acknowledged enormous dangers in ecstatic acting. Besides risking possible psychological damage, the ecstatic actor could also appear comical at times or produce a pseudo-ecstasy reminiscent of nerve-acting.

Of course, it is unlikely that the majority of the theatrical Expressionists would have agreed to all of Emmel's tenets of Expressionist acting and his division into nerve and blood acting. (Certainly, most of the roots Emmel ascribed to the actor of nerves, like masking, were claimed by some Expressionists.) Yet, Emmel's further detailed and high praise of Kortner's dynamic-speech—"He compresses Fate into a single word or lets it zoom through his sentences . . . His pauses reveal an overwhelming pressure of movement and inner tension . . . His tonal strength is an echo of the soul's movement"—and Krauss's ecstatic-gestures—"Almost every one of his movements signifies an ecstatic bodily transformation"—were very much in line with the other late analyses of Expressionist acting that frequently appeared in theatre reviews.

MODES OF EXPRESSIONIST ACTING AND PERFORMANCE

Although later critics and historians of the Expressionist theatre have long recognized its non-monolithic, changing nature and have been sensitive to the differences in Expressionist stage decor, many of these same critics also treated Expressionist styles of production and acting as a single entity—and, not surprisingly, discovered ingenious contradictions: for instance, in the dramatic quest for pure human emotionalism and pure abstraction. Yet, to point up these discrepancies in the Expressionist theatre movement, rather than in individual artists, belies a misunderstanding of the philosophical and physical range of theatrical Expressionism.

At the center of the Expressionist universe was Man. All other objective or conceptual phenomena—every physical property, theory, idea, formal grammar, science, or methodology—that precluded Man was eliminated or diminished. This emphasis on Man, and Man alone, produced a variety of different performance and acting styles since the theatrical Expressionists themselves strongly disagreed as to the concept or mode of presentation of their Man-centered art. Once the curtains were drawn and the stage-space revealed, the post-war German audiences could expect to viscerally experience one of several kinds of Expressionist utopias.

Borrowing some of the terminology from Bernhard Diebold's influential study, *Anarchy in the Drama* (Frankfurt, 1921), that was used to describe models of pre-Expressionist and Expressionist dramas, German Expressionist performances can be sub-divided into three general styles based on their expressive relationship to the audience—the creation of ecstasy through induction, association, or identification—and their overall approach to acting. These three categories are 1) the *Geist* (purely spiritual or abstract) *performance*, which could be viewed as an ultimate vision of pure expression without the conventional intervention of dramatic characters or intricate plot—a sort of absolute communication between the playwright/director's *Seele*-mind and his audience; 2) the *Schrei* (scream or ecstatic) *performance*, which could be likened to an actual, if hazy, intense dream-state where movement, exteriors, language, motivation, and inner logic were uniformly and bizarrely warped; and 3) the *Ich* (I or ego) *performance*, which resembled the second type in certain ways, but focused upon a central performer who acted less—*or more*—grotesquely than the other, often stereotypical, characters and who was the subject of the playwright's and audience's identification—a kind of dream told to another person, or a dream remembered.

(As with Diebold's general divisions, there is a necessary, but dangerous, arbitrariness in differentiating all, particularly the late, Expressionist performances according to this system. For instance, Martin's well-known production of Toller's *The Transfiguration* shared characteristics of both the second and third types, due to the nature of the play and the tiny staging-area. Other productions of the time, such as the Deutsches Theater's *Lonely Lives* (1920), utilized the talents of actors from three theatrical generations—those of Otto Brahm, Reinhardt, and the Expressionists. However, the theatrical intent of most Expressionist directors was, by and large, clearly articulated in their contemporary writings and announcements.)

I. THE GEIST PERFORMANCE

Historically, the *Geist* play precedes all other forms of Expressionist drama, with the possible exception of Kokoschka's *Murderer, Hope of Women* (1909), which can be seen as the progenitor of all three types. As early as 1909, the Russian painter Vassily Kandinsky wrote the scenario *The Yellow Sound*, later published with an introduction in the *Blaue Reiter Almanac* (Munich, 1912). Kandinsky's theory of performance was based on the production of "delicate vibrations" that effect the "strings" of the audience's souls. In part, Kandinsky's program was a further development of Symbolist and neo-Symbolist theatrical tendencies in Germany, France, and Russia. But, unlike Wagner's idea of the *Gesamtkunstwerk*, which greatly influenced the French Symbolists, Kandinsky's theory called for a production style that abstracted and separated the various theatrical elements, rather than allowing them to overlap and reinforce one another. Each expressive feature of the performance—like the music, "the physical-psychical sound and its movement," or color-tone—while existing independently of the others, functioned only as a means to the artist's ultimate goal. In the text of the second picture of *The Yellow Sound*, for example, actors, dressed in assorted primary colors, were instructed to speak ecstatically in unison, then repeat themselves individually in various tones, keys, and tempos. Sometimes they were to shout as if possessed, then hoarsely, before their voices and costumes faded into the sounds of orchestra and stage-lights.

Although *The Yellow Sound* was not staged, Ball, a theatrical producer in Munich in 1914, asserted that Kandinsky's abstract performance theories would be the basis of "The Expressionst Theatre." Also about this time, August Stramm began to compose his telegraphically-worded and grotesquely violent plays that were soon printed in the periodical, *Der Sturm*, founded by the Expressionist Herwarth Walden. The technical influence of Italian Futurist poetry on Stramm has been noted, yet Stramm's dramatic tensions and abstract characterizations were unlike anything the literary Expressionists had read. Lothar Schreyer, who joined the *Sturm*-circle in 1916, arranged for dynamic recitals of Stramm's and Kokoschka's plays, and poetry by Rudolf Blümner and Walter Mehring at the *Sturm*-evenings during the war.

A production of Stramm's *Sancta Susanna*, the first *Geist*-performance, was staged by members of the *Sturmbühne*, a section of Walden's *Sturm*-school, under the direction of Schreyer on 15 October 1918. Performances of *Sancta Susanna* continued through October of that year for audiences limited to subscribers of *Der Sturm* and were met with mixed reactions. Although Schreyer claimed otherwise, at least some Berlin theatre critics were sympathetic to and impressed by the production.

After the war, in 1919, Schreyer journied to his native Hamburg and established the *Kampfbühne*, a sister theatre to the *Sturmbühne*. With help of two hundred supporters, Schreyer was able to mount premiere performances of

Walden's *Transgression*, Stramm's *Powers* and *The Bride of the Moor*, as well as Expressionist adaptations of Hölderlin's *Death of Empedocles* and a German folk play. In 1920, Schreyer returned to Berlin to present his play *Man* with the *Sturmbühne* group at Reinhardt's Deutsches Theater. It was there, according to Huntley Carter, that the actors represented "Tones and Movement, Form and Color." However, Reinhardt felt that the production was too cultish and declined to promote other *Sturmbühne* projects. Schreyer's most abstract work, *Crucifixion*, was presented on 12 April 1920. Later that year in September, Walden directed *Geist*-performances of *Impulse* and his pantomime The Four Deaths of Framettia in Dresden. In 1921, Schreyer directed his best known play *Child-Deaths*.

Many of the *Sturmbühne*'s scenic ideas were derived from the Zurich Dadas—the Berlin and Hanover Dadas, Mehring and Kurt Schwitters were frequent contributors to *Der Sturm*—and Futurism. Thus, we find in the *Sturmbühne* performances: brightly-colored backdrops of black, yellow, green, and red (*Sancta Susanna*); oversized cylindric costumes made from geometrically-painted cardboard and wire (*Child-Deaths*); gigantic—ten-foot high—masks (*Transgression*); bizarre instrumentation, like a West African xylophone (*The Bride of the Moor*), glass harmonica (*Child-Deaths*), or a violin-solo (*The Death of Empedocles*)—all dramatic elements of other avant-garde theatres.

Like Kandinsky, whose search always led to the "inner music" of a theatrical component, Schreyer was most concerned with the *sound* of a performance. The earlier work of modernist composers like Scriabin, Arnold Schönberg, and Paul Hindemith, and the unique word-formations of Stramm, were of the utmost importance to him. According to Schreyer, the actor was only the bearer of "form, color, movement, and sound"; and he trained his students at the *Sturm*-school to be "sound-speakers," who could reproduce any "vibration of the soul" with their mouths and throats. Hidden behind yards of thick paper and cardboard, however, the *Sturmbühne* actors were probably less successful in achieving this than in any other aspect of their acting.

Although Schreyer was appointed to direct the stage-workshop of the Weimar Bauhaus in 1921 and obviously influenced the more purely abstract director, Oskar Schlemmer, he always considered himself an Expressionist. In fact for this reason, besides being thought something of a mystic among functionalists, Schreyer resigned from his post in 1923. Like Walden, Schreyer maintained that only the *Sturmbühne* exemplified Expressionism in the theatre; everything else was pseudo-Expressionism. The *Geist*-performance's position is best summed up in Schreyer's statement in the final number of the *Sturmbühne* magazine.

Art is the artistically logical formulation of optical and acoustic relations. Art comes from the senses and appeals to the senses. It has

nothing to do with understanding. The theatre is the form[...]
focal color forms.

(October [...]

II. THE SCHREI PERFORMANCE

Most critics associate the *Schrei*-performance with the bulk of Expressionist productions. Certainly, the premise of much of the Expressionist theories on acting was directed toward this style. As in the 1919 German film, *The Cabinet of Dr. Caligari*, the performer's acting constantly shifted from a kind of cataleptic stasis to a powerful, if epileptic, dynamism. The decor was marked by buildings and objects indicated with irregular, nonparallel lines and often shaded with impossible shadows. In terms of acting and scenography, the comparison of *Caligari* with the *Schrei*-performance is useful, despite the fact that there is some question whether *Caligari* should be thought of as an "Expressionist" film. Photographs of *Schrei*-performances, even posed ones, show the heightened states of the actors as they performed against a background of distorted stage properties and painted backdrops. Many early definitive descriptions of Expressionist acting were from *Schrei*-performances ("[in him] sounds became corporal and movements aural") yet the roots and development of the *Schrei*-performance differed from the *Geist* and *Ich* varieties.

The *Schrei*-directors and actors freely borrowed from the contemporary middle-European dancers and painters, just as the *Geist*-directors incorporated elements from the pre-Expressionist/Expressionist musicians and poets. Most of the *Schrei*-directors came from cities outside Berlin—cities such as Dresden, Frankfurt, Mannheim, and Munich—where the grip of the professional, commercial theatre was considerably looser, and where there was a greater access to German Expressionist and Swiss dance and art. Many of the *Schrei*-actors were university students selected or hired for the occasion. Consequently, there was often a free, spontaneous atmosphere in *Schrei*-performances that did not exist in the other types. (For example, in Heinrich George's Dresden production of three Kokoschka plays [3 June 1917], a cabaret-dancer, much to the audience's surprise and outrage, appeared naked in her role as Eve.)

Two of the best-known *Schrei*-directors were Gustav Hartung and Richard Weichert, both of whom staged their most important works at the Frankfurt *Schauspielhaus* between 1917-21 and then directed Expressionist productions in Berlin. One of Hartung's Frankfurt productions, Fritz Unruh's *A Generation* (16 June 1918) was particularly noted for its "total" intensity in the acting, the simple Expressionist settings, and its religious attitude—some of the performances were given on Sunday mornings, for instance. Weichert established himself as an Expressionist director with an early production of Hasenclever's *The Son* (18 January 1918) in Mannheim. In many of Weichert's later Frankfurt productions, such as *Penthesilea* (17 September 1921), there was a stylistic emphasis on emotive, primitive abstraction, more akin to Expressionist woodcuts the Futurist-inspired abstractions of the *Sturmbühne*.

t, if there was a less professionally rigid, programmed quality to these performances, the *Schrei*-directors were more doctrinaire—and more democratic—in their devotion to Expressionist philosophy; that is, in the molding of each ecstatic actor in the cloak of the New Man. Working with basically untrained performers, this creation of ecstatic-states in the actors had its dangers: speaking-lines were sometimes swallowed or lost; actors frequently had to be restrained in their relations with other actors and the audience. The actress Leontine Sagan later claimed in *Cinema Quarterly* (Summer 1933) that Expressionist acting began to have adverse psychological effects on the off-stage behavior of the performers.

III. THE ICH PERFORMANCE

Theatrical Expressionism came to Berlin in the fall of 1919. Since the *Sturmbühne* performances of the previous year hardly met with the mass expectations that were fed by the Berlin reviews of the *Schrei*-performances from Dresden, Frankfurt, Munich, and Leipzig, the theatre-going public was most anxious to view theatrical Expressionism first-hand. At that time, the entire theatre structure in Berlin vastly differed from other German cities, being long dominated by Reinhardt and his co-directors. Indeed, when Expressionism became established in the Berlin theatre, it was in conjunction with Symbolist and Neo-Romantic aesthetics.

The marriage of the *Schrei* acting style with Reinhardt's star system and mass choruses formed the basis of the *Ich*-performance. Characteristically, an *Ich*-performance focused upon the single ecstatic actor surrounded by or confronted with dozens of choral-performers who moved in unison, creating grotesque, but picturesque, poses. Frequently, the central actor, like Kortner or Alexander Granach, received his earliest training in both *Schrei* and Reinhardt productions. For the most part, *Ich*-directors absorbed much of Reinhardt's use of *mise-en-scène*, whether they worked in competition with him or under his auspices. The best known of these were Karl-Heinz Martin, Leopold Jessner, and Jürgen Fehling.

Beginning as a revolutionary director at the small leftist theatre, the *Tribüne*, Martin expressionistically attempted to bridge the gap between performer and audience. At the time of his first production, *The Transfiguration* (30 September 1919), Kortner's performance was thought to be the first standard by which all Expressionist acting could be judged. Martin soon became known as both an Expressionist and a "mass-director"—in the footsteps of Reinhardt. His Berlin productions of *Antigone, Europa* (5 November 1920), *Florian Geyer* (5 January 1921), *The Maid of Orleans* (22 February 1921), *The Robbers* (26 September 1921), and Toller's *The Machine-Wreckers* (30 June 1922) demonstrated a scenic trend away from Neo-Romanticism toward a Central-European abstraction. (This trend would culminate in an Expressionist/Constructivist collaboration with the Viennese architect Friedrick Kiesler in 1924.) However, Martin retained a purified *Ich*-style of acting in the later performances. Thus, we find in his stage directions for *The Maid of Orleans*, instructions for the title character to rant, not only in changing tempos, but also to perform as if she were "speaking in tongues."

A few months after the opening of the *Tribüne*, Jessner mounted a version of Schiller's *William Tell* (12 December 1919) at the State Theatre with Kortner in the lead role. Kortner's ecstatic performance — his shrill manner of speaking and frenzied gesticulation — again, and Emil Pirchan's sparse *mise-en-scène* were both highly praised. In other productions, *Marquis of Keith* (12 March 1920), *Richard III* (5 November 1920), *Othello* (11 November 1921), and *Macbeth* (10 November 1922), Jessner retained this unique and celebrated combination of Kortner and Pirchan.

Heavily influenced by the scenic experiments of Appia and Delacroze, Jessner reduced and abstracted all the dramatic elements that could be used to spotlight the essential poetic, human, Expressionistic vision, namely the soul-states of his central characters.

> The historical becomes the abstract, the human focuses itself into the symbolic, external fades into an adumbration, space and the scene are reduced to the simplest common denominator, costumes are resolved into masses of color. The poetry, the characters, and passions remain dominant, but with a treble, a tenfold force and meaning. It is indeed an expressionistic summary, but also a compressionistic one.
>
> Herman Scheffauer, *The New Vision in the German Arts*
> (New York, 1924)

In his desire to intensify the emotive aspects of classical and proto-Expressionistic plays, Jessner was accused of abandoning every dramatic component except one, and then "hammering that point to death." Jessner accomplished many of his mathematically-calculated effects through an unswerving reliance on heightened Symbolism: pure colored lights and carpeted-platforms of red, gold, white, and black that signified the protagonist's mood and ultimate destiny; oversized, austere stage properties; distorted shadows projected across vast spaces; and abstract, Appia-like levels called *Jessnertreppen*. It was this last Symbolist feature that caught the critics' attention. For instance, Lee Simonson enthusiastically described their use in *Richard III*:

> How immensely the movement of the second part was enhanced by the staircase when Richard appeared at the summit, when his men in red and Richmond's in white moved up and down it with all the sym-

bolism of opposing forces, groups mounting toward its apex in immi-
nent struggle. And what a contrast to all heightened movement as
Richard descends slowly at the end in utter lassitude, to dream his last
dream at its base.

"Down to the Cellar," *Theatre Arts Monthly*, VI (April 1922)

The *Jessnertreppen* served many Expressionist purposes. It signified the relationships between characters and their individual psychic states; it increased
the actor's plastic possibilities, allowing him to be more easily perceived in
depth; it rhythmically heightened the impact of slow, fast, or disjointed
movements; and it created a novel aesthetic unity that was thought to be lacking in other Expressionist productions. Yet, an otherwise comic anecdote
points up the peril of Jessner's multi-leveled scenery: at the premiere of *Macbeth*,
Kortner, in a "possessed" state of mind, lost his footing on the stairs and went
sliding down the length of the platforms. While mass actors could be precisely
choreographed in the negotiation of the complex staging, an ecstatic actor
could not.

Formerly an actor at the *Volksbühne*, Fehling achieved renown with his *Ich*-
production of Toller's *Mass-Mensch* (29 September 1921). Both his work before
and after that production reflected late theatrical Expressionism's growing interest in the conventional grotesque and comic irony—modeled after the
fairground booth performance, circus, variety-stage, and the popular
cinema—especially in *Marriage* (1 March 1920) and in *The Rats* (10 March
1922). Although it would be difficult to assess Fehling's major histrionic and
scenic techniques, except for his central use of the *Ich*-performance style of production and rhythmic choruses, in *Mass-Mensch*, which is superbly
documented in Kenneth Macgowan's and Robert Edmond Jones's *Continental
Stagecraft*, there are a number of innovations: characters are set off against a
background of black curtains and intense beams of light. As in the Jessner productions, the abstract *mise-en-scène* and highly choreographed groups of actors
allowed the audience to focus upon the expressions of a single performer (Mary
Dietrich) or situation. Unlike Jessner, Fehling varied his formal sets for each
scene and was not as insistent on the perfection of his actors' tonal qualities.
Fehling's later successes with Expressionist plays from 1923 to 1930 marked the
very last vestiges of pure Expressionism in the German theatre.

EXPRESSIONIST TEXTS

Mary Wigman (1919)

Laban Group demonstrating *eukinetics*

The Wigman group (1919)

Gustav Hartung's production of A *Generation* (Frankfurt, 1918)

Fritz Kortner in Leopold
Jessner's production of *Richard III*
(Berlin, 1920)

Sphinx and Strawman

a curiosity

[1907]

Oskar Kokoschka

Translation by Victor H. Meisel

Better known for his graphic art, Oskar Kokoschka (1886-1980) is often credited with the invention of the Expressionist drama. His Viennese trilogy, *Sphinx and Strawman*, *Murderer, Hope of Women*, and *The Burning Bush* were not only performed and published long before any other Expressionist plays, they also provided earliest artistic impetus for many Expressionist poets and dramatists. The son of an Austrian goldsmith, Kokoschka studied at the School of Arts and Crafts in Vienna. Like the Cubists before him, Kokoschka chose pre-nineteenth-century artists and non-European cultures for his influences in painting and sculpture. Problems with his teachers and an innately rebellious personality probably led Kokoschka to theatre. In 1907 he drafted a script of *Sphinx* (all of Kokoschka's plays exist in several versions), which was performed at the School of Arts and Crafts in some improvised manner. A rewritten *Sphinx* was staged in March 1909 at Vienna's Cabaret Fledermaus.

In July of 1909, Kokoschka once again mounted *Sphinx and Strawman* but this time with his notorious sketch, *Murderer, Hope of Women*. Performed out of doors between two buildings at the Kunstschau, *Murderer* utilized a percussion orchestra of four musicians, hand-held torches, and the ranting actions of students, on whose bodies Kokoschka painted nerves, veins, and muscle fibers. Accounts vary but some kind of riot ensued during *Murderer* with Bosnian soldiers, irate intellectuals, confused students, and friends of Kokoschka mixing it up. Either the mythic, sado-masochistic violence, which resulted in real bruises on the performers' bodies, or the verbal unintelligibility of *Murderer*—or both—caused the sensation. In any case it is not clear what happened to the dramatization of dream-like *Sphinx* on that evening.

Kokoschka continued his artistic career, painting avant-garde portraits. In 1910 he temporarily moved to Berlin, becoming a contributor to *Der Sturm*, which published his dramatic sketches. An emotionally devastating affair with Alma Mahler-Werfel brought about a mental crisis, and Kokoschka went about cafés in the evening carrying a mannequin of Mahler, often seating it or ordering drinks for it. When a monograph of Kokoschka's paintings and plays appeared in 1913, each of the plays were rewritten with the love-hate relationship between the central male and female characters made more bitter still.

With the outbreak of the First World War in 1914, Kokoschka joined the Austro-Hungarian cavalry. Severely wounded in the head and chest, he very nearly died after his single year in the service. While convalescing in Dresden in 1917, the Zurich Dadas staged the 1913 version of *Sphinx and Strawman*. A modern painter, like Kokoschka, Marcel Janco found the extreme dislocation of images and language—almost schizophrenic in its odd comic intensity—ideal to express the age-old sexual conflict in a novel and disturbing manner. Meanwhile, Kokoschka himself produced his trilogy in Dresden with a newer version of *Sphinx*, entitled *Job*.

Kokoschka's association with theatre diminished after 1919. His plays, while miniature in length, were generally successful throughout Germany. Although lacking in professional experience, even his directing abilities were highly praised; the little he knew or cared to know about acting was overcome with his sense of high spectacle and dramatic feeling. Except for his directorial assistance with Paul Hindemith's opera of *Murderer, Hope of Women* in 1927, Kokoschka abandoned the stage until 1955, when he returned to his native Austria to design for the opera. After decades of exile in Prague, London, Italy, and Switzerland, Kokoschka died in 1980.

Kokoschka's poster for
Murderer, Hope of Women and
Sphinx and Strawman
(Vienna, 1909)

Kokoschka's *Job* directed by
Heinrich George
(Frankfurt, 1920)

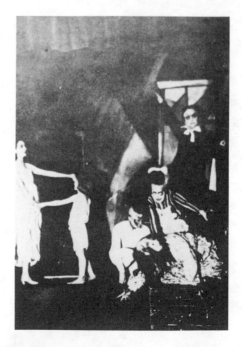

CHARACTERS:

Mr. Firdusi,* a gigantic, revolving straw head with arms and legs. He carries a pig's bladder on a string.
Mr. Rubberman, an accomplished contortionist.
Female Soul, called "Anima."
Death, a normal, living person.
Parrot

FIRDUSI: (*His gigantic head rocking back and forth on his legs; talks to the parrot.*) Who are you? What is your name?
PARROT: The female soul, Anima, sweet Anima.
FIRDUSI: (*Turns away.*) I had a wife, I treated her like a goddess and she left my bed. She said to our sad little chambermaid, "Help me on with my traveling cloak" and then disappeared with a healthy muscleman. I had created a human soul but the ground vanished from beneath its feet. Now my creation floats in the air like a pig's bladder—*Horror vacui!* What kind of God steals words out of my own mouth in order to make me believe that they are his words of wisdom? Just like a sponge drinks up vinegar only to give it back without swallowing a drop.
PARROT: Anima, sweet Anima!
FIRDUSI: At first she was a woman. Then I found myself dining with a ghoul, in the ecstasies of love with a ghost and then I solved the mystery of certain vocal phenomena. A nightmare entered my skull, it strangled my consciousness. Vitality, essentiality, reality, help! That poor Adonis! She will feed on his mind until he begins to speak with my voice. She is a woman who lost her virginity for a soul and now she wanders from one man into another, she spins and wraps herself into a cocoon, she devours men's brains

---

*The name of a tenth-century Persian poet who wrote the national epic of Persia, and the title of a poem from Goethe's *West-östlicher Divan*.

and she only leaves their empty skulls, as a magnificent butterfly, in order to lay her egg. Anima, Anima, the nucleus from one, protoplasm from the other, and we all recognize ourselves in the result. Resurrection from life. I want to die.

(*Death, who looks like an ordinary person, appears in thunder and lightning. He gestures threateningly, but with a smile and then disappears without doing anything.*)

FIRDUSI: (*To the public.*) When I grab my handkerchief you all start to cry, how touching. But why do you look at me now so coolly, one hundred indifferent people against a single desperate person? Only a nuance separates the hero from the audience. Do you believe in a bluff? I am only exploiting your intelligence and your nerves and our mutual romantic interest in ghosts.

RUBBERMAN: (*Enters and touches Firdusi's leg.*) Hey there, I'm a doctor. You say you want to die! Let's talk awhile, you know, to exchange impressions is not to explain insights but to interchange outlooks. You don't die as easily as you're born. However, I have something for you in case your last little hour should give you any trouble. I know a woman . . . (*Anima peeks in the door*) who is slowly murdering her husband in such a way that no court in the world could prove a thing. "Fear of adultery" is a poison which works with absolute certainty. And how can I serve you?

FIRDUSI: Thanks—thanks. (*Lost in thought.*) I don't think—things have gone that far—yet—. But you are a doctor, and you don't try to stop crime?

RUBBERMAN: Oh, I'm interested in experimentation. I'm no practicing doctor, just a modest priest of science.

ANIMA: (*Half aloud.*) A man, magnificence and modesty combined, anything spectacular like that fascinates me.

FIRDUSI: (*Embarrassed, he puts a rubber figure on his finger and lets it nod back and forth.*) May I introduce my child, Emanuel, my hope—Mr. Rubberman!

RUBBERMAN: Be a credit to your father Mr. Emanuel, my dear sir. (*To Firdusi.*) But to be frank with you, if you want your offspring to be legitimate —legal—you have to declare at least who its most important producers were.

FIRDUSI: (*He becomes confused and pulls the figure from his finger.*) Oh my dear sir don't talk so loosely, my child is still pure. But you're right, Emanuel's progress might be hurt by not having a mother.

PARROT: Anima, sweet Anima.

ANIMA: (*In a light blue conventional angel's costume, wings, hands folded, she approaches the men.*) Oh Lord, if I could only save a man's soul! They say that men suffer so from the mysteries of their delicate and cultivated eroticism. (*Pointing to Rubberman.*) You must be worthy, you have powerful muscles. (*Rubberman, pleased, shows off his thigh muscles. She looks down at her own feet coquettishly, one placed a little ahead of the other.*) Horrors! Don't you think that one of my footsies is shorter than the other?

RUBBERMAN: (*Gallantly.*) Perspective is an optical swindle invented by art experts.

ANIMA: (*Acts reassured.*) And that's why I'll have to limp for the rest of my life! (*She lifts her dress and gives Firdusi, who has not paid any attention to her, a light kick in the pants with her graceful leg.*)

FIRDUSI: (*Grumbling.*) Women should only be looked down upon. (*He turns his head slowly without moving his body. Anima, moving step by step, keeps out of his line of sight until Firdusi's head has turned completely round; in spite of great effort he is then unable to get his head back where it belongs. Thus right to the end Firdusi never sees Anima. Whining.*) If you are kind and considerate in love, those raging Amazons feel themselves cheated, but if you are rough and domineering your own sensibility is violated. (*Backing up to the door like a crab, he rings for the butler.*) Johann, bring a mirror, a red rose and the photograph, also the cockatoo, bring them into the Rose room. (*The servant brings the rose and the mirror. Firdusi, going backwards as before, storms to the armchair, sits down backwards. He puts the rose first in his back, then on his necktie, puts the mirror to his rump and then to his face.*)

ANIMA: (*In new, exquisitely luxurious clothes, singing with a book in her hand.*) Oh, where is the man who is worthy of me, the man I dreamed of as a girl? Oh, no man like that proved himself worthy of me! I took a feature from one man, another from the next, to my lover I offered resigned lips, to my husband scorn and melancholy. I am forced to wander and wander, eternally, from one to the other. (*To Firdusi.*) Hello handsome!

FIRDUSI: (*Without being able to see her.*) Who are you? What's your name? Angel.

ANIMA: The female soul, Anima, sweet Anima.

PARROT: (*Repetitiously.*) Anima, sweet Anima.

FIRDUSI: (*Pulls a larva out, like a dentist.*) I've been through all this once already. Women have an earthly body but an immortal soul.

ANIMA: (*Pointing to his figure.*) You have an interesting view. (*Firdusi, thinking that she is referring to what he has said, proudly puffs his chest out.*) Oh, I believe that I only love you.

FIRDUSI: (*Smiling pathetically.*) If I could only respond out of my loneliness to your secret confessions, oh, to be able to place a rainbow of reconciliation over shocked sexes, (*becoming hysterical*) my feelings are like so many falling stars, stars falling into the narrow fields of my soul to be extinguished—but the Word which reaches out far beyond me like a huge gesture means nothing to you.

ANIMA: Oh, but I do so love grand gestures! My dear, sweet big head. My light, my wisdom. (*Shrieking, she jumps on top of him.*) My master, dear sweet Mr. Firdusi.

FIRDUSI: My self-respect grows by leaps and bounds. (*Rubberman panting; Anima pulls his leg up to his nose and he trembles gently.*)

ANIMA: (*Quietly.*) Oh, Rubberman, I think I'm in love but I'm not sure. Do you gentlemen know each other—Mr. Rubberman.

FIRDUSI: (*Involuntarily.*) Fir-du-si!

RUBBERMAN: The pleasure is all mine! (*A very deep and very odd bow; Firdusi bows facing the other way for obvious reasons.*)

FIRDUSI: Emanuel is getting a mother.

PARROT: Anima, sweet Anima.

(*Death appears in thunder and lightning; Firdusi is horrified.*)

FIRDUSI: (*Screams.*) *Entreprise des pompes funèbres!* Sex murder for ever! If you think about the future the present disappears. (*Searching for Anima.*) I don't even have her photograph.

DEATH: (*Knocks with a bone on the proscenium. Firdusi becomes rheumatic.*) In spite of the spectacular stage effects I want to reassure the audience that death has lost all its horror now that the masculine imagination in Europe is obsessed by gynolatry.

FIRDUSI: (*Still upset but a little quieter.*) The human soul is like a magic lantern, in the past it projected devils on the wall, now it projects our women over the whole world. (*Shudders like an electric eel and destroys the pig's bladder.*) That used to be the soul. (*Resigned.*) Oh, I'll never ever again disbelieve in fairytales, but I will laugh a little. (*Laughs louder, a hundred-voiced resonance, a rushing echo, then quiets down.*) My method for restoring my body's balance. (*He hitches up his trousers. Death follows him. Anima screams and flees with Rubberman into the Rose room. Firdusi gropes after them clumsily but he is unable to find his way. Meanwhile, the Rose room is lit up. Two shadows can be seen kissing.*)

PARROT: Oh, my Anima, sweet Anima. (*Very clearly.*) Oh my sweet Mr. Rubberman! Oh my sweet Mr. Rubberman! Oh my sweet Mr. Rubberman!

FIRDUSI: (*His head snaps back as he hears the unexpected additional remarks of the Parrot; he notices the shadows, and then rushes to the telephone.*) Who are you?

ANIMA: Anima, your dear sweet Anima, the female soul.

FIRDUSI: What are you up to?

ANIMA: Experiments in spiritualism, exorcism. I am having myself saved.

FIRDUSI: Who am I?

PARROT: Oh my sweet Mr. Rubberman.

(*Firdusi staggers to the middle of the stage, lies down flat on the floor and shoots himself with an air pistol. He sprouts horns. Johann opens a curtain which hangs below the Rose room. On it there is a painting of a gigantic cat catching a mouse. There is another curtain. On it are painted a group of gentlemen dressed in black with top hats. Instead of faces there are holes through which heads pop out. First one gentleman speaks and then quickly another answers and so on to the end.*)

FIRST GENTLEMAN: The Enlightenment will come to a bad end. The brain is too heavy and the pelvis much too frivolous.

SECOND GENTLEMAN: And there is no conscience to keep things balanced.

THIRD GENTLEMAN: Death gave all his power to a woman.

FOURTH GENTLEMAN: This is the way a great fantast takes all the magic out of culture.

FIFTH GENTLEMAN: Mr. Firdusi, who was supposed to have been born of woman, gave his inheritance, his masculine imagination back to his wife, and now her soul suffers.

SIXTH GENTLEMAN: He persuaded a woman to swallow her miscarriage under the impression that she could still give it a proper birth.

SEVENTH GENTLEMAN: Eat this you bird people, or die!

EIGHTH GENTLEMAN: Can't modern science help.

NINTH GENTLEMAN: It's become shameful since everyone in the elementary schools knows its ancestors.

TENTH GENTLEMAN: Man must be willing to suffer the anguish which woman causes him because he knows why she is so different from him. He wisely compensates for the "it is" through the better "it could be" and so rounds out the horizon of his experience. (*Anima throws herself on Firdusi weeping.*)

FIRDUSI: (*Stirs himself for the last time.*) I forgot! — Quick, a priest!

RUBBERMAN: (*Chases after Anima; his tie is gone.*) What about the wedding? (*Sings.*) Joy reigns supreme, conscience is dead. Yes, marriage reform, marriage reform and let us make love in front of scientists!

FIRDUSI: (*Stirs himself for absolutely the last time.*) Passion needs spirit as a filter or else it floods over the entire body and soul and dirties them both. I have faith in the genius of mankind, Anima, amen.

DEATH: (*With lightning and thunder.*) A good, strong faith is like blindness. It covers over unpleasant things, but those things never disappear. (*Death goes away with Anima.*)

END

August Stramm

Sancta Susanna

[1911]

August Stramm

*Translation by Henry Marx**

---

*This translation is indebted to an earlier English version by Edward J. O'Brien.

August Stramm (1874-1915) was among the earliest and most radical of the Expressionist playwrights. Born to a petty bourgeois family in Münster, Stramm seemed destined for a similar life-style although his Catholic mother and Protestant father had conflicting claims to his choice of careers. Devoted to civil service, as his father wanted, Stramm rose to the rank of postal secretary and later as a captain in the German army. Even his 1909 dissertation topic at the University of Halle appeared to be aggressively unexciting: "Historical, Critical, and Cameralistic Investigation of the Letter Postage Rates of the Universal Postal Union and their Foundations."

Only at age twenty-eight, after establishing a career and family, did Stramm begin to write. His total output was tiny. Between 1902 and 1915, he completed ten plays as well as a small amount of poetry and short prose, much of which is lost today. Stramm's dialogues consisted of violent, impossible neologisms and voiced choppy, schizophrenic-like thoughts. It reminded many critics of Italian Futurism or the sometimes strange titling of silent movies. Some detractors suggested that Stramm's long apprenticeship as a postal clerk was really responsible for his "telegraphic" word style. Singled-word threats of torture, declarations of dominance, and murderous mutilation seemed to guide his characters' hellish actions. Like Oskar Kokoschka's *Murderer, Hope of Women*, Stramm's plays were fueled by the sexually-bound and sado-masochistic struggle between men and women.

Killed in combat in 1915, Stramm never lived to see any of his work on the stage. In 1918, the leader of the Berlin Sturmbühne, Lothar Schreyer, mounted Stramm's *Sancta Susanna*. A second series of Stramm plays—*The Bride of the Moor* and *Powers*—followed in 1919 at Schreyer's Kampfbühne in Hamburg. Only Max Reinhardt's 1921 production of *Powers* proved to be successful. However, Stramm's use of language was greatly influential in the development of an Expressionist dramatic vocabulary.

CHARACTERS:

Susanna
Clementia
A Maid
A Servant
Choir of Nuns
A Spider
Nightingales, Moonlight, Wind, and Blossoms

(*The Convent Church. Trembling streaks of moonlight; in the rear of the high altar, the eternal light. A large candle is burning in a wall niche to the left in front of a larger-than-life image of Christ on the Cross. Susanna lies in prayer in front of the flower-adorned altar of the Virgin, which stands in a niche at a right angle to the crucifix altar. Her forehead rests on the lowest step, her arms are spread over the upper steps.*)

CLEMENTIA: (*A few steps behind Susanna.*) Sancta Susanna! . . . (*She lays her hands on Susanna's shoulders. Susanna gets up.*) Night has begun! . . .

SUSANNA: (*Her spirit far away.*) It sounds . . . a tone . . .

CLEMENTIA: The organ re-echoes! . . .

SUSANNA: To me it is . . . like the ringing . . . of bottomless depths . . . heavenless heights . . .

CLEMENTIA: You come from there . . . You were with God! . . .

SUSANNA: (*Meditating.*) I . . . was . . .

CLEMENTIA: You are sick . . . you pray . . . you scarcely live on this earth any longer . . . you have a body, too! (*Susanna gets up, stares at her terrified. Clementia puts her arm around her.*) Come! (*The belfry clock strikes once clearly; the night wind rattles the windows, the branches rustle. To herself.*) Ave Maria! . . .

SUSANNA: (*Startled.*) Who is speaking?! . . .

CLEMENTIA: The night wind flings the blossoms against the windows . . .

SUSANNA: Something called . . .

CLEMENTIA: The belfry clock struck . . . I spoke the Ave . . . (*A window opens, the night wind enters, singing in a tone that dies away; leaves and branches rustle and whisper down to a murmuring.*)

(*Susanna turns with hands stretched down, away from her body toward the dark choir, silently, rigidly.*)

CLEMENTIA: A window opened! . . . I will close it!

SUSANNA: Let it . . . (*She breathes heavily.*)

CLEMENTIA: The great lilac bush, do you smell its blossoms? (*She inhales.*) . . . They smell sweetly even here! It blooms in white and red clusters . . . oh . . . such clusters. . . ! I will have it uprooted . . . tomorrow . . . if it disturbs you!

SUSANNA: It is not disturbing . . . it blooms! . . . (*A woman's voice chokes in moaning desire.*)

CLEMENTIA: The meadow ridge below the blossoms! I will close the road . . .

SUSANNA: (*Listening.*) . . . she . . . is . . . not . . . alone . . .! (*Clementia crosses herself. Susanna breathes heavily, starts making the sign of the cross, but her motion freezes.*) Will . . . she . . . perhaps . . . come?!

CLEMENTIA: Who?! . . .

SUSANNA: . . . (*Clementia, frightened, folds her hands.*)

SUSANNA: (*Her hand heavy on the pew.*) I . . . will . . . appeal . . . to . . . her conscience . . . (*Clementia folds her hands, bows her head, and goes away. A catch door rattles softly.*) The . . . (*The terrified scream of a woman dies away; branches rustle. Wincing.*) Lilac . . . blooms! . . . (*The catch door rattles softly with a wafting echo; softly shuffling steps approach. The Maid, behind Clementia, trembles with timid glances, her hands folded.*)

SUSANNA: Ave Maria! . . . (*The Maid sinks on her knees, bowing low to the ground.*) Child! . . .

MAID: (*Lifts her head helplessly, staring at her.*) I . . . I . . . don't know! (*She breaks out in frightened crying and, with folded hands, slides toward the middle pillar to hide behind it.*)

SUSANNA: I am not angry with you . . . you . . . were . . . under . . . the . . . lilac?! . . .

MAID: (*Becoming very quiet, stares at Susanna.*) I . . . I . . . nothing . . . ! . . . he . . . he . . . wants . . . (*She hangs her head very low.*)

SUSANNA: (*Gravely.*) He . . . ?!

MAID: (*Lifts her head and stares at her, then bursts out laughing loudly.*) My Bill . . . holy . . . (*She pauses in fright, bowing shyly, the laughter and the words resound from the vaults . . . twice . . . three times . . . in a jumble . . . in a vanishing ghostly echo.*)

SUSANNA: (*Looks at her motionless; then she is shaken by a sudden, silvery laughter*

*that encompasses her whole figure; the laughter dies away in the vaults as if in
small silver bells and dissolves in trembling vibrations. She goes toward the Maid,
puts a hand on her shoulder, lifts up her head, and looks into her face.)* Get
up! . . . *(The Maid gets up with hands folded.)* Do you love him?

MAID: *(Twists her fingers, shy, laughing quietly, bashful.)* Oh . . . holy mother . . .
Oh . . .

SUSANNA: I . . . would like . . . to . . . see him . . . *(Clementia raises her hand.)*

*(The Maid stares at Clementia and shudders. A loud knock at the door in the choir
. . . three times . . . and a voice calling. All are frightened. Clementia lets her arm
fall.)*

MAID: *(In relieved, restrained rejoicing.)* That's him!

*(Clementia goes into the choir; a key turns heavily; a door opens creakily and falls shut
with a dull sound; a man's repressed voice speaks angrily. Heavy steps try in vain to
tread softly.)*

A SERVANT: *(Young, stocky, turning his cap in one hand, in the nave between the
pillars, his eyes looking downward, with shy defiance.)* I want to fetch my girl!

*(Clementia emerges from behind him out of the darkness. Susanna stares at him, then
turns abruptly and walks to the altar. Complete stillness. The Maid sneaks toward the
Servant who puts his arm around her; both exit with shyly thundering steps, followed
by Clementia. The key turns. The door creaks. A gust of wind whisks blusteringly between the pews. The door falls shut with a loud thud. The key cries out. The candle in
front of the crucifix goes out with a sudden flare and shiver.)*

SUSANNA: *(Stares, startled, into the darkness where, between the pews, the white
face of Clementia now floats closer. She screams.)* Satanas! . . . Satanas! . . .

CLEMENTIA: *(Remains motionless for a moment as if paralyzed, then rushes forward
and, with hands convulsively twisting, stands before Susanna.)* Susanna!!! *(Susanna puts her hand on Clementia's shoulder and bows her head, exhausted.)*

CLEMENTIA: *(Shocked.)* Sister Susanna!! . . . Sister! . . . You must rest . . . *(She
tries to lead her away.)*

SUSANNA: *(Sits down on the steps of the altar.)* Light the candle! . . .

CLEMENTIA: . . .

SUSANNA: Light it . . . *(Clementia takes a wax taper out of the niche and goes into
the choir. She turns around in her confused haste, the eyes behind her.)*

SUSANNA: What is. . . ?! . . .

CLEMENTIA: *(In panting fear.)* I . . . can . . . not! . . . *(She presses quite close to
Susanna. Susanna rises and gazes into the darkness.)*

CLEMENTIA: *(Sits on the steps of the altar.)* I do not . . . know . . . it blows . . .

it moves . . .

SUSANNA: The night wind . . .

CLEMENTIA: It hums . . . it taps . . .

SUSANNA: The organ . . . the blossoms . . . (*Takes the wax taper away from her.*)

CLEMENTIA: Sancta Susanna . . . (*Cowers and convulsively claps her hands in front of her face. Susanna walks slowly forward between the pews and vanishes in the darkness; the eternal light goes out behind her. Out of the darkness, a light approaches slowly at the same height: the light of the wax taper Susanna carries before her. She lights the candle.*)

CLEMENTIA: (*Leans her head in one hand.*) There was a night . . . there was a night . . . like this . . . thirty, forty years ago . . . it was a night like this. (*She stands up staring, looks into the void, and raises her hand imploringly. Susanna turns around, stares at Clementia under her sway.*)

CLEMENTIA: The night wind sang . . .

SUSANNA: The . . . night wind . . . sang. . . ?

CLEMENTIA: The . . . blossoms . . . tapped . . .

SUSANNA: The . . . blossoms . . . tapped. . . ?

CLEMENTIA: And I was young . . .

SUSANNA: Young. . . ?

CLEMENTIA: Dedicated to the Lord . . . (*Susanna lets her head sink on her breast.*) Here I was lying on my knees just as . . . you do . . . (*A nightingale warbles. She cries out hoarsely.*) Beata! . . . (*She covers her face with her arms in terror and lets her arms fall again. Susanna raises her head, staring at her with large, fearful eyes. Clementia speaks with a choking voice, staring into the void.*) Pale . . . without breast veil or headband . . . naked . . . thus, she came . . . (*A nightingale calls from far away.*) Thus . . . (*Her rigid arm pointing to the right.*) She mounted the steps . . . and saw me not . . . she ascended the altar . . . and saw me not . . . (*In hot haste.*) She pressed her naked, sinful body against the crucified image of the Redeemer . . . and saw me not . . . she embraced him with her white-hot arms . . . and kissed His head . . . and kissed . . . and kissed . . . (*The two nightingales rejoice near and far, loud and persistently. Crying out.*) Beata . . . I called . . . I only called. . . ! (*Weary.*) Then she fell down . . . fell down . . . (*Suddenly, the nightingales fall silent.*) We carried her away . . . (*In horror, the upper part of her body half turning toward the image of the crucifixion and stretching out her hands as if warding off something.*) Ever since the light is burning . . . eternally . . . the candle for atonement . . . ever since the cloth girds the loins . . . the loins . . . there . . . (*Points to the darkness behind the crucifix.*) There they have her . . . flesh and blood . . . imbedded her . . . in a stoned wall . . . (*Hoarsely.*) Do you hear her?! . . . do you hear . . . ?! I have . . . heard her . . . for a long time . . . always . . . just before . . . (*Points to the darkness around the high altar.*) . . . there . . . just now. (*Clasps her hands in front of her face.*) . . . Almighty Father in Heaven! . . . the candle has gone out!

SUSANNA: (*Rigidly.*) I have lit it again! . . . (*She leans with her hand on the altar.*)

CLEMENTIA: (*Lets her hands sink slowly and stares at her. A spider the size of a fist creeps forth out of the darkness behind the altar. Terrified, she goes down on her knees, pointing to the insect.*) The . . . spider!

SUSANNA: (*Turns her head toward the spider and remains standing, paralyzed and trembling. The spider runs across the altar and disappears on the other side behind the crucifix. After a while she turns to Clementia; trembling and shuddering, she lifts her hand mechanically from the altar, hands stretched from her body toward the floor, stiff with terror.*) Do you hear her . . . ?!

CLEMENTIA: (*Terrified.*) Do . . . you . . . hear . . .

SUSANNA: Do . . . you . . . hear . . .

CLEMENTIA: . . .

SUSANNA: The voice . . .

CLEMENTIA: I . . . hear . . . nothing . . .

SUSANNA: . . .

CLEMENTIA: (*Attempts to scream, but remains hoarse with terror.*) I hear . . . nothing!

SUSANNA: (*Speaking in the same ghostly voice.*) Confess . . . confess . . . (*She stands with her back turned to the cross.*) Does . . . he say . . . something?! . . .

CLEMENTIA: (*In utmost terror.*) . . . ?! (*Susanna motions with her head toward the crucifix.*)

CLEMENTIA: (*Folds her hands, stammering.*) Ave . . . Maria . . .

SUSANNA: Does he say nothing. . . ?! . . . (*Clementia, in dumb terror, shakes her head. Susanna extinguishes the wax taper with her hand and puts it on the altar, performing all motions mechanically; then she descends from the altar . . . step by step . . . silently . . . remains standing close in front of Clementia. She bursts out laughing happily and silver-clear . . . a tender, many-voiced echo mingles with the dying song of the wind and the rustle of the branches. She tears off her veil, kerchief, and band; her long hair falls over her naked shoulders.*) Sister Clementia . . . I am beautiful . . . ! . . . (*The wind pushes hard; the branches rustle mightily and the nightingales warble together. Clementia, her folded hands raised high, sinks to her knees.*)

SUSANNA: Sister Clementia . . . I am beautiful . . .

CLEMENTIA: Sancta Susanna . . .

SUSANNA: Sister Clementia . . . I am . . .

CLEMENTIA: (*Rises stiffly and rigidly, with each word becoming more resolute.*) Chastity . . . poverty . . . obedience . . .

(*Susanna stares at her silently, her hand heavily on a pew. Clementia passes her firmly to go into the darkness; the window slams shut; the jubilant song of the nightingales, the rustle of the trees, and the song of the wind all die suddenly. She returns.*)

SUSANNA: (*Jumps up and grabs her.*) Open the window! . . . the window . . .

(*Clementia raises the great cross of the rosary against her.*)

SUSANNA: (*Reels back, staring at the cross, step by step back to the altar.*) I . . . I . . . see the . . . shining body . . . ! . . . I see . . . Him stooping down . . . I . . . feel Him spread his arms . . .

CLEMENTIA: (*Holding the cross high.*) Chastity . . . poverty . . . obedience . . . (*Each word re-echoes clearly in the vault. In the end, all three words coalesce into one and die out.*)

SUSANNA: (*Screaming and staring around her.*) Who speaks here?! . . .

CLEMENTIA: I!

SUSANNA: I . . . I . . . I . . . never said that!! . . . (*Clementia holds up the cross in front of her. Susanna rips off the loin cloth from the great crucifix in one single pull.*) Thus, my savior helps me against yours . . . ! (*She sinks on her knees and looks up to Him. The spider falls down behind the arm of the cross and into her hair. She screams shrilly and hits the altar with her forehead. The spider creeps across the altar and disappears behind it. The hour bell sounds shrilly through the vault, recording the hollow strokes of the twelfth hour. She rouses herself, runs her hands wildly through her hair, and creeps on all fours down the altar steps, fleeing in horror from herself. With the last stroke of the hour, the bell dies down.*)

CLEMENTIA: (*Lets the cross sink.*) Ave Maria! . . . a new day! . . . (*Susanna crouches with a vacant look on the first altar step. Soft steps shuffle and prayers are murmured. A procession of nuns enters.*)

PRECENTRESS: Kyrie eleison . . .

CHORUS: Kyrie eleison . . .

PRECENTRESS: Regina coeli sancta . . .

CHORUS: Ora pro nobis . . .

PRECENTRESS: Virgo virginum sancta . . .

CHORUS: Ora pro nobis . . .

(*The moonlight that fell in clear streaks through the windows and cast a bluish light on the pews disappears; it becomes completely dark. The nuns come forward to the holy water font, but stop when they catch sight of Clementia, who stands immobile in the nave between the pillars and looks at Susanna. The prayer ends; the nuns assemble in a wide semi-circle around Susanna, moving silently; finally they all stand still, motionless in mute awe.*)

OLD NUN: (*Silently makes a step forward.*) Sancta . . . Susanna! . . . (*Susanna jumps up straight as a bolt.*)

OLD NUN: (*Bows her head.*) Sancta Susanna. . . !

SUSANNA: There are stones behind the yard . . . (*The Old Nun looks up.*)

SUSANNA: (*In a firm voice.*) You must get the wall ready for me! . . . (*The Old Nun, spreading her arms, slowly sinks on her knees. The Chorus follows her. Clementia stands rigidly, staring at Susanna.*)

SUSANNA: (*Suddenly forceful.*) No! . . . (*The Old Nun jumps up; the Chorus follows her. *The Old Nun holds the cross of the rosary over her head. The Chorus follows her.*)

OLD NUN: Confess! . . .

SUSANNA: . . . (*Clementia raises the cross.*)

CLEMENTIA AND OLD NUN: (*Severely urgent.*) Confess!!!

SUSANNA: No!!! . . .

CLEMENTIA, OLD NUN, AND CHORUS: (*Shrill.*) Confess!!! (*The word echoes three times in the vault; the church windows are shaking; the storm howls outside.*)

SUSANNA: No!!! (*The echo of the word is submerged in the earlier echoes.*)

OLD NUN: (*Ecstatically.*) Satana!!!

OLD NUN AND CLEMENTIA: Satana!!!

OLD NUN, CLEMENTIA, AND CHORUS: Satana!!! (*Shrill, confused echo.*)

(*Susanna draws herself up to full height, in untouched dignity. All stand quiet and motionless.*)

END

Cesar Klein's design for the Berlin production of
From Morn to Midnight (1921)

Viktor Barnowsky's production of Kaiser's *Hell, War, Earth*
Sets by Cesar Klein (Berlin, 1920)

From Morn to Midnight

a modern mystery in seven scenes

[1912]

Georg Kaiser

Translation by Ashley Dukes

With over forty plays produced, Georg Kaiser (1878-1945) was clearly the most prolific of Expressionist playwrights. He was also one of the most personally complicated, generating hordes of followers and detractors. The celebrated Berlin theatre reviewer, Alfred Kerr, once denounced him as "half bluffer, half Expressionist," which revealed a critical truth about Kaiser's career: it always was on a zig-zag course away from pure dramatic Expressionism and then an immediate return. Kaiser also felt a curious contempt for his audiences and directors; like Plato, he claimed, he wrote philosophical dialogue without regard to any real production needs.

Brought up in a middle-class Prussian environment, Kaiser resisted all attempts to conform to a normal adolescence. A poor student beset with psychosomatic illnesses, Kaiser began a career as a bookseller, then as a clerk in Buenos Aires. Returning to Germany after three years in South America, Kaiser's ship smashed up against the coast of Africa. Sick with malaria, he was forced to travel through Spain and Italy on his way home. Like other young and alienated intellectuals of his generation, Kaiser took up the spiritually-heroic mantles of Schopenhauer and Nietzsche. Further discoveries of Georg Büchner and Frank Wedekind caused him to develop a life-long interest in the new drama. In fact, Kaiser's first works swung between Strindberg-like Naturalism and a kind of Neo-Romanticism, with plays set in the distant past, where self-sacrificing characters confronted their cowardly contemporaries.

Rejected from war duties because of his psychological instabilities, Kaiser had only seen two of his twenty-five completed plays mounted before 1917. But as the jingoism of the World War began to wind down, his pacific drama *The Citizens of Calais* was successfully mounted in Frankfurt. A few months later in April of 1917, *From Morn to Midnight*, written in 1912 and denied a Berlin premiere by the censors, was produced in Munich after the intervention of the Naturalist playwright Gerhardt Hauptmann. Divided into seven scenes, or stations, *From Morn to Midnight* featured the flight of a Bank Cashier, who unexpectedly embezzles 60,000 Marks. His "soul journey" takes him from a bourgeois existence into a world of high excitement and decadence, and then finally into utter disillusionment and suicide. The play proved so popular that it received ten major productions between 1917 and 1925 in Germany alone. It also was among the first Expressionist plays to be translated and staged in the non-German speaking countries.

Despite numerous publications, new productions, and even film rights to his works, Kaiser himself was under constant financial ruin; in 1920 and 1921, he served time in prison for embezzlement of funds. His defense that artists were above the law failed to move any of the Weimar magistrates. Between 1922 and 1938, over twenty new Kaiser plays and libretti were seen on the German stage. Elected to the Prussian Academy of Arts and Letters in 1926, Kaiser soon felt the wrath of the National Socialist revolution. His plays and operas were protested and disrupted and in 1933, all of his books publicly burned and his

Academy membership revoked. Threatened with arrest by the Gestapo, he fled Germany five years later. Unable to procure a visa to the United States because of his anti-fascist activities, he remained in Switzerland until his death in 1945.

CHARACTERS:

Bank Cashier
Mother
Wife
First and Second Daughters
Bank Manager
Clerk
Porter
Stout Gentleman
Muffled Gentleman
Messenger Boy
Serving Maid
Lady
Son
Waiter (*in hotel*)
Five Jewish Gentlemen
Four Female Masks
Waiter (*in cabaret*)
Gentlemen in Evening Dress
Salvation Lass
Officers and Soldiers (*of Salvation Army*)
Penitents
Crowd (*at Salvation Meeting*)
Policemen

SYNOPSIS OF SCENES:

I. Interior of a small bank
II. Writing-room of a hotel
III. Field deep in snow
IV. Parlor in cashier's house
V. Steward's box at a velodrome, during cycle races
VI. Private supper room in a cabaret
VII. Salvation Army hall

In a small town and a city, at the present time.

SCENE ONE

(*Interior of a provincial bank. On the left, pigeon-holes and a door inscribed Manager. Another door in the middle marked Strong Room. Entrance by swing-doors in the right background. At the right hand side is a cane sofa, and in front of it a small table with a water-bottle and glass. The Cashier at the counter and the Clerk at a desk, both writing. On the cane sofa sits a Stout Gentleman, wheezing. In front of the counter stands a Messenger Boy staring at the door, through which someone has just gone out. The Cashier raps on the counter. The Messenger Boy turns, hands in a check. The Cashier examines it, writes, takes a handful of silver from a drawer, counts it, pushes a small pile across the counter. The Messenger Boy sweeps the money into a linen bag.*)

STOUT GENTLEMAN: (*Rising.*) Now the big men take their turn. (*He pulls out a bag. Lady enters; expensive furs; rustle of silk. Stout Gentleman stops short.*)
LADY: (*Opens the swing door with difficulty and smiles involuntarily in his direction.*) At last! (*The Stout Gentleman makes a wry face. The Cashier taps the counter impatiently. The Lady looks at the Stout Gentleman.*)
STOUT GENTLEMAN: (*Giving place to her.*) The big men can wait. (*The Lady bows distantly, comes to the counter. The Cashier taps as before.*)
LADY: (*Opens her handbag, takes out a letter and hands it to Cashier. A letter of credit.*) Three thousand, please. (*The Cashier takes the envelope, turns it over, hands it back.*)
LADY: I beg your pardon. (*She pulls out the folded letter and offers it again. The Cashier turns it over, hands it back.*)
LADY: (*Unfolds the letter, handing it to him.*) Three thousand, please. (*The Cashier glances at it, puts it in front of the Clerk. The Clerk takes the letter, rises, goes out by the door inscribed Manager.*)
STOUT GENTLEMAN: (*Retiring to sofa.*) I can wait. The big men can always wait. (*The Cashier begins counting silver.*)
LADY: In notes, if you don't mind. (*The Cashier ignores her.*)
MANAGER: (*Youthful, plump, comes in with the letter in his hand.*) Who is—? (*He

stops short on seeing the Lady. The Clerk resumes work at his desk.)

STOUT GENTLEMAN: Ahem! Good morning.

MANAGER: (*Glancing at him.*) How goes it?

STOUT GENTLEMAN: (*Tapping his belly.*) Oh, it rolls along, you know.

MANAGER: (*Laughs shortly. Turning to Lady.*) I understand you want to draw on us?

LADY: Three thousand marks.

MANAGER: I would pay you three (*glancing at letter*) three thousand with pleasure, but—

LADY: Is anything wrong with the letter?

MANAGER: (*Suave, important.*) It's in the proper form. "Not exceeding twelve thousand"—quite correct (*spelling out the address*) b-a-n-c-o-

LADY: My bank in Florence assured me—

MANAGER: Your bank in Florence was quite in order.

LADY: Then I don't see why—

MANAGER: I suppose you applied for this letter?

LADY: Of course.

MANAGER: Twelve thousand payable at such places—

LADY: As I should visit on my journey.

MANAGER: And you gave them duplicates of your signature?

LADY: Certainly. To be sent to the banks mentioned in the list.

MANAGER: (*Consults letter.*) Ah! (*Looks up.*) We have received no letter of advice. (*The Stout Gentleman coughs; winks at the Manager.*)

LADY: That means I must wait until—

MANAGER: Well, we must have *something* to go upon! (*The Muffled Gentleman, in fur cap and shawl, comes in and takes his place at the counter. He darts angry glances at the Lady.*)

LADY: I was quite unprepared for this—

MANAGER: (*With a clumsy laugh.*) As you see, madam, we were also unprepared.

LADY: I need the money so badly— (*The Stout Gentleman laughs aloud.*)

MANAGER: There again we're in the same boat. (*The Stout Gentleman neighs with delight.*

MANAGER: (*Looking round for an audience.*) Take myself for instance—or these gentlemen here . . . (*To the impatient muffled customer.*) You're not half so busy as I am. But you see I can find time for the lady. (*Turning.*) Now, ma'am, what do you expect? Am I to pay you on your own word? (*The Stout Gentleman titters.*)

LADY: (*Quickly.*) I'm staying at the Elephant. (*The Stout Gentleman wheezes with laughter.*)

MANAGER: An excellent house. I generally lunch there.

LADY: Can the hotel people vouch for my—for my—?

MANAGER: Your character, madam? I hope so, indeed. (*The Stout Gentleman rocks with delight.*)

LADY: Of course I have luggage with me—

MANAGER: Would you like me to search your trunks?

LADY: I'm in the most unlucky position.

MANAGER: We can shake hands upon that. (*He returns the letter.*)

LADY: What do you advise me to do?

MANAGER: This is a snug little town of ours—in a charming neighborhood. The Elephant is a well-known house; you'll make pleasant acquaintances—the time will slip away, take my word for it.

LADY: I don't in the least mind passing a few days here.

MANAGER: Your fellow guests will be delighted.

LADY: But I happen to need the money urgently this morning!

MANAGER: (*To Stout Gentleman.*) Will anybody here go bail for a lady from abroad, who needs three thousand marks?

LADY: I couldn't dream of accepting that—I shall be in my room at the hotel. When the letter of advice arrives, will you please inform me at once by telephone?

MANAGER: Personally, madam, if you wish.

LADY: As you please, but as quickly as possible. (*She folds up the letter, replaces it in the envelope, and puts both into her handbag.*) I shall call again in any case this afternoon.

MANAGER: At your service. (*The Lady bows coldly, goes out. The Muffled Gentleman moves up to the counter, on which he leans, crackling his check impatiently. The Manager ignores him, looks merrily at the Stout Gentleman, who sniffs the air. The Manager laughs.*) All the fragrance of Italy, eh? Straight from the bottle. (*The Stout Gentleman fans himself with his hand.*) What do you say?

STOUT GENTLEMAN: (*Pours out water.*) Three thousand is not bad. (*Drinks.*) I guess three hundred would be gratefully received.

MANAGER: Perhaps you'd like to make an offer, at the Elephant?

STOUT GENTLEMAN: No use to us big fellows.

MANAGER: Our morals are protected by Nature, eh? (*The Muffled Gentleman raps impatiently on the counter.*)

MANAGER: (*Indifferently.*) Well? (*He takes the check, smooths it out and hands it to the Cashier. The Messenger Boy enters, stares after the departed Lady, then at the last speakers; finally stumbles over the Stout Gentleman on the sofa.*)

STOUT GENTLEMAN: (*Robbing him of his wallet.*) There, my boy, that's what comes of making eyes at pretty ladies! Now you've lost your wallet. (*The Messenger Boy looks shyly at him.*) What are you going to do about it? (*The Messenger Boy laughs. Stout Gentleman returns the wallet.*) Mark my words. You're not the first young fool whose eyes have run away with him—with the whole body rolling after? (*The Messenger Boy goes out. The Cashier has counted out some small silver.*)

MANAGER: And they trust money to young jackanapes like that! A born embezzler!

STOUT GENTLEMAN: The loser pays.

MANAGER: But employers can't see it, until one fine day the boy takes his chance. (*To Muffled Gentleman.*) Is anything wrong? (*The Muffled Gentleman examines every coin.*) That's a twenty-five pfennig piece. Forty-five pfennigs altogether; do you want any more? (*The Muffled Gentleman pockets his money with great ceremony; buttons his coat over the pocket.*)

STOUT GENTLEMAN: (*Ironically.*) You ought to patronize the strong room. (*Rising.*) Now the big men can unload a trifle. (*The Muffled Gentleman turns away from the counter and goes out.*)

MANAGER: (*To Stout Gentleman.*) Well, what's your little game?

STOUT GENTLEMAN: (*Sets his attaché case on the counter and takes out a pocket book.*) Is your confidence in the public shaken? (*He offers his hand.*)

MANAGER: (*Taking it.*) It's true we're not at home to pretty faces in business hours.

STOUT GENTLEMAN: (*Counting out his money.*) How old was she, would you say?

MANAGER: I haven't seen her yet without the paint.

STOUT GENTLEMAN: What's the woman doing in the town?

MANAGER: We shall hear that tonight at the Elephant.

STOUT GENTLEMAN: But who's the attraction?

MANAGER: All of us, perhaps.

STOUT GENTLEMAN: What can she want with three thousand, in this little place?

MANAGER: That's her affair. She wants it badly.

STOUT GENTLEMAN: I wish her luck. Let her pick it up if she can.

MANAGER: From me?

STOUT GENTLEMAN: That's her affair. (*They laugh.*)

MANAGER: I'm curious to see when that letter of advice from Florence will arrive.

STOUT GENTLEMAN: If it arrives!

MANAGER: Ah, if it arrives!

STOUT GENTLEMAN: We might take a collection for her benefit.

MANAGER: I dare say that's what she has in mind.

STOUT GENTLEMAN: Eh?

MANAGER: Perhaps you won a prize in the last lottery? (*They laugh.*)

STOUT GENTLEMAN: (*To Cashier.*) Take this little pile off my hands. (*To Manager.*) It's as well in your strong room as in my safe—not to mention the interest. Give me a credit note for the Building Society.

MANAGER: (*Sharply to Clerk.*) The Building Society credit note.

STOUT GENTLEMAN: Sixty thousand marks, then—in paper money. (*The Cashier begins counting.*)

MANAGER: (*After a pause.*) And how are things with you, on the whole?

STOUT GENTLEMAN: (*To Cashier, who pauses to examine a note.*) Yes, that one's patched.

MANAGER: We'll accept it, of course. We shall soon be rid of it. I'll reserve it for our fair client from Florence. She wore patches too.

STOUT GENTLEMAN: But behind these you find a thousand marks.

MANAGER: The face value.

STOUT GENTLEMAN: (*Laughing immoderately.*) The face value! That's good!

MANAGER: The face value! Here's your receipt. (*Choking with laughter.*) Sixty thousand —

STOUT GENTLEMAN: (*Takes it, reads.*) Sixty thou —

MANAGER: The face —

STOUT GENTLEMAN: Value. (*They shake hands.*)

MANAGER: (*In tears.*) We shall meet tonight.

STOUT GENTLEMAN: (*Nods.*) The face — the face value! (*He buttons his overcoat and goes out, laughing. The Manager wipes the tears from his pince-nez; then goes into the inner room. The Cashier fashions together the notes in bundles.*)

MANAGER: (*Returning.*) Well, what did you think of our Italian customer? You don't see a picture like that behind your counter every morning. Wrapped in furs, perfumed. (*Sniffs.*) She still hangs on the air, this lady. You breathe adventures. Italy casts a spell; there's magic in the name. But lift her veil, and you see the Riviera — Mentone — Nice — Monte Carlo! The land of orange-blossoms, the home of fraud! There the robber gangs make up their train. There the birds of prey cluster, and circle, and scatter. They prefer little towns — like ours, well off the beaten track. There they swoop down — rustling, frothing in furs and silk! Yes, women are the sirens of today; they sing of the South! One glance at them, and you're lost. Stripped bare down to your shirt, down to your naked, naked skin! (*He drums with a pencil on the Cashier's back.*) Depend upon it, this bank in Florence knows as much about the lady as the man in the moon. The whole affair is a swindle, carefully arranged. And the web was woven not in Florence, but in Monte Carlo. This was one of the gay parasites who spawn in the hotbed of the Casino. Mark my words, we shall never see her any more. The first attempt missed fire; she'll scarcely risk a second! Oh, you have to be pretty sharp in the banking business, I can tell you! You may be easy-going, you may have your little joke now and then, but you must keep both eyes wide open! Perhaps I might have given a nod to the superintendent of police. But after all, it's no concern of mine. The attempt failed; that's good enough. And banks are pledged to secrecy. (*At the door of his room.*) You might keep an eye on the papers — in the police-court columns, that's where we shall hear of our lady from Florence again! (*Exit. The Cashier seals up rolls of banknotes.*)

PORTER: (*Enters with letters, hands them to Clerk.*) One registered letter. I want the receipt. (*The Clerk stamps receipt form, hands it to Porter. The Porter rearranges glass and water-bottle on the table, and goes out. The Clerk takes letters into Manager's room, and returns.*)

LADY: (*Re-enters; comes quickly to the counter.*) I beg your pardon. (*The Cashier stretches out his hand, without looking at her. Louder.*) If you please! (*The Cashier raps on the counter.*) Please tell me—would it be possible for me to leave you the letter of credit for the whole sum, and to receive an advance of three thousand in part payment? (*The Cashier raps impatiently.*) I shall be willing to deposit my diamonds as security if required. Any jeweller in the town will value them for you.

(*The Lady takes off a glove and pulls at her bracelet. The Serving Maid comes in quickly, plumps down on sofa, and begins rummaging in her market-basket. The Lady, startled by the commotion, looks round. As she leans on the counter her hand sinks into the Cashier's. The Cashier bends over the hand which lies in his own. His spectacles glitter; his glance travels slowly upward from her wrist. The Serving Maid, with a sigh of relief, discovers the check she is looking for. The Lady nods kindly in her direction. The Serving Maid replaces vegetables, etc., in her basket. The Lady turns again to the counter, meets the eyes of the Cashier. The Cashier smiles at her.*)

LADY: (*Drawing back her hand.*) Of course I shall not ask the bank to do anything irregular. (*She puts the bracelet on her wrist; the clasp refuses to catch. Stretching out her arm to the Cashier.*) Would you be so kind? I'm clumsy with the left hand. (*The Cashier stares at her as if mesmerized. His spectacles, bright points of light, seem almost to be swallowed up in the cavity of his wide-open eyes.*)

LADY: (*To Serving Maid.*) You can help me, mademoiselle. (*The Serving Maid does so.*) Now the safety catch. (*With a little cry.*) Oh, that grips my arm! Ah, that's better. Thank you so much. (*She bows to the Cashier and goes out. The Serving Maid, coming to the counter, planks down her check. The Cashier takes it in trembling hands; the slip of paper flutters and crackles, he fumbles under the counter then counts out money.*)

SERVING MAID: (*Looking at the pile of money.*) Is all that mine? (*The Cashier writes. The Clerk becomes observant. The Serving Maid speaks to Clerk.*) But it's too much! (*The Clerk looks at Cashier. The Cashier rakes in part of the money.*) Still too much!(*The Cashier ignores her and continues writing. The Serving Maid, shaking her head, puts the money in her basket and goes out.*)

CASHIER: (*Hoarsely.*) Fetch me—glass—water! (*The Clerk hurries from behind the counter, comes to table.*) That's been standing. Fresh water, cold water from the tap! (*The Clerk hurries out with glass. The Cashier goes quickly to electric bell, and rings. the Porter enters from the hall.*) Get me fresh water.

PORTER: I'm not allowed to leave the door.

CASHIER: (*Hoarsely.*) Water. For me. Not those dregs there. Bring water from the tap. (*The Porter seizes water-bottle and hurries out. The Cashier quickly crams his pockets with bank notes. Then he takes his coat from a peg, throws it over his arm, and puts on his hat. He lifts a flap in the counter, passes through, and goes out.*)

MANAGER: (*Absorbed in reading a letter, enters from his room.*) Here's the letter of advice from Florence after all! (*The Clerk enters with a glass of water. The Porter enters with full water-bottle. The Manager looks up.*) What the devil—?

SCENE TWO

(*Writing room of a hotel. Glass door in background. On the left, desk with telephone. On the right, sofa and armchairs with table and newspapers. The Lady writes. The Son, in hat and cloak, enters carrying under his arm a large flat object wrapped in green baize.*)

LADY: (*With surprise.*) Have you brought it with you?

SON: Hush! The wine merchant is downstairs. The queer old chap thinks I shall rob him of his treasure.

LADY: But I thought this morning he was glad to get rid of it.

SON: And now he scents mischief everywhere.

LADY: You must have given yourself away.

SON: Perhaps I showed him I was pleased with the bargain.

LADY: (*Smiling.*) That would open the eyes of the blind!

SON: Believe me, they will be opened. But don't be afraid, Mamma, the price remains the same.

LADY: Is the man waiting for his money?

SON: We can let him wait.

LADY: But, my dear boy, I must tell you—

SON: (*Kissing her.*) Hush, Mamma. The hush of a great moment. You must only look when I give you the word. (*He takes off his hat and cloak, puts the picture on a chair and lifts the green baize covering.*)

LADY: Are you ready?

SON: (*In a low tone.*) Mamma. (*The Lady turns in her chair. The Son comes to her, puts his arm round her neck.*) Well?

LADY: That was surely never meant to hang in a wine shop?

SON: Its face was to the wall. On the back the old fellow had pasted his own photograph.

LADY: Was that included in the price?

SON: (*Laughs.*) Tell me, what do you think of it?

LADY: I find it—very naive.

SON: Delightful, isn't it? Marvelous!

LADY: Do you really think so highly of it as a painting?

SON: As a painting—Of course! But just look at the wonderful quality of the treatment. Epoch-making, simply. This handling of the subject—where can you find such a gift? In Pitti—Uffizi—the Vatican? Even the Louvre has hardly anything to compare with it. In this picture we have the one and only erotic vision—yes, vision—of the pair in the Garden of Eden. Here the apple has rolled away upon the grass—there the serpent still peeps from the magical leaves. You see that the drama is played on the green lawns of Paradise itself, and not in the desert of banishment. There's original sin for you—the real fall! Cranach painted dozens of Adams and Eves, standing on either side of the apple-bough. In them he says coldly, stiffly: they knew each other! But here he cries blithely, exultantly: they loved each other! Here he shows himself a master. (*In front of the picture.*) And yet mark the restraint in his ecstasy! This line of the manly arm which slants across the curving womanly hip. The horizontal, which never for a moment wearies the eye. This grouping and these tones bring love to life.—Don't you feel it to be so?

LADY: I find you as naive as your picture.

SON: What does that mean?

LADY: I beg you to put it away in your room.

SON: When we reach home perhaps I shall value it most. Florence and this masterpiece! Think of finding it here!

LADY: But you guessed almost to a certainty that it must be in the neighborhood.

SON: I'm dazed nevertheless to find myself right. Mamma, I'm one of Fortune's children.

LADY: This is only the reward of your own careful research.

SON: But how could I gain it without your help? Your goodness?

LADY: I find my happiness in yours.

SON: Your patience is endless. I tear you from your beautiful quiet life in Fiesole. Warm southern blood runs in your veins, but I drag you through Germany in mid-winter. You pass the night in sleeping-cars or second-rate hotels, you have to rub against all kinds of people—

LADY: (*Smiling.*) Yes, there you are certainly right!

SON: But now I promise you the work is nearly finished. I'm all impatience myself to bring the treasure home. Let's take the three o'clock train. Will you give me the three thousand marks?

LADY: I haven't them.

SON: But the owner is here, in the hotel.

LADY: The bank couldn't pay me. The letter of advice has somehow been delayed.

SON: I've promised him the money.

LADY: Then you must return the picture until the letter arrives.

SON: Can't we hurry it in any way?

LADY: I've written a telegram; here it is ready to send. You see we traveled so quickly that— (*The Waiter knocks at the door.*) Come in!

WAITER: A gentleman from the bank wishes to speak to the lady.

LADY: (*To Son.*) That will be the money, sent by hand. (*To Waiter.*) Show him in. (*The Waiter exits.*)

SON: You can call me when it's ready. I must keep an eye on the old man.

LADY: I shall ring you up.

SON: Then I'll wait downstairs. (*The Son leaves. The Lady closes her portfolio. The Waiter and the Cashier are seen behind the glass door. The Cashier overtakes the other, and opens. The Waiter turns and retires. The Cashier, cloak over arm, enters. The Lady points to a chair and seats herself on the sofa. The Cashier still holding his cloak seats himself.*)

LADY: I hope the bank— (*The Cashier sees the picture and starts violently.*) My visit to the bank was closely connected with this picture.

CASHIER: (*Staring.*) You!

LADY: Do you notice any similarities?

CASHIER: (*Smiling.*) In the wrist.

LADY: Are you a connoisseur?

CASHIER: I should like to be.

LADY: Do these pictures interest you?

CASHIER: I'm in the picture!

LADY: Are these others of the same school in private collections here? If so, can you find them for me? You would do me a great service—greater even than bringing me money.

CASHIER: I've brought the money.

LADY: I fear at this rate my letter of credit will soon be exhausted.

CASHIER: (*Producing a roll of banknotes.*) This will last longer!

LADY: I can only draw twelve thousand marks in all.

CASHIER: I have sixty thousand!

LADY: But—how did you—?

CASHIER: That's my business.

LADY: How am I to—?

CASHIER: We shall bolt.

LADY: Bolt? Where?

CASHIER: Abroad. Anywhere. Pack your trunk, if you've got one. You can start from the station. I'll take a car to the next stop and jump the train. We stay the first night in—give me a time-table! (*He finds it.*)

LADY: Have you brought more than three thousand from the bank?

CASHIER: (*Preoccupied with the time-table.*) I took sixty thousand.

LADY: And my share of that is—

CASHIER: (*Opens a roll of notes and counts them with professional skill, then lays a bundle of them on the table.*) Your share? Take this. Put it away. We may be noticed. The door has a glass panel. That's five hundred.

LADY: Five hundred?

CASHIER: More to come. All in good time. When we're in a safer place. Here we must be careful.—Cash received—Now let's be off. No time for love-making. The wheel spins. An arm outstretched will be caught in the spokes. (*He springs to his feet.*)

LADY: But I need three thousand marks.

CASHIER: If the police find them on you, it's all up!

LADY: What have the police to do with it?

CASHIER: You were in the bank. Your scent hung in the air. They'll suspect you; the link between us is as clear as daylight.

LADY: I went to your counter—

CASHIER: As cool as a cucumber—

LADY: I made a request—

CASHIER: An attempt.

LADY: I tried—

CASHIER: You tried it on. With your forged letter.

LADY: (*Taking a paper from her handbag.*) Is this letter not genuine?

CASHIER: As false as your diamonds.

LADY: I offered them as a pledge. Why should my pretty stones be paste?

CASHIER: Ladies of your complexion only dazzle.

LADY: What do you take me for? I'm dark, it's true: a southerner, a Tuscan.

CASHIER: From Monte Carlo!

LADY: (*Smiles.*) No, from Florence!

CASHIER: (*His glance lighting upon the son's hat and cloak.*) Ha! Have I come too late?

LADY: Too late?

SON: Where is he? I'll bargain with him; he'll be open to a deal. I have the ready money. How much shall I offer? How high do you put the indemnity? How much of this stuff shall I cram into his pockets? I'll go up to fifteen thousand. Is he asleep? Still rolling in bed? Where's your room? Twenty thousand—five thousand extra for instant withdrawal! (*Picking up hat and cloak.*) I'll take him his clothes.

LADY: (*In astonishment.*) The gentleman is sitting in the lounge.

CASHIER: Downstairs? Too risky; too many people down there. Call him up; I'll settle with him here. Ring for him; let the waiter hurry. Twenty thousand, cash down! (*He begins counting the money.*)

LADY: Can my son speak for me?

CASHIER: (*Bounding back.*) Your—son!!!

LADY: I'm traveling with him. He's collecting material for a book on the history of art.

CASHIER: (*Staring at her.*) Son?

LADY: Is that so dreadful?

CASHIER: But—but—this picture—

LADY: A lucky find of his. My son is buying it for three thousand marks; this was the amount I needed so urgently. The owner is a wine merchant whom you will know by name.

CASHIER: Furs . . . silk . . . you glistened and rustled. The air was heavy with your scent!

LADY: This is midwinter. As far as I know, my mode of dress is not exceptional.

CASHIER: The forged letter—

LADY: I was about to wire to my bank.

CASHIER: Your bare wrist—stretched out to me with the bracelet—

LADY: We're all clumsy with the left hand.

CASHIER: (*Dully to himself.*) And I—have taken the money—

LADY: (*Diverted.*) Will that satisfy you? If you want further proofs, my son is not unknown in the academic world.

CASHIER: Now—at this very moment—they've discovered everything! I called for water to get the clerk out of the way—and again for water to clear the porter from the door. The notes are gone; I'm missing. I mustn't show myself in the streets: the police are warned. Sixty thousand! I must slip away across the fields—through the snow—before the whole town is on my track!

LADY: (*Shocked.*) For Heaven's sake, stop!

CASHIER: I took the money. It was because you filled the bank. Your scent hung on the air. You glistened and rustled—you put your naked hand in mine—your breath came warm across the counter—warm—

LADY: (*Silencing him.*) Please!—I am a lady.

CASHIER: But now you must—

LADY: (*Controlling herself.*) Tell me, are you married? Yes? (*Violent gesture from Cashier.*) Ah, that makes a difference. You gave way to a foolish impulse. Listen. You can make good the loss. You can go back to your counter and plead a passing illness—a lapse of memory. I suppose you still have the full amount?

CASHIER: I've embezzled the money—

LADY: (*Abruptly.*) That really doesn't interest me.

CASHIER: I've robbed the bank.

LADY: You grow tedious, my dear sir.

CASHIER: And now you must—

LADY: Preposterous.

CASHIER: I've stolen for you. I've given myself into your hands, broken with the world, destroyed my livelihood. I've blown up every bridge behind me. I'm a thief and a criminal. (*Burying his face in his hands.*) Now you must—! After this you must!

LADY: (*Movement.*) I shall call my son. Perhaps he—

CASHIER: (*With a change of tone, springs nimbly to his feet.*) Aha! Call him, would you? Rouse the hotel, give the alarm? A fine plan! A clumsy trick. You don't catch me so easily. Not in that trap. I have my wits about me, ladies and gentlemen. Yours come fumbling afterwards, tapping like a blind man—but I'm always ahead of you. Don't stir. Sit where you are without a word, until I—(*he puts the money in his pocket*)—until I—(*he presses his hat over his eyes*)—until I—(*he wraps his coat closely about him*)—until I—(*Softly he opens the glass door and slips out. The Lady rises, stands motionless.*)

SON: (*Entering.*) The man from the bank has just gone out. You're looking worried, Mamma. Is the money—?

LADY: I found this interview trying. You know, my dear boy, how money matters get on my nerves.

SON: Is there some difficulty again about the payment?

LADY: I'm not thinking of that—

SON: But that's the chief question!

LADY: I think I ought to give information at once.

SON: What information?

LADY: Send this telegram to my bank. In future I must have proper documents that will satisfy everyone.

SON: Isn't your letter of credit good enough?

LADY: Not quite. Go to the post office for me. I prefer not to send the porter with an open wire.

SON: And when shall we have the three thousand marks? (*Telephone bell rings.*)

LADY: (*Recoils.*) They're ringing me up already. (*At the phone.*) Oh! The letter has arrived? And I am to call for the money myself? Very good. (*Change of tone.*) Not at all. Pray don't mention it. One is easily mistaken. Yes, of course. (*Change of tone.*) Florence is a long way off. And then the Italian post—I beg your pardon? Oh, via Paris; then one can easily understand . . . Not in the least. Thank you. In ten minutes. Goodbye. (*To Son.*) All settled, my dear boy. Never mind the telegram. (*She tears up the form.*) You shall have the picture. Call a cab, and put your wine merchant in it; he can drive with us and collect his money at the bank. Pack up your treasure. We go straight from the bank to the station. (*Telephoning while the Son wraps up the picture.*) The bill, please. Rooms 14 and 16. Yes, immediately. Please.

SCENE THREE

(*Aslant a field deep in snow, through a tangle of low-hanging branches, blue shadows are cast by the midday sun.*)

CASHIER: (*Comes backward, shoveling snow with his hands, and covering his footprints. He stands upright.*) How wonderful a toy is every man! The mechanism runs silently in his joints. Suddenly the faculties are touched and transformed into a gesture. What gave animation to these hands of mine? A moment ago they were straining to heave the masses that the drifting snowflakes had strewn! My footprints across the field are blotted out. With my own hands I have accomplished nothingness. (*Takes off his wet shirtcuffs.*) Frost and damp breed chills; fever comes unaware and works upon the mind. The mechanism creaks and falters; the control is lost; and once a man is thrown upon a sick bed, he's as good as done for. (*He unfastens his sleeve-links and throws the cuffs away.*) Soiled. There they lie. Missing in the wash. The mourners will cry through the kitchen: a pair of cuffs are lost! A catastrophe in the boiler! A world in chaos! (*He picks up the cuffs and thrusts them into his overcoat pocket.*) Queer. Now my wits begin to work again. I see with infallible clearness. I'm drudging here in a snowdrift, fooling with two bits of dirty linen. These are the gestures which betray a man. Hop-la! (*He swings into a comfortable seat in a forked bough.*) But I'm inquisitive. My appetite is whetted. My curiosity is hugely swollen. I feel that great discoveries lie before me. To-day's experiences open up the road. This morning I was still a trusted employee. Fortunes were passing through my hands: the building society made a big deposit. — At noon I'm a cunning scoundrel, an expert in embezzlement, a leaf in the wind, a cork on the water. Wonderful ac-complishment! — And but half the day gone by!

(*He props his chin on his clenched hand.*) I'll open my breast to Fate; all comers are welcome. I can prove that I'm free man. I'm on the march — there's no turning back, no falling out. No shuffling either — so out with your trumps! Ha! ha! I've put sixty thousand on a single card — it must be trumps. I'm playing too high to lose. Out with them — cards on the table — none of your sharping tricks — d'ye understand? (*He laughs hoarsely.*)

After this you must, pretty lady! Yes indeed, silken lady! Your cue, bright lady; you must play up to me, or the scene will fall flat. — Heavy! — Clumsy! And such gawks are called comedians! Pay your debts, perform your natural duties, breed children — and don't box the prompter's ears!

Ah, forgive me, you have a son? That alters the case completely. I withdraw all aspersions on your character. You are acquitted. Goodbye to you, and give my respects to the Manager. His bullock eyes will cover you with slime, but let that pass. He's been touched for sixty thousand; his roof leaks and rattles in the wind. The building society will mend it for him, never fear.

I release you, silken lady. I waive all claims; you're free, you can go. — Stop! Take my thanks with you on your journey. — What do you say? There's no occasion? Oh, but you're wrong! Not worth mentioning? Why, you're my sole creditor. I owe you my life! You think I exaggerate? — No, pretty lady. It's you who have loosened my creaking joints. In one stride behind you I have entered a land of miracles; with one leap I'm at the heart of the universe, the focus of unimagined brightness. And with this load in my breast-pocket I'm paying cash — cash down for everything! (*With a negligent gesture.*)

You can make yourself scarce; vanish, evaporate! You're outbid and outplayed. Your means are too limited. Remember that son of yours.

(*He pulls out his bundle of notes and slaps it on the palm of his hand.*) I'm pay-ing cash down! Here are my liquid assets; the buyer is waiting. What's for sale? (*Looking across the field.*) Snow. Sunlight. Stillness. (*He shakes his head and puts away the money.*) Blue snow is dear at the price; I won't encourage shameful profiteering. I decline the bargain. The proposition's not serious! (*Stretching his arms to heaven.*) But I must pay! I must spend! I have the ready money! Where are the goods I can buy for cash on the nail? For the whole sixty thousand — and the whole buyer thrown in, flesh and bone, body and soul! (*Crying out.*) Deal with me! Sell to me! I have the money, you have the goods; bring them together! (*The sun is overcast. He climbs out of the forked bough.*)

The earth is in labor—spring storms are threatening. It comes to pass, it comes to pass! I knew my cry would not be in vain. The call was pressing. Chaos is affronted, and shudders at this morning's monstrous deed.—Of course I know such cases can't be overlooked. It's down with your trousers, and a good hard whipping at the least! Pardon me, sir, to whom do I lift my hat so politely? (*His hat has been blown off by a sudden squall. Snowflakes, shaken from the branches, stick in the tree-top and form a skeleton with grinning jaws. A branching arm holds the lost hat.*)

Were you sitting all the while behind me, eavesdropper? What are you? A detective? Shall we say—one of Fate's policemen? Are you the staggering answer to my emphatic question? Does your rather well-ventilated appearance announce the final truth—that you are worn out? The information is scanty. Very scanty. It amounts in fact to nothing at all. I reject the argument as too elliptical. Your philosophy, my friend, is full of gaps. Your services are not required. You can shut your rag-and-bone shop. I'm not the first who has peeped into your window—and passed on!

My crime was remarkably simple, it's true; and you would skip the rest of the plot. You'd jump to the conclusion, would you? Ha, ha! But I prefer the complications. So good-day to you.

A soldier on the march can't halt on every doorstep not even at the warmest invitation. I see stretching ahead of me a host of calls to pay, before this evening. It's impossible that you should be the first. The last you may be; but even then, only the last resort. A miserable makeshift, a poor lodging at the journey's end. But as a last resort—well, we may come to terms. Ring me up again toward midnight. Ask the exchange for my number; it will change from hour to hour.—And excuse the coldness of my tone. We should be on a friendlier footing, I know. We are closely bound. I think even now one of your branches is sticking into my back. Free yourself from this tangle of undergrowth, my friend, and envelop me, make me one with you. You'll save me the labor of first covering my footprints. But first give me back my hat! (*He takes his hat from the branch, which is bent toward him by the wind. Bowing deeply.*)

I see we have come to a sort of understanding. That will do to begin with. Mutual trust will follow, and support us in the whirl of coming great events. You won't find me ungrateful. (*With a flourish.*) My very best respects—(*After a peal of thunder, a last gust of wind sweeps the snow from the tree. The sun comes out; all is bright as at the opening of the scene.*)

There, I said it would soon pass!

(*He puts on his hat, turns up his coat collar and strides away across the snow.*)

SCENE FOUR

(*Parlor in Cashier's house. In the window-boxes are blown geraniums. Two doors at right and left in the background. Table and chairs, piano. Mother (hard of hearing) sits near the window. First Daughter is embroidering at the table. Second Daughter is practising the overture to "Tannhäuser." Wife comes and goes in the background.*)

MOTHER: What's that you're playing?

FIRST DAUGHTER: Oh, Grandmamma! The overture to *Tannhäuser*.

MOTHER: *O Tannenbaum* is another pretty piece.

WIFE: (*Entering.*) It's time I began to grill the chops.

FIRST DAUGHTER: Oh, not yet, Mamma.

WIFE: No, it's not yet time to grill the chops. (*Goes out.*)

MOTHER: What are you embroidering there?

FIRST DAUGHTER: The carpet slippers, Grandmamma.

WIFE: (*Coming to Mother.*) Today we have mutton chops for dinner.

MOTHER: Have you begun grilling them?

WIFE: Plenty of time. It's not twelve o'clock yet.

FIRST DAUGHTER: Not nearly twelve, Mamma.

WIFE: No, not nearly twelve.

MOTHER: When he comes, it will be twelve.

WIFE: He's not due yet.

FIRST DAUGHTER: When Father comes, it will be twelve o'clock.

WIFE: Yes. (*Goes out.*)

SECOND DAUGHTER: (*Stops playing, listens.*) Is that Father?

FIRST DAUGHTER: (*Listens.*) Father?

WIFE: (*Enters.*) Is that my husband?

MOTHER: Is that my son? (*Cashier enters, hangs up hat and cloak.*) Where have you been?

CASHIER: In the graveyard.

MOTHER: Has somebody died suddenly?

CASHIER: (*Patting her on the back.*) You can have a sudden death, but not a sudden burial.

WIFE: Where have you come from?

CASHIER: Out of the grave. I burrowed through the clods with my forehead. See, here's a lump of ice. It was a big struggle to get through. Quite hard work. You notice I've dirtied my hands. You want long fingers to work your way through, for you lie there deep embedded. — In a lifetime they shovel lots of earth over you. They overturn mountains on your head — all the dustmen and scavengers — like a great rubbish-shoot. The dead men lie three yards under the soil, but the living are always being buried deeper, deeper down.

WIFE: You're frozen from head to foot.

CASHIER: Thawed. Shaken by storms, like the spring. The wind whistled and

and roared; it plucked the flesh from me, and my bones sat naked, knuckles and ribs—bleached in a twinkling. A rattling boneyard! At last the sun melted me together again; from the soles of my feet upward. And here I stand.

MOTHER: Did you say you had been out in the open air?

CASHIER: In deep dungeons, Mother! In bottomless pits beneath monstrous towers; deafened by clanking chains, blinded by darkness.

WIFE: The bank must be closed today. The manager's been drinking with you. Has there been a happy event in his family?

CASHIER: He has his eye on a new mistress. An Italian beauty, in silk and furs—from the land of orange-blossoms. Wrists like polished ivory. Black tresses—olive complexion. Diamonds. Real—all real.

Tus—tus—the rest sounds like Canaan. Fetch me an atlas. Tus—Canaan. Is that right? Is there an island of that name? A mountain? A swamp? Geography can tell us everything.

But he'll burn his fingers. He'll have a nasty fall. He'll be brushed away like a cinder. There he lies—sprawling on the carpet—legs in the air—our fat little manager!

WIFE: Is the bank still open?

CASHIER: Always, wife. Prisons are never closed. The procession of customers is endless. One at a time they hop through the open door, like sheep into a shambles. Inside they stand closely wedged together. There's no escaping, unless you make a saucy jump over all the backs!

MOTHER: Your coat's torn.

CASHIER: And look at my hat! A tramp would never own it.

SECOND DAUGHTER: The lining's all tattered.

CASHIER: Feel in my pockets. Left—right. (*First and Second Daughter pull out cuffs.*) Well?

DAUGHTERS: Your cuffs.

CASHIER: But no sleeve-links. I took them out. A triumph of coolness. Hat and coat were bound to go in tatters in those leaps from back to back. The other beasts grab at you, clutch you with their horny feet. Silence in the pen! Order in the fold! Equal rights for all! But one jump for dear life, and you're out of the sweating, jostling crowd. One bold stroke—and here I am. Behind me nothing and before me—what? (*He looks around him. The Wife stares at him.*)

MOTHER: (*Half whispering.*) He's ill. (*The Wife goes quickly toward the door on the right.*)

CASHIER: (*Stops her. To one of the Daughters.*) Fetch my jacket. (*To the other.*) My slippers. (*To the first.*) My cap. (*To the other.*) My pipe. (*All are brought.*)

MOTHER: You oughtn't to smoke, when you've already been—

WIFE: (*Motioning her to be silent.*) Shall I give you a light?

CASHIER: (*In jacket, slippers, and embroidered skull-cap, with pipe in hand, seats himself comfortably at the table.)* Light up!

WIFE: (*Anxiously.*) Does it draw?

CASHIER: (*Looking into pipe.*) I shall have to send it for a thorough cleaning. There must be some bits of stale tobacco in the stem. I oughtn't to have to pull so hard.

WIFE: Shall I take it now?

CASHIER: No, leave it. (*Blowing great smoke-clouds.*) It draws after a fashion. (*To Second Daughter.*) Play something. (*Second Daughter, at a sign from her Mother, sits at piano and plays.*) What piece is that?

SECOND DAUGHTER: Overture to *Tannhäuser*.

CASHIER: (*Nods approval. To First Daughter.*) Are you sewing or darning?

FIRST DAUGHTER: Working your carpet-slippers, Papa.

CASHIER: Good. And you, Grandma?

MOTHER: (*Feeling the universal dread.*) I was just—just having forty winks.

CASHIER: Forty winks. In peace and quiet.

MOTHER: Yes, my life is quiet now.

CASHIER: (*To Wife.*) And you, wife?

WIFE: I was going to grill the chops.

CASHIER: (*Nodding.*) The cook.

WIFE: I'll grill yours now. (*Goes out.*)

CASHIER: (*Nodding as before.*) The cook. (*To First Daughter.*) Open wide the doors. (*First Daughter opens doors in background; on the right the Wife is seen busily employed at her kitchen range, on the left is a bedroom with twin beds.*)

WIFE: (*In the kitchen doorway.*) Are you too warm in there? (*She returns to her task.*)

CASHIER: (*Looking round him.*) Grandmother nodding in an armchair. Daughters: one busy with embroidery, the other playing the piano. Wife at cooking-range. Build four walls about this scene, and you have a family life.—Comfortable, cosy, contented. Mother—son—grandchildren under one roof. The magic of familiar things—the household spell. Let it work. Parlor with table and hanging lamp. Window with geraniums. Piano, music stool. Hearth—home fires burning. Kitchen, daily bread. Chops for dinner. Bedroom, four-poster—in—out. The magic of familiar things. Then one day—on your back, stiff and white. The table pushed back against the wall—cake and wine. In the middle a slanting yellow coffin—screw like, adjustable stand. A band of crepe hangs round the lamp—the piano stands untouched for a year— (*The Second Daughter stops playing and runs sobbing into the kitchen.*)

WIFE: (*On the threshold.*) She's still practicing the new piece.

MOTHER: Why doesn't she try something simpler?

WIFE: (*As the Cashier knocks out his pipe and begins putting on his hat and overcoat.*) Are you going to the bank? Have you an appointment there?

CASHIER: Not at the bank.

WIFE: Then where must you go?

CASHIER: Where must I go? That's a hard question, wife. I've climbed down from windswept trees to look for an answer. This was my first call. It was bound to be the first. Warm and cosy, this nest of yours; I won't deny its good points; but it doesn't stand the final test. No! The answer is clear. This is not a halting-place, but a signpost; the road leads further on. (*He is now fully dressed.*)

WIFE: (*Distraught.*) Husband, how wild you look!

CASHIER: Like a tramp, as I told you. Never mind. Better a ragged wayfarer than an empty road!

WIFE: But it's just dinner time.

CASHIER: I smell mutton chops.

MOTHER: And you're going out, just before a meal!

CASHIER: Full stomach, drowsy wits. (*The Mother beats the air suddenly with her arms, and falls senseless.*)

FIRST DAUGHTER: Grandmamma—

SECOND DAUGHTER: (*From the kitchen.*) Grandmamma! (*Both fall on their knees beside her. The Wife stands motionless.*)

CASHIER: (*Going to Mother's chair.*) She dies because a man goes out of the house before a meal. (*He brushes the Daughters aside and regards the body.*) Grief? Mourning? Overflowing tears? Are the bonds drawn too close for these? Mother and son! Are they so tightly knit that the very pain is clenched, the very suffering numbed, when they are torn apart? (*He pulls the roll of banknotes out of his pocket and weighs it in his hand, then shakes his head and puts the money away.*) Pain brings no paralysis. The eyes are dry, but the mind runs on. There's no time to lose, if my day is to be well spent. We must take the road. (*He lays his well-worn purse on the table.*) Provide for yourselves. There's money honestly earned. That may be worth remembering. Do your best with it. (*He goes out on the right. The Wife stands motionless. The Daughters bend over the dead Mother.*)

MANAGER: (*Coming through the open doorway.*) Is your husband at home? Has your husband been here? I have to bring you the painful news that he has absconded. We missed him some hours ago; since then we have been into his books. The sum involved is sixty thousand marks deposited by the Building Society. So far I've refrained from making the matter public, in the hope that he would come to his senses and return. This is my last attempt. You see I've made a personal call. Has your husband been here? (*He looks round him, and observes jacket, pipe, etc.*) It looks as though— (*His glance lights upon the group at the window. He nods.*) I see that affairs have already reached an advanced stage. In that case— (*He shrugs his shoulders, puts on his hat.*) It remains only to express my private sympathy, you can rely on that. The rest must take its course. (*He leaves.*)

DAUGHTERS: (*Coming to Wife.*) Mother—

WIFE: (*Savagely.*) Don't screech in my ears! Don't stand gaping at me! Who are you? What do you want? Ugly brats, monkey-faces—What have you to do with me? (*Breaking down.*) My husband has left me! (*The Daughters stand shyly, holding hands.*)

SCENE FIVE

(*Velodrome during a cycle race meeting. Arc lamps. Jewish gentlemen, stewards come and go. They are all alike; little animated figures in dinner jackets, with silk hats tilted back and binoculars slung in leather cases. Whistling, cat-calls, and a restless hum from the crowded tiers of spectators. Music. In the background, a wooden bridge or raised platform.*)

FIRST GENTLEMAN: (*Entering.*) Is everything ready?

SECOND GENTLEMAN: See for yourself.

FIRST GENTLEMAN: (*Looking through glasses.*) The palms—

SECOND GENTLEMAN: What's the matter with the palms?

FIRST GENTLEMAN: I thought as much!

SECOND GENTLEMAN: But what's wrong with them?

FIRST GENTLEMAN: Who arranged them like that?

THIRD GENTLEMAN: Perfect madness!

SECOND GENTLEMAN: Upon my soul, you're right!

FIRST GENTLEMAN: Was nobody responsible for arranging them?

THIRD GENTLEMAN: Ridiculous. Simply ridiculous.

FIRST GENTLEMAN: Whoever it was, he's as blind as a bat!

THIRD GENTLEMAN: Or fast asleep.

SECOND GENTLEMAN: Asleep, you say? But this is only the fourth night of the race.

FIRST GENTLEMAN: The palm-tubs must be pushed on one side.

SECOND GENTLEMAN: Shall I give the order?

FIRST GENTLEMAN: Right against the wall. There must be a clear view of the course.

THIRD GENTLEMAN: And of the royal box.

SECOND GENTLEMAN: I'll come with you. (*They all go out. (The Fourth Gentleman enters, fires a pistol shot, then withdraws. The Fifth Gentleman enters with a red lacquered megaphone.*)

THIRD GENTLEMAN: How much is the prize?

FIFTH GENTLEMAN: Eighty marks. Fifty to the winner, thirty to the second.

FIRST GENTLEMAN: (*Re-enters.*) Three times round, no more. We're tiring them out.

FOURTH GENTLEMAN: (*Through megaphone.*) A prize is offered of eighty marks for the next race. The winner to receive fifty marks, the second thirty marks. (*Applause. The Second and Third Gentlemen return, one carrying a red flag.*)

FIRST GENTLEMAN: Now we can get them off.

SECOND GENTLEMAN: Not yet. Number seven has a new mount.

FIRST GENTLEMAN: Off!

(*The Second Gentleman lowers his red flag, then goes out. The race begins. Rising and falling volume of applause, with silent intervals.*)

THIRD GENTLEMAN: The one on the left moves well.

FOURTH GENTLEMAN: The other's only waiting his chance.

FIFTH GENTLEMAN: We shall see some sport presently.

THIRD GENTLEMAN: The riders are pretty excited.

FOURTH GENTLEMAN: And no wonder.

FIFTH GENTLEMAN: Depend upon it, the championship will be settled tonight.

THIRD GENTLEMAN: The Americans are still fresh.

FIFTH GENTLEMAN: Our lads will hustle them.

FOURTH GENTLEMAN: Let's hope our visitor will see a popular victory.

FIRST GENTLEMAN: (*Looking through glasses.*) The box is still empty. (*Outburst of applause.*)

THIRD GENTLEMAN: The result!

VOICE: Prizes in cash—fifty marks No. 11, thirty marks for No. 4. (*The Second Gentleman enters with Cashier. The latter is in evening clothes, with silk hat, patent shoes, gloves, cloak, his beard trimmed, his hair carefully brushed.*)

CASHIER: Just explain the idea of the thing—

SECOND GENTLEMAN: I'll introduce you to the stewards.

CASHIER: My name is of no concern of anybody's.

SECOND GENTLEMAN: But you have a right to be introduced to the management.

CASHIER: I prefer to remain incognito.

SECOND GENTLEMAN: You're a good sportsman.

CASHIER: I know nothing about it. What are they doing down there? I can see a round track with a bright moving line, like a snake. Here and there one joins in; another falls out. Why is that?

SECOND GENTLEMAN: The riders race in pairs. While one partner is pedaling—

CASHIER: The other sleeps?

SECOND GENTLEMAN: He undergoes massage.

CASHIER: And you call that a relay race?

SECOND GENTLEMAN: Certainly.

CASHIER: It might as well be called a relay rest.

FIRST GENTLEMAN: (*Approaching.*) Ahem! The enclosure is reserved for the management.

SECOND GENTLEMAN: This gentleman offers a prize of a thousand marks.

FIRST GENTLEMAN: (*Change of tone.*) Allow me to introduce myself.

CASHIER: On no account.

SECOND GENTLEMAN: The gentleman wishes to preserve his incognito.

CASHIER: Impenetrably.

SECOND GENTLEMAN: I was just explaining the sport to him.

CASHIER: Yes, don't you find it funny?

FIRST GENTLEMAN: How do you mean?

CASHIER: Why, this relay rest.

FOURTH GENTLEMAN: A prize of a thousand marks then. For how many circuits of the course?

CASHIER: As many as you please.

FOURTH GENTLEMAN: How much shall we allot to the winner?

CASHIER: That's your affair.

FOURTH GENTLEMAN: Eight hundred and two hundred. (*Through the megaphone.*) An anonymous gentleman offers the following prizes for a race of ten circuits; eight hundred marks to the winner, two hundred marks to the second; one thousand marks in all. (*Loud applause.*)

SECOND GENTLEMAN: But tell me, if the sport only tickles you, why do you offer such a big prize?

CASHIER: Because it works like magic.

SECOND GENTLEMAN: On the pace of the riders, you mean?

CASHIER: Rubbish.

THIRD GENTLEMAN: (*Entering.*) Are you the gentleman who is offering a thousand marks?

CASHIER: In five mark notes.

SECOND GENTLEMAN: That would take too long to count.

CASHIER: Watch me. (*He pulls out a roll of banknotes, slips off the elastic band, moistens his finger and counts rapidly.*) That's one bundle the less.

SECOND GENTLEMAN: I see you're an expert.

CASHIER: A mere detail, sir. (*Handing him the money.*) Accept delivery.

SECOND GENTLEMAN: With acknowledgements.

FIFTH GENTLEMAN: (*Approaching.*) Where is the gentleman? Allow me to introduce—

CASHIER: Certainly not.

THIRD GENTLEMAN: (*With red flag.*) I shall give the start. (*General movement to the platform.*)

FIFTH GENTLEMAN: Now we shall see a tussle for the championship.

THIRD GENTLEMAN: (*Joining group.*) All the cracks are in the race.

FOURTH GENTLEMAN: Off! (*Outburst of applause.*)

CASHIER: (*Taking First and Second Gentlemen by the collars and turning them round.*) Now I'll answer your question for you. Look up!

SECOND GENTLEMAN: But you must keep your eye on the track, and watch the varying course of the struggle—

CASHIER: Childish, this sport. One rider must win because the others lose— Look up, I say! It's there, among the crowd, that the magic works. The wine ferments in this vast barrel of spectators. The frothing is least at the bottom, among the well-bred public in the stalls. There you see nothing but looks—but what looks! Round stares. Eyes of cattle!—One row higher the bodies sway and vibrate, the limbs begin to dance. A few cries are heard. Your respectable middle class!—Higher still all veils are dropped. A wild fanatic shout, a bellowing nakedness, a gallery of passions!—Just look at that group! Five times entwined; five heads dancing on one shoulder, five pairs of arms beating time across one howling breast! At the heart of this monster is a single man. He's being crushed—mangled—thrust over the parapet! His hat, crumpled, falls through the rising smoke—flutters into the middle balcony, lights upon a lady's bosom. She pays no heed. There it rests daintily—so daintily! She'll never notice the hat; she'll go to bed with it; year in, year out, she'll carry this hat upon her breast! (*The applause swells.*)

FIRST GENTLEMAN: The Dutchman is putting on a spurt.

CASHIER: The middle row joins in the shout. An alliance has been made; the hat has done the trick. The lady crushes it against the rails. Pretty lady, your bosom will show the marks of this! There's no help for it. Madness to struggle. The throng presses you against the rails, and you must yield. You must grant all!—

SECOND GENTLEMAN: Do you know the lady?

CASHIER: See now, the five up there have thrust their one over the balustrade. He swings free, he loosens his hold, he drops, he sails down into the stalls. What has become of him? Vanished! Swallowed, stifled, absorbed! A raindrop in a maelstrom!

FIRST GENTLEMAN: The Hamburger is making up ground.

CASHIER: The stalls are frantic. The falling man has set up contact. Restraint can go to the devil! Dinner-jackets quiver. Shirt fronts begin to split. Studs fly in all directions. Lips are parted, jaws are rattling. Above and below—all distinctions are lost. One universal yell from every tier. Pandemonium. Climax.

SECOND GENTLEMAN: (*Turning.*) He wins! He wins! The German wins! What do you say to that?

CASHIER: Stuff and nonsense!

SECOND GENTLEMAN: A marvelous spurt!

CASHIER: Marvelous trash!

FIRST GENTLEMAN: (*About to leave.*) We'll just make certain.

CASHIER: (*Holding him back.*) Have you any doubts about it?

SECOND GENTLEMAN: The German was leading, but—

CASHIER: Never mind that, if you please. (*Pointing to the audience.*) Up there you have the staggering fact. Watch the supreme effort, the last dizzy height of accomplishment. From stalls to gallery one seething flux, dissolving the individual, recreating—passion! Differences melt away, veils of nakedness are stripped; passion rules!—Look from this window, it's a sight worth seeing.—Gates and barriers vanish in smoke. The trumpets blare and the walls come tumbling down. No restraint, no modesty, no motherhood, no childhood—nothing but passion! There's the real thing. That's worth the search. That justifies the price!

THIRD GENTLEMAN: (*Entering.*) The ambulance column is working splendidly.

CASHIER: Is the man hurt who fell?

THIRD GENTLEMAN: Crushed flat.

CASHIER: There must be dead, where many live in fever.

FOURTH GENTLEMAN: (*Through megaphone.*) Result: eight hundred marks won by No. 2; two hundred marks by No. 1. (*Wild applause.*)

FIFTH GENTLEMAN: The riders are tired out.

SECOND GENTLEMAN: You could see the pace dropping.

THIRD GENTLEMAN: They need rest.

CASHIER: I've another prize to offer.

FIRST GENTLEMAN: Presently, sir.

CASHIER: No interruptions, no delays.

SECOND GENTLEMAN: We must give the riders a chance to recover.

CASHIER: Bah! Don't talk to me of those fools! Look at the public, blazing with excitement. This power mustn't be wasted. We'll feed the flames; you shall see them leap into the sky. I offer fifty thousand marks.

SECOND GENTLEMAN: Are you serious?

THIRD GENTLEMAN: How much did you say?

CASHIER: Fifty thousand! Everything.

THIRD GENTLEMAN: It's an unheard-of sum—

CASHIER: The effect will be unheard-of. Warn your ambulance men on every floor.

FIRST GENTLEMAN: We accept your offer. The contest shall begin as soon as the box is occupied.

SECOND GENTLEMAN: Capital idea!

THIRD GENTLEMAN: Excellent!

FOURTH GENTLEMAN: This is a profitable visitor.

FIFTH GENTLEMAN: (*Digging him in the ribs.*) A paying guest.

CASHIER: (*To First Gentleman.*) What do you mean—as soon as the box is occupied.

FIRST GENTLEMAN: We'll talk over the conditions in the committee room. I suggest thirty thousand to the winner; fifteen thousand to the second; five thousand to the third.

THIRD GENTLEMAN: (*Gloomily.*) Downright waste, I call it.

FIFTH GENTLEMAN: The sport's ruined for good and all.

FIRST GENTLEMAN: Directly the box is occupied.

(*All go out leaving Cashier alone. Enter Salvation Lass. Laughter and cat-calls from some spectators.*)

SALVATION LASS: The War Cry; ten pfennigs, sir.

CASHIER: Presently, presently.

SALVATION LASS: The War Cry, sir.

CASHIER: You're too late. Here the battle's in full swing.

SALVATION LASS: (*Shaking tin box.*) Ten pfennings, sir.

CASHIER: Will you start a war for ten pfennings?

SALVATION LASS: Ten pfennings, sir.

CASHIER: I'm paying a war-bill of fifty thousand marks.

SALVATION LASS: Ten pfennings.

CASHIER: Yours is a wretched scuffle. I only subscribe to pitched battles.

SALVATION LASS: Ten pfennings.

CASHIER: I've only bank notes on me.

SALVATION LASS: Ten pfennings.

CASHIER: Bank—

SALVATION LASS: Ten—

CASHIER: (*Seizing megaphone, bellows at her through it.*) Banknotes! Banknotes!! (*Salvation Lass goes out. Handclapping and hoarse laughter from the spectators. Many gentlemen enter.*)

FOURTH GENTLEMAN: Would you care to announce your offer yourself?

CASHIER: No, I'm a spectator. (*Handing him the megaphone.*) You shall speak. You shall communicate the final shock.

FOURTH GENTLEMAN: (*Through the megaphone.*) A new prize is offered by the same anonymous gentleman. (*Cries of "Bravo!"*) The total sum is fifty thousand marks. (*Deafening applause.*) Five thousand marks to the third. Fifteen thousand to the second. The winner to receive thirty thousand marks. (*Ecstasy.*)

CASHIER: (*Stands apart, nodding his head.*) There we have it. The pinnacle. The summit. The climbing hope fulfilled. The roar of a spring gale. The breaking wave of a human tide. All bonds are burst. Up with the veils—down with the shams! Humanity—free humanity, high and low, untroubled by class, unfettered by manners. Unclean, but free. That's a reward for my imprudence. (*Pulling out a bundle of notes.*) I can pay with a good heart! (*Sudden silence. The gentlemen have taken off their silk hats and stand with bowed heads.*)

FOURTH GENTLEMAN: (*Coming to Cashier.*) If you'll hand me the money, we can have the race for your prize immediately.

CASHIER: What's the meaning of this?

FOURTH GENTLEMAN: Of what, my dear sir?

CASHIER: Of this sudden unnatural silence everywhere?

FOURTH GENTLEMAN: Unnatural? Not at all. His Royal Highness has just entered his box.

CASHIER: Highness—the royal box—the house full—

FOURTH GENTLEMAN: Your generous patronage comes at the most opportune moment—

CASHIER: Thank you! I don't intend to waste my money.

FOURTH GENTLEMAN: What do you mean?

CASHIER: I find the sum too large—as a subscription to the Society of Hunchbacks!

FOURTH GENTLEMAN: But pray explain—

CASHIER: This glowing fire extinguished—trodden out by the patent-leather boot of his Highness! You take me for crazy, if you think I will throw one single penny under the snouts of these grovelling dogs, these crooked lackeys! A kick where the bend is greatest, that's the prize they'll get from me!

FOURTH GENTLEMAN: But the prize has been announced. His Royal Highness is in his box. The audience is showing a proper respect. What do you mean?

CASHIER: If you don't understand my words, let deeds speak for me! (*With a violent blow he crushes the other's silk hat down upon his shoulders. Leaves. There is a prevailing silence and heads are bowed respectfully.*)

SCENE SIX

(*Private supper room in a cabaret. Darkness, with a lighted doorway. Subdued dance music. A Waiter opens the door, and switches on red shaded lamps. The Cashier enters, evening clothes, coat, silk muffler, gold-headed bamboo cane.*)

WAITER: Will this room suit you, sir?

CASHIER: Well enough. (*The Waiter takes his coat, etc. The Cashier turns his back and looks into a mirror.*)

WAITER: How many places shall I lay, sir?

CASHIER: Twenty-four. I'm expecting my grandma, my mamma, my wife and several aunts. The supper is to celebrate my daughter's confirmation. (*The Waiter stares at him. The Cashier speaks to the other's reflection in the mirror.*) Donkey! Two places! Else why do you furnish these discreet little cabins with a sofa and a dim red light?

WAITER: What brand would you prefer?

CASHIER: Leave that to me, my oily friend. I shall know which flower to pluck in the ballroom—round or slender, a bud or a full-blown rose. I shall not require your invaluable services. No doubt they are invaluable—or have you a fixed tariff?

WAITER: What brand of champagne, if you please?

CASHIER: Ahem! Grand Marnier.

WAITER: That's a liqueur, sir.

CASHIER: Then I leave it to you.

WAITER: Two bottles of Pommery—extra dry. (*Producing menu card.*) And for supper?

CASHIER: Pinnacles.

WAITER: Oeufs pochés Bergère? Poulét grillé? Steak de veau truffé? Parfait de foie gras en croute? Salade coeur de laitue?

CASHIER: Pinnacles, pinnacles from the soup to the savoury.

WAITER: Pardon?

CASHIER: (*Tapping him on the nose.*) A pinnacle is the point of perfection — the summit of a work of art. So it must be with your pots and pans. The last word in delicacy. The menu of menus. Fit to garnish great events. It's your affair, my friend; I'm not the cook.

WAITER: (*Sets a large menu-card on the table.*) It will be served in twenty minutes. (*He rearranges glasses, etc. Heads with silken masks peep through the doorway.*)

CASHIER: (*Sees them in the mirror. Shaking a warning finger at them.*) Wait my mother! Presently I shall have you in the lamplight! (*The masks vanish, giggling. The Waiter hangs a notice RESERVED on the outside of the door, then withdraws and closes it behind him.*)

CASHIER: (*Pushes back his silk hat, takes out a gold cigarette case, strikes a match, sings.*) "Tor-ea-dor, Tor-ea-dor." Queer, how this stuff comes to your lips. A man's mind must be cram full of it — cram full. Everything. Toreador — Carmen — Caruso. I read all this somewhere — it stuck in my head. There it lies, piled up like a snowdrift. At this very moment I could give a history of the Baghdad railway. And how the Crown Prince of Rumania married the Czar's second daughter Tatjana. Well, well, let them marry. The people need princes. (*Sings.*) "Tat-tat-ja-na, tat-ja-na —" (*Twirling his cane, he goes out. The Waiter enters with bottles on ice. Uncorks them, pours out wine. Leaves. The Cashier re-enters, driving before him a female Mask in a harlequin's red and yellow quartered costume.*) Fly, moth! Fly, moth!

FIRST MASK: (*Running round the table.*) Fizz! (*She drinks both of the filled glasses, and throws herself on the sofa.*) Fizz!

CASHIER: (*Pouring out more wine.*) Liquid powder. Load your painted body.

FIRST MASK: (*Drinking.*) Fizz!

CASHIER: Battery mounted, action front.

FIRST MASK: Fizz!

CASHIER: (*Putting aside the bottles.*) Loaded. (*Coming to sofa.*) Ready to fire. (*The First Mask leans drunkenly toward him. The Cashier shakes her limp arm.*) Look brighter, moth. (*The First Mask does not respond.*) You're dizzy, my bright butterfly. You've been licking the prickly yellow honey. Open your wings, enfold me, cover me up. I'm an outlaw; give me a hiding-place; open your wings.

FIRST MASK: (*With a hiccup.*) Fizz.

CASHIER: No, my bird of paradise. You have your full load.

FIRST MASK: Fizz.

CASHIER: Not another drop, or you'll be tipsy. Then what would you be worth?

FIRST MASK: Fizz.

CASHIER: How much are you worth? What have you to offer?

FIRST MASK: Fizz.

CASHIER: I gave you that. But what can you give me? (*The First Mask falls asleep.*) Ha! You'd sleep here, would you? Little wag! But I've no time for the joke; I find it too tedious. (*He rises, fills a glass of wine and throws it in her face.*) Good morning to you! The cocks are crowing!

FIRST MASK: (*Leaping to her feet.*) Swine!

CASHIER: A quaint name. Unfortunately I'm traveling incognito, and can't respond to the introduction. And so, my mask of the well-known snoutish family—get off my sofa!

FIRST MASK: I'll make you pay for this!

CASHIER: I've paid already. It was cheap at the price. (*The First Mask goes out. The Cashier drinks champagne, also goes out. The Waiter enters with caviar; collects empty glasses. Exits. The Cashier enters with two black Masks.*)

SECOND MASK: (*Slamming the door.*) Reserved!

THIRD MASK: (*At the table.*) Caviar!

SECOND MASK: (*Running to her.*) Caviar?

CASHIER: Black as your masks. Black as yourselves. Eat it up; gobble it, cram it down your throats. (*Seating himself between them.*) Speak caviar. Sing wine. I've no use for your brains. (*He pours out champagne and fills their plates.*) Not one word shall you utter. Not a syllable, not an exclamation. You shall be dumb as the fish that strewed this black spawn upon the Black Sea. You can giggle, you can bleat, but don't talk to me. You've nothing to say. You've nothing to shed but your finery. Be careful; I've made one clearance already! (*The Masks look at one another, sniggering. The Cashier takes Second Mask by the arm.*) What color are your eyes? Green—yellow? (*Turning to Third Mask.*) And yours? Blue—red? A play of glances through the eye-holes. That promises well. Come, I'll offer a beauty prize! (*The Masks laugh. The Cashier speaks to Second Mask.*) You're the pretty one. You struggle hard, but wait! Presently I'll rip up your curtain and look at the play! (*Second Mask breaks away from him. The Cashier speaks to Third Mask.*) You have something to hide. Modesty's your lure. You dropped in here by chance. You were roving in search of adventure. Well, here's your adventurer! Off with your mask! (*Third Mask slips away from him.*) Is this the goal? I sit here trembling. You've stirred my blood. Now let me pay. (*He pulls out a bundle of notes and divides it between them.*) Pretty mask, this for your beauty. Pretty mask, this for your beauty. (*Holding his hand before his eyes.*) One-two-three! (*The Masks lift their dominoes. The Cashier looks at them, laughs hoarsely.*) Cover them—cover them up! (*He runs round the table.*) Monsters—horrors! Out with you this minute—this very second or I'll— (*He lifts his cane.*)

SECOND MASK: But you told us—

THIRD MASK: You wanted us—

CASHIER: I want to get at you! (*The Masks run out. The Cashier shakes himself, drinks champagne.*) Sluts! (*He leaves. The Waiter enters with fresh bottles. He leaves. The Cashier kicks the door open and enters dancing with Fourth Mask, a Pierrette in a domino cloak reaching to her shoes. He leaves her standing in the middle of the room and throws himself on the sofa.*) Dance! (*The Fourth Mask stands still.*) Dance! Spin your bag of bones. Dance, dance! Brains are nothing. Beauty doesn't count. Dancing's the thing, twisting, whirling! Dance, dance, dance! (*The Fourth Mask comes halting to the table. The Cashier waves her away.*) No interval, no interruptions. Dance! (*The Fourth Mask stands motionless.*) Why don't you leap up in the air? Have you never heard of Dervishes? Dancing-men. Men while they dance, corpses when they cease. Death and dancing—signposts on the road of life. And between them— (*The Salvation Lass enter.*) Hallelujah!

SALVATION LASS: The War Cry.

CASHIER: I know—ten pfennigs. (*Salvation Lass holds out her box.*) When do you expect me to jump into your box?

SALVATION LASS: The War Cry.

CASHIER: I suppose you do expect it?

SALVATION LASS: Ten pfennigs.

CASHIER: So you mean to stick to my coat-tails, do you? (*The Salvation Lass shakes her box.*) Very good, then— (*To Mask.*) Dance! (*The Salvation Lass goes out. The Fourth Mask comes to sofa.*) Why were you sitting in a corner of the ballroom, instead of dancing in the middle of the floor? That made me look at you. All the others went whirling by, and you were motionless. Why do you wear a long cloak, when they are dressed like slender boys?

FOURTH MASK: I don't dance.

CASHIER: You don't dance like the others.

FOURTH MASK: I can't dance.

CASHIER: Not to music, perhaps; not keeping time. You're right; that's too slow. But you can do other dances. You hide something under your cloak—your own particular spring, not to be cramped by steps and measures! You have a nimbler leap. (*Pushing everything off the table.*) Here's your stage. Jump on to it. A boundless riot in this narrow circle. Jump now. One bound from the carpet. One effortless leap—on the springs that are rooted in your joints. Jump. Put spurs to your heels. Arch your knees. Let your dress float free, over the dancing limbs!

FOURTH MASK: (*Nestling closer to him on the sofa.*) I can't dance.

CASHIER: You lash my curiosity. Do you know what price I can pay? (*Showing her a roll of banknotes.*) All that!

FOURTH MASK: (*Takes his hand and passes it down her leg.*) You see—I can't.

CASHIER: (*Leaping to his feet.*) A wooden leg! (*He seizes the champagne cooler and upsets it over her.*) I'll water it for you! We'll make the buds sprout!

FOURTH MASK: Now you shall be taught a lesson!

CASHIER: I'm out to learn!

FOURTH MASK: Just wait! (*Goes out. The Cashier leaves. Puts a banknote on the table, takes cloak and stick. Guests in evening dress enter.)*

FIRST GUEST: Where is the fellow?

SECOND GUEST: We should like a closer look at him.

FIRST GUEST: A blackguard who entices away our girls—

SECOND GUEST: Stuffs them with caviar—

THIRD GUEST: Drenches them in champagne—

SECOND GUEST: And then insults them!

FIRST GUEST: We'll find out his price—

SECOND GUEST: Where is he?

THIRD GUEST: Given us the slip!

SECOND GUEST: Vamoosed!

FIRST GUEST: He smelt trouble!

SECOND GUEST: The place was too hot for him.

THIRD GUEST: (*Finding the banknote.*) A thousand mark note!

SECOND GUEST: Good God!

FIRST GUEST: He must stink of money.

SECOND GUEST: That's to pay the bill.

THIRD GUEST: He's bolted. We'll do a vanishing trick too. (*He pockets the money.*)

FIRST GUEST: That's the indemnity for our girls.

SECOND GUEST: Now let's give *them* the slip.

THIRD GUEST: They're all drunk.

FIRST GUEST: They'll only dirty our shirt-fronts for us.

SECOND GUEST: Let's go out on the tiles.

THIRD GUEST: Bravo! While the money lasts! Look out, here comes the waiter! (*The Waiter enters with full tray, halts dismayed.*)

FIRST GUEST: Are you looking for anyone?

SECOND GUEST: You might serve him under the table. (*Laughter.*)

WAITER: (*In an outburst.*) The champagne—the supper—the private room— nothing paid for. Five bottles of Pommery, two portions of caviar, two special suppers—I have to stand for everything. I've a wife and children. I've been four months out of a place, on account of a weak chest.— You won't see me ruined, gentlemen?

THIRD GUEST: What has your chest to do with us? We all have wives and children.

SECOND GUEST: Did *we* bilk you? What next?

FIRST GUEST: But what is this place? Where are we? It seems to be a common swindlers' den. And you lure customers into such a house! We're respectable people who pay for our drinks. (*To others.*) What do you say?

THIRD GUEST: (*After changing the doorkey to the outer side.*) Look on the floor there. You'll find our bill too! (*He gives the Waiter, who turns round, a push which sends him sprawling. The Waiter staggers, falls. The Gentlemen all go out. The Waiter rises, runs to the door, finds it locked. Beating his fists on the panels.*)

Let me out! You needn't pay me! I'm going into the river!

SCENE SEVEN

(*The Salvation Army hall, seen in depth. The background is formed by a yellow curtain embroidered with a black Cross, the height of a man. In front of this stands the low platform, in which are the penitent form, on the right, and the band—trombones and kettledrums—on the left. In the body of the hall, the benches are crowded. A great hanging lamp, with a tangle of wires for electric lighting, is above the audience. In the foreground, on the right, is the entrance. Music. From a corner, applause and laughter centering in one man. Salvation Lass goes to this corner and sits near the disturber. She takes his hand in hers and whispers to him.*)

VOICE: (*From the further side.*) Move up closer. Be careful, Bill! Ha, ha! Move up there! (*Salvation Lass goes to the speaker, a young workman.*)

WORKMAN: What are you after? (*Salvation Lass looks at him, shaking her head gravely. Merriment.*)

OFFICER: (*Woman of thirty, coming on to the platform.*) I've a question to ask you all.

SOME: (*Cry "Hush," or whistle for silence.*)

OTHERS: Speech—None of your jaw! Music!—The band!

VOICE: Begin!

VOICE: Stop!

OFFICER: Tell me—why are you sitting crowded there?

VOICE: Why not?

OFFICER: You're packed like herrings in a barrel. You're fighting for places—shoving one another off the forms. Yet one bench stands empty.

VOICE: Nothing doing!

OFFICER: Why do you sit squeezing and crowding there? Can't you see it's a nasty habit? Who knows his next-door neighbor? You rub shoulders with him, you press your knees against his, and for all you know he may be ill. You look into his face—and perhaps his mind is full of murderous thoughts. I know there are sick men and criminals in this hall. So I give you warning! Mind your next-door neighbor! Beware of him! Those benches groan under sick men and criminals!

VOICE: Next to me?

VOICE: Or me?

OFFICER: I give you this word of advice: steer clear of your neighbor! In this asphalt city, disease and crime are everywhere. Which of you is without a scab? Your skin may be smooth and white, but your looks give you away. You have no eyes to see, but your eyes are wide open to betray you. You haven't escaped the great plague; the germs are too powerful. You've been sitting too long near bad neighbors. —Come up here, come away from those benches, if you would not be as your neighbors are in this city of asphalt. This is the last warning. Repent. Repent. Come up here, come to the penitent form. Come to the penitent form, come to the penitent form! (*Music; trombones and kettledrums. The Salvation Lass leads in the Cashier. The Cashier, in evening dress, arouses some notice. The Salvation Lass finds Cashier a place among the crowd, seats herself next to him and explains the procedure. The Cashier looks around him, amused. The music ceases. Ironical applause.*)

OFFICER: (*Coming forward again.*) One of our comrades will tell you how he found his way to the penitent form. (*The First Soldier, a young man, steps on to the platform.*)

VOICE: So that's the mug! (*Some laughter.*)

FIRST SOLDIER: I want to tell you of my sin. I led a life without giving a thought to my soul. I cared only for my body. I built up my body like a strong high wall; the soul was quite hidden behind it. I sought for glory with my body, and made broader the shadow in which my soul withered away. My sin was sport. I practiced it without a moment's pause for reflection. I became a professional cyclist. I was vain of the quickness of my feet on the pedals, and the strength of my arms on the handle-bars; I forgot everything in the applause of the spectators. I sent out many a challenge; I won many a prize. My name was printed on every hoarding; my portrait was in all the papers. I was in the running for the world championship . . . At last my soul spoke to me. Its patience was ended. I met with an accident. The injury was not fatal. My soul wanted to leave me with time for repentance. My soul left me strength enough to rise from those benches where you sit, and to climb up here to the penitent form. There my soul could speak in peace. What it told me I can't tell you now. It's all too wonderful, and my words are too weak to describe it. You must come yourselves, and hear the voice speak within you! (*He steps down. A Man laughs obscenely. Several cry "Hush."*)

SALVATION LASS: (*To Cashier, in a low voice.*) Do you hear him?

CASHIER: Let me alone.

OFFICER: (*Coming forward.*) You've heard our comrade's testimony. Can anything nobler be won than a soul? And it's quite easy, for the soul is there within you. You've only to give it peace—once, just once. The soul wants to sit with you for one quiet hour. Its favorite seat is on this form. There must be one among you who sinned like our comrade here. Our comrade will help him. The way has been opened up. So come. Come to the penitent form. Come to the penitent form. Come to the penitent form! (*Silence. The First Penitent, of powerful build, with one arm in a sling, rises in a corner of the hall and makes his way through the crowd, smiling nervously. He mounts the platform. The Man laughs obscenely.*)

ANOTHER: (*Indignantly.*) Where is that dirty lout? (*The Man rises abashed, and makes his way toward the door.*)

OTHERS: That's the fellow! (*The Salvation Lass hurries to Soldier and leads him *back to his place.*)

VOICE: (*Facetiously.*) Oh, let me go, Angelina!

SEVERAL OTHERS: Bravo!

FIRST PENITENT: (*On the platform.*) In this city of asphalt there's a hall. Inside the hall is a cycle-track. This was my sin. I was a rider too. I was a starter in the relay races. On the second night I met with a collision. I was thrown; my arm was broken. The race goes hurrying on, but I am at rest. I have time to reflect in peace. All my life I have been riding hard without a thought. I want to think of everything. (*Loudly.*) I want to think of my sins at the penitent form! (*Led by a soldier, he sinks on to the bench; Soldier remains at his side.*)

OFFICER: A soul has been won! (*Music. Soldiers throughout the hall stand up and exult with outstretched arms. Music ceases.*)

SALVATION LASS: (*To Cashier.*) Do you see him?

CASHIER: The cycle races.

SALVATION LASS: What are you muttering?

CASHIER: That's my affair. My affair.

SALVATION LASS: Are you ready?

CASHIER: Hold your tongue.

OFFICER: (*Stepping forward.*) Another comrade will testify. (*A Man hisses.*)

OTHERS: Be quiet there!

SECOND SOLDIER: (*Girl, mounts the platform.*) Whose sin is my sin? I'll tell you of my sin without shame. I had a wretched home, if you could call it a home. The man drank—he was not my father. The woman—who was my mother—went with smart gentlemen. She gave me all the money I wanted; her bully gave me all the blows—I didn't want. (*Laughter.*) No one thought of me; least of all did I think of myself. So I became a lost woman. I was blind in those days, I couldn't see that the miserable life at home was only meant to make me think of my soul and dedicate myself to its salvation. One night I learned the truth. I had a gentleman with me, and he asked me to darken the room. I turned out the gas, though I wasn't used to such ways. Presently I understood why he had asked me; for there was a deformity at my side. Then horror took hold of me. I began to hate my body; it was only my soul that I could love. And now this soul of mine is my delight. It's so perfect, so beautiful; it's the bonniest thing I know.—I know too much of it to tell you here. If you ask your souls they'll tell you all—all! (*She steps down. Silence.*)

OFFICER: (*Coming forward.*) You've heard our sister testify. Her soul offered itself to her, and she did not refuse. Now she tells you her story with joyful lips. Isn't a soul offering itself now, at this moment, to one of you? Let it come closer. Let it speak; here on this bench it will be undisturbed. Come to the penitent form. Come to the penitent form! (*There is a movement in the hall. Some turn round.*)

SECOND PENITENT: (*Elderly prostitute begins to speak as she comes forward.*) What do you think of me, ladies and gentlemen? I was just tired to death of street-walking, and dropped in here for a rest. I'm not shy—oh dear no! Take a good look at me, from tip to toe; it's your last chance; enjoy the treat while you can! It's quite all right; never mind me; I'm not a bit shy; look me up and down.—Thank you, my soul's not for disposal. I've never sold that. You could offer me as much as you pleased, but my soul was always my own.—I'm obliged to you for your compliments, ladies and gentlemen. You won't run up against me in the streets again. I've not a minute to spare for you. My soul leaves me no peace. (*She has taken off her hat. A Soldier leads her to the penitent form.*)

OFFICER: A soul has been won! (*Music. Jubliation of the Soldiers.*)

SALVATION LASS: (*To Cashier.*) Do you hear all?

CASHIER: That's my affair. My affair.

SALVATION LASS: What are you muttering about?

CASHIER: The wooden leg.

SALVATION LASS: Are you ready?

CASHIER: Not yet. Not yet.

A MAN: (*Standing upright in the middle of the hall.*) Tell me my sin! I want to hear my sin!

OFFICER: (*Coming forward.*) Our comrade here will tell you.

VOICES: (*Excitedly.*) Sit down! Keep quiet! Give him a chance!

THIRD SOLDIER: (*Elderly man.*) Let me tell you my story. It's an everyday story; and that's how it came to be my sin. I had a snug home, a contented family, a comfortable job. Everything was just—everyday. In the evening, when I sat smoking my pipe at the table, under the lamp, with my wife and children round about me, I felt satisfied enough. I never felt the need of a change. Yet the change came. I forget what started it; perhaps I never knew. The soul knocks quietly at your door. It knows the right hour and uses it.—However that might be, I couldn't pass the warning by. I stood out at first in a sluggish sort of way, but the soul was stronger. More and more I felt its power. All my born days I'd been set upon satisfaction; now I knew that nothing could satisfy me fully but the soul. I don't look for contentment any longer at the table under the lamp, with a pipe in my mouth; I find it here alone at the penitent form. That's my everyday story. (*He stands down.*)

OFFICER: (*Coming forward.*) Our comrade has told you—

THIRD PENITENT: (*Elbowing his way up.*) My sin! My sin! (*From the platform.*) I'm the father of a family. I have two daughters. I have a wife. My mother is still with us. We live in four rooms. It's quite snug and cozy in our house. One of my daughters plays the piano, the other does embroideries. My wife cooks. My old mother waters the geraniums in the window-boxes. It's cozy in our house. Coziness itself. It's fine in our house—it's grand—first-rate—it's a model—a pattern of a home— (*With a change of voice.*) Our house is loathsome—horrible—mean—paltry through and through! It stinks of paltriness in every room; with the piano-playing, the cooking, the embroidery,

the watering-pots—(*Breaking out.*) I have a soul! I have a soul! I have a soul!
(*He stumbles to the penitent form.*)

OFFICER: A soul has been won! (*Jubilant music. Loud uproar in the hall.*)

MANY: (*Standing upright, clambering on benches, and stretching out their hands.*)
What's my sin? My sin? I want to know my sin! Tell me my sin!

OFFICER: (*Coming forward.*) Our comrade will tell you. (*Deep silence.*)

SALVATION LASS: (*To Cashier.*) Do you see him?

CASHIER: My daughters. My wife. My mother.

SALVATION LASS: What do you keep mumbling in your beard?

CASHIER: My affair. My affair.

SALVATION LASS: Are you ready?

CASHIER: Not yet. Not yet. Not yet.

FOURTH SOLDIER: (*Middle-aged, comes forward.*) My soul had a hard struggle to
win the victory. It had to take me by the throat and shake me like a rat. It
was rougher still with me. It sent me to jail. I'd stolen the money that was entrusted to me. I'd absconded with a big sum. They caught me; I was tried and
sentenced. In my prison cell I found the rest my soul had been looking for.
At last it could speak to me in peace. At last I could hear its voice. Those
days in the lonely cell became the happiest in my life. When my time was
finished I couldn't part from my soul. I looked for a quiet place where we two
could meet. I found it here on the penitent form; I find it here still, each
evening that I feel the need of a happy hour! (*He stands aside.*)

OFFICER: (*Coming forward.*) Our comrade has told you of his happy hours at
the penitent form. Who is there among you who wants to escape from this
sin? Here he will find peace! Come to the penitent form!

ALL: (*Standing up, shouting and gesticulating.*) Nobody's sin! That's nobody's sin! I
want to hear mine! My sin! My sin!

CASHIER: My sin!

SALVATION LASS: (*Above the uproar.*) What are you shouting?

CASHIER: The bank. The money.

SALVATION LASS: (*Shaking him.*) Are you ready?

CASHIER: Yes, now I'm ready!

SALVATION LASS: (*Taking his arm.*) I'll lead you up there. I'll stand by you—
always at your side. (*Turning to the crowd, ecstatically.*) A soul is going to
speak. I looked for this soul. I found this soul! (*The tumult ebbs into a quiet
hum.*)

CASHIER: (*On the platform, Salvation Lass by his side.*) I've been on the road since
this morning. I was driven out on this search. There was no chance of turning back. The earth gave way behind me; all bridges were broken. I had to
march forward on a road that led me here.

I won't weary you with the halting-places that wearied me. None of them
were worth my break with the old life; none of them repaid me. I marched
on with a searching eye, a sure touch, a clear head. I passed them all by,

stage after stage; they dwindled and vanished in the distance. It wasn't this, it wasn't that, or the next—or the fourth, or the fifth!

What is the goal, what is the prize, that's worth the whole stake? This hall, humming with crowded benches, ringing with melody! This hall! Here, from stool to stool, the spirit thunders fulfillment! Here glow the twin crucibles: confession and repentance! Molten and free from dross, the soul stands like a glittering tower, strong and bright!

You cry fulfillment from those benches. I'll tell you my story.

SALVATION LASS: Speak, I'm with you. I'll stand by you.

CASHIER: I've been all day on the road. I confess: I'm a bank cashier; I embezzled the money that was entrusted to me. A good round sum, sixty thousand marks! I fled with it into your city of asphalt. By this time they're surely on my track; perhaps they've offered a big reward. I'm not hiding any more. I confess! You can buy nothing worth having, even with all the money of all the banks in the world. You get less than you pay, every time. The more you spend, the less the goods are worth. The money corrupts them; the money veils the truth. Money's the meanest of the paltry swindles in this world! (*Pulling rolls of banknotes out of his breast pocket.*) This hall is a burning oven; it glows with your contempt for all mean things. I throw the money to you; it shall be torn and stamped underfoot! So much less deceit in the world! So much trash consumed! I'll go through your benches and give myself up to the first policeman; after confession comes atonement. So the cup is filled!

(*With gloved hands he scatters banknotes broadcast into the hall. The money flutters down; all hands are stretched upward; a scrimmage ensues. The crowd is tangled into a fighting skein. Musicians, instruments in hand, leap from the platform; benches are overturned, blows of fisticuffs resound above the shouting. At last the cramped mass rolls to the door and out into the street. The Salvation Lass, who has taken no part in the struggle, stands alone among the overturned benches.*)

CASHIER: (*Smiling at her.*) You are standing by me. You are with me still! (*Picking up an abandoned kettledrum and a pair of sticks.*) On we go. (*Roll of drums.*) The crowd behind us. The yelping pack outrun. A stretch of emptiness. Elbow room! Breathing-space! (*Drumtaps.*) A maid remains—standing upright, standing fast! (*Drumtaps.*) A man and a maid. The old garden is reopened. The clouds are rolled back. A voice cries from the silent treetops. All's well. (*Drumtaps.*) Maiden and man—eternal constancy. Maiden and man—fullness in the void. Maiden and man—the beginning and the end. Maiden and man—the seed and the flower. Maiden and man—sense and aim and goal! (*Rapid drumtaps, then a long roll. The Salvation Lass draws back to the door and slips out. The Cashier beats a tattoo.*)

SALVATION LASS: (*Throws the door open. To Policeman.*) There he is! I've shown him to you! I've earned the reward!

CASHIER: (*Letting fall the drumsticks in the middle of a beat.*) Here I am. Up here. There's only room for one.—Loneliness gives breathing-space. Coldness brings sunshine. The body burns in fever, freezes in fever too. A desert in green fields. Ice in the growing roots.—Who would escape? Where is the door?

POLICEMAN: Is this the only entrance? (*The Salvation Lass nods. The Cashier feels in his pocket.*) He's got a hand in his pocket. Switch off that light. We're a target for him! (*The Salvation Lass obeys. All the lights of the hanging lamp are put out, except one. This illuminates the tangle of wires, forming a skeleton in outline.*)

CASHIER: (*Feeling with his left hand in his breast pocket, grasps with his right a trumpet, and blows a fanfare toward the lamp.*) Found! I overtake you, my pursuer! My huntsman, you're run to earth! (*Fanfare.*) This morning, among the snowy boughs, I mocked at you. Now, in that tangled wire, you are welcomed as an old friend! (*Fanfare.*) I salute you! (*Fanfare.*) The road is behind me. The last steep curves climb upward—to you. My forces are spent. I've spared myself nothing! (*Fanfare.*) I've made the path hard where it might have been easy. I took the longest way round. Your short cut would have simplified the journey. This morning, when we sat on one branch together, you should have been more pressing in your invitation. How many hours of drudgery that would have saved! How easy it would have been just to sit there with you, in the snow-laden tree! (*Fanfare.*) Why did I climb down? Why did I take the road? Where does it lead me now? (*Fanfare.*) From first to last you sit there, naked as a bone. From morning to midnight I run raging in a circle—and now your beckoning arm shows me the way—whither? (*He shoots the answer into his breast. The trumpet-note dies on his lips.*)

POLICEMAN: Switch the light on.

(*The Salvation Lass does so. The Cashier has fallen back with arms outstretched against the Cross on the back wall. His husky gasp is like an Ecce, his heavy sigh is like a Homo. One second later all the lamps explode with a loud report.*)

POLICEMAN: There must be a short circuit in the main. (*All is in darkness.*)

END

Ithaka

[1914]

Gottfried Benn

Translation by J. M. Ritchie

Not usually thought of as a playwright, although he wrote many short plays and dramatic sketches, Gottfried Benn (1886-1956) represents a complicated and "black" side of literary Expressionism. Cynical and rebellious to friends and foe alike, Benn has been frequently compared to Louis-Ferdinand Céline and th post-war French Existentialists. His early support for the Nazis and "their transformation of values," added to his attack on fellow Expressionists in exile, could be seen as one more "against the grain" feature of his radical personality. Still he was the very opposite of an opportunist. In 1945, Benn refused to take part in the de-Nazification program instituted by the victorious Allies although he was among the first German intellectuals to desert Nazi culture in the halcyon year of 1935. Both decisions brought about material hardship but for Benn certain artistic and psychological needs had to be served first, no matter what the cost.

The son of a minister and a Romanisch-speaking woman from Switzerland, Benn studied theology and philosophy before turning to medicine and army service. Already writing poetry in his off-hours, he was forced to leave the military because of a kidney disorder in 1912. A specialist in skin and venereal diseases, Benn immediately set up practice in the poorhouses, sanatoriums, and brothels of Berlin. His poems, written in the after-hours, were among the most graphic and indelicate ever penned in German: the gold-encrusted molar of a nameless and dead whore; the specific smell of rotting bodies in a cancer ward; the drowned peasant girl, in whose breasts a nest of rats live, were all central images for his Expressionist poetry. Even the bright red color of a poppy only reminded Benn of death and menstrual blood.

During the First World War, Benn served as a medical officer in a Belgian brothel. It was here that his nihilistic writings blossomed. His alter ego character, Rönne, appeared over and over. In one prose piece, when Rönne is greeted on the street, he becomes thoroughly stunned. What is the correct reply to "How are you?" For Rönne, as for Benn, it was both a petty and cosmic question; Rönne's brain cannot fix an adequate response, so he just walks on. In Berlin after the war, Benn's writings began to find a wide readership. Curiously, his greatest literary support was from left-wing Expressionists and Jews, the very groups that Benn's Nazi comrades would persecute and destroy in the coming decades.

Although the Nazis welcomed Benn's support in the early thirties, for them Expressionism—even his kind—was a decadent, Bolshevik-Jewish invention. By 1935, it became clear to Benn that the cultural cleansing the National Socialists had promised was nothing more than a return to the bourgeois values of the eighteenth and nineteenth centuries. He retired to army life and once again passed the war period as a physician. Only in the last years before his death in 1956 was Benn again honored as a great German poet and intellectual.

CHARACTERS:

Albrecht, a professor of pathology
Dr. Rönne, his assistant
Medical students
Kautski, a student
Lutz, a student

(*In the professor's laboratory. At the end of a course. The professor and medical students.*)

PROFESSOR: And now, gentlemen, to the special surprise I have saved for you as a final treat. As you see here, having stained pyramidal cells from the cornu ammonis in the left hemisphere of the cervical cortex of a fourteen day rat of a special strain, what do we find—they are stained not red but pink with a tinge of brownish violet, just verging on green. A most fascinating observation. You are aware that not long ago the Graz Institute brought out a paper disputing this, notwithstanding the detailed nature of my own investigations on this subject. Far be it from me to make any general comment on the Graz Institute, but I must say that the paper in question struck me as immature in the extreme. And now, as you see, I have the proof here in front of me. The possibilities this opens up are quite staggering. One would be able to tell rats with long black hair and dark eyes from those with short rough hair and light eyes by the additional means of this sensitive color-index, given that the rats are similar in age, fed on candy-sugar, that they play for half an hour daily with a puma kitten and defecate spontaneously twice nightly at a body temperature of 37-36°C. Naturally, the fact that similar phenomena have also been observed under other conditions must not be ignored, but even so this observation seems to me worth publishing in full—indeed, I would almost regard it as a new step towards the understanding of the vast complex of forces which control the universe. And so, good evening, gentlemen, good evening.

LUTZ: And supposing, Professor, that one does examine this preparation carefully, can one say anything more than: I see, so this is not red, but pink, tinged with brownish violet, verging on green?

PROFESSOR: Gentlemen, please! In the first place there is the three volume encyclopedia by Meyer and Müller on the staining of rats' brains. As a first step one would have to go through that.

LUTZ: And supposing that was done, would it be possible to draw any conclusions? To come up with practical consequences?

PROFESSOR: Conclusions! My good man, we are not Thomas Aquinas, ha ha ha! Have you never heard of the new age of conditionalism which has dawned for our science? We established the conditions in which something happens. We vary the conditions which make certain changes possible. Theology is a different case entirely.

LUTZ: And supposing one day your whole student audience got to its feet and bellowed at you that it would prefer mysticism of the blackest hue to the dusty creakings of your mental acrobatics, suppose they sent you flying from the rostrum with a kick in the backside, what would you say to that? (*Enter Dr. Rönne.*)

RÖNNE: Here is your book on the perforation of the peritoneum in infants. I have no interest whatsoever in describing the state of an abdominal cavity as found on autopsy to an audience of people I do not know, already trained in what to expect. And my brain revolts at this game, this wish to destroy, to break up the simple, self-contained naivete of an individual case.

PROFESSOR: Your reasons are foolish in the extreme, but as you wish, give it to me. There are plenty other gentlemen interested in the paper. If you were rather less short-sighted than you seem to be in my opinion, you would understand that it's not a question of this individual case. On the contrary, with every particular examination the systematization of all knowledge, the organization of experience—in a word, science itself is at stake.

RÖNNE: Science had its rightful place two hundred years ago when it could prove God's wisdom from the perfection of organs and the extent of His intelligence and goodness from the mouths of locusts. But in two hundred years from now, Professor, will it not seem just as ludicrous that you spend three years of your life establishing whether the stain to be used on a particular type of fat is osmium or Nile blue.

PROFESSOR: I have not the slightest intention of discussing general principles with you. You do not wish to do this piece of work. Right, I shall give you another one.

RÖNNE: Nor do I wish to describe the result of the catheterization of Frau Schmidt's uterus—whether the intestinal coils passed through the gap in question in the sixth or the eighth month. Nor to tell them how much the diaphragm of a drowned man was distended next morning. The collection, the systematization of knowledge—is the most puerile brainwork imaginable! For a century now you have been encouraging the stupidity of the population to the point where the plebs will gawk in respectful silence at any old B.F. who knows how to work an incubation chamber, but in so doing you have yet to come up with as much as a grain of thought of less than total banality. Get one lot hatched after another; keep your thoughts on the navel and don't forget the placenta—that's all you can think of—you bunch of moles and ape-brains—you make me spew, the lot of you!

LUTZ: What are you really doing? Now and again you grab up a fact, so-called. In the first place it's been discovered already, but not published, by a colleague ten years ago. Another ten years and it'll all be in the dustbin. And what do you really know? That earthworms don't need knives and forks and ferns don't get sores on their backsides. That's the extent of your achievements. Is there anything else you know?

PROFESSOR: In the first place, it is completely beneath my dignity to reply to the tone of your remarks.

LUTZ: Dignity? Whose dignity? Who are you? Go on, answer.

PROFESSOR: I'll frame my reply to suit the occasion. Right, gentlemen, you talk disparagingly about theories, that's no concern of mine. But in a subject of such eminently practical implications, you must admit that serum and salvarsan are not just speculation?

LUTZ: Are you trying to argue that what you're working for is to let Frau Meier do her daily shopping for two months longer or to let Krause, the chauffeur, carry on at the wheel for another two months? Anyway, if that is what you enjoy, the fight to keep these nobodies alive, you carry on. And just to forestall you, Professor, don't bring up the argument about the universal human drive. There are whole civilizations where the people lie in the sand all day playing bamboo flutes.

PROFESSOR: And humane values? Saving a child's life for its mother or a breadwinner's for his family? The gratitude shining in their eyes.

RÖNNE: Let it shine, Professor! Infant mortality and every other kind are as much a part of life as winter is of the year. Don't let us reduce life to trivialities.

LUTZ: Anyway these practical aspects are of very superficial interest. The question which we want to hear answered is this: where do you get the courage to introduce youth to a science which you know to be incapable of any greater insight than a confession of its own ignorance? Just because it suits your shit-like lump of a brain to work out the statistics of bowel-blockages when you're not hard at it fucking? What kind of brains do you think you've got in front of you?

PROFESSOR: . . .

RÖNNE: . . . O.K.! O.K.! The commanding heights of the intellect! A thousand years of optics and chemistry! O.K.! O.K.! There are not so many color-blind people in the world, so you have a certain advantage. But let me tell you, I've stomached your lies till they make me sick—if you dare to come out with them just once more I shall strangle you with my own hands. I've chewed the whole cosmos to pieces inside my head. I've sat and thought till I slavered at the mouth. I've been so out and out logical I nearly vomited shit. And once the mists had cleared, what was left? Words and the brain. Over and over again this same terrifying, everlasting brain. Nailed to this cross. Caught in this incest. In this rape of things—if you only knew my existence, this torment, this terrible sense that we're at an end, betrayed before God by the beasts, and God and beast alike destroyed by thought and spewed out, a random throw in the mists of this land, I tell you you would resign quietly without fuss and be glad that you are not being called to account for the brain damage you have caused.

PROFESSOR: I am extremely sorry if you should be feeling unwell. But if your degeneracy or neurosis or for all I know these medieval mists of yours are causing you to go to pieces, what has that got to do with me? Why get worked up at me? If you really haven't got the strength to join us on the road to the new knowledge, why not just stay behind? Give up your anatomy. Go in for mysticism. Use formulae and corollaries to calculate the location of the soul; but leave us out of it. We are spread out over the world like an army: heads to rule with and brains to conquer with. The force that cut axes from stone, that kept fire alive, that gave birth to Kant, that created machines—is ours to conserve. The prospects ahead are infinite.

RÖNNE: The prospects ahead infinite; an enormous cervical cortex with a fold in the middle takes a little stroll; fingers stand up like calipers; teeth have grown into computers—mankind will turn into a maw with a machine on top, systematizing—what perspectives! What infinite perspectives ahead! For all I care we could have stayed jelly-fish. For me the whole history of evolution is useless. The brain is a blind alley. A bluff to fool the middle-classes. Whether one walks vertically or swims horizontally is all a matter of habit. The totality of life, its overall structures have been destroyed for me by thought. The cosmos roars past on its way. I stand on the bank: gray, steep, barren. My branches hang down into the living water; but their gaze is turned inwards, on the waning flow of their blood and the numbing chill in their limbs. I am set apart, my self. I make no move now.

Where, where will it lead? Why make the long journey? What center is there for us to gather round? When I stopped thinking for a moment, surely my limbs fell off?

Something finds associations inside one. Some process takes place inside one. All I can feel now is my brain. It lies on my skull like a lichen. It gives me from above a feeling of nausea. It lies everywhere ready to pounce: yellow, yellow, brain, brain. It hangs down between my legs . . . I can feel it distinctly knocking against my ankles.

Oh, if I could return to the state of being a grassy field, sand dotted with flowers, a vast meadow. With the earth bearing everything to one on waves that are warm or cool. No forehead left. A state of being lived.

KAUTSKI: But can you not see the dawn all around our bodies? There since eternity, since the primal stage of the world? A century is at an end. A sickness is conquered. A dark journey, the sails straining; now the music of home is heard across the sea.

Who is to say what has driven you away? A curse, the Fall, or something else. For thousands of years there were no more than mere beginnings of it. For thousands of years it lay hidden. But then, a century ago it suddenly exploded and like a pestilence engulfed the world 'til nothing was left but that animal, large, greedy and power-hungry: the man of intellect; he stretched from heaven to heaven, he conjured the world out of his mind. But we are older. We are blood; from the warm seas, the mothers who gave   birth to life. You are a small channel of this same sea. Come home now. I call you.

PROFESSOR: Don't let Rönne mislead you. All this thinking with no clearly defined objective has crushed him. Such casualties will be inevitable on our path.

RÖNNE: The Mediterranean was there; from primeval times; and it is there still. Perhaps it is the most human thing there has ever been? What do you think? . . .

PROFESSOR: (*Continuing*) But, gentlemen, all these strange feelings and the other things you talked about—myth and knowledge, could it not be that these are age-old poisons in our bloodstream, which will be cast off in the course of evolution, just as we no longer possess a third eye looking backwards to warn us of enemies. In the hundred years during which the sciences and their application have existed, how life has changed! Has not Man's mental activity largely abandoned speculation and the transcendental to concentrate entirely on the shaping of material things, to satisfy the needs of a self-renewing soul? Is it not already possible to talk about a homo faber instead of a homo sapiens as hitherto? Is it not right that in the course of time all Man's speculative-transcendental needs will be refined and purified out of existence? Could scientific research and the teaching of knowledge not be justified from that point of view?

KAUTSKI: If you want to produce a race of plumbers, certainly.

But there was a country once: full of the whirring of doves' wings, with the thrill of marble from sea to sea, dream and ecstasy . . .

RÖNNE: . . . Brains, soft and rounded; dull and white.

A rosy flush spreading and rustling groves of blue.

Forehead soft and blooming. All tension eased in yearning towards shores.

The banks piled high with oleander, then lost to view in fragrant, gentle bays.

. . . Blood now seems ready to burst. Temples to surge with hope.
In my forehead, the coursing of waters about to take flight.
Oh, the rush of ecstasy like a dove to my heart: laughing, laughing—
Ithaca!—Ithaca! . . .

Oh stay! stay! Don't send me back! Such a path to tread, homewards at last, as the blossom falls sweet and heavy from all the worlds . . . (*Goes up to the Professor and takes hold of him.*)

PROFESSOR: Gentlemen, what are you trying to do? I am more willing to meet your wishes. You have my assurance that in the future I shall invariably give out in my lectures that we in this faculty cannot teach ultimate wisdom and that lectures in philosophy should be followed at the same time. I shall not fail to emphasize that the nature of our knowledge is open to question . . .

(*Shouting*) Listen to me, gentlemen! After all, we are all scientists, we must avoid fantasy. Why should we get involved in situations which the structure of modern society is—let's say—not equipped to cope with . . . We are doctors after all, don't let us overdo questions of belief. No one will ever know what took place here!

Murder! Murder!

LUTZ: (*Also taking hold of him.*) Murder! Murder! Fetch some shovels. Back to the ground with this lump of clay! Lash this scum with our foreheads!

PROFESSOR: (*Choking.*) You callow youths! You murky dawn! Your life blood will be shed and the mob will feast in triumph over it! Go on, trample the north under foot! Logic will triumph! On every side the same abyss: Ignorabimus! Ignorabimus!

LUTZ: (*Smashing him repeatedly with his forehead.*) Ignorabimus! Take that for your ignorabimus! Your researches weren't deep enough! Go deeper into things if you want to teach us! We are the young generation. Our blood cries out for the heavens and the earth and not for cells and invertebrates. Yes we're trampling the north underfoot. The hills of the south are swelling up already. Oh soul, open wide your wings; soul! soul! We must have Dream. We must have Ecstasy. Our cry is Dionysos and Ithaca!

END

The Son

a drama in five acts

[1914]

Walter Hasenclever

Translation by Henry Marx

Born in Aachen, the son of a Jewish physician, Walter Hasenclever (1890-1940) created the generational-play genre within German Expressionism. A rebellious child, like many of his protagonists, Hasenclever studied at universities in Oxford, Lausanne, and Leipzig. During his stay in Great Britain in 1908, he published his first play, which he claimed was paid for out of his poker winnings. Influenced by Wedekind and the Expressionist poets at Leipzig, Hasenclever wrote *Youth* in 1913 and the semi-autobiographical *The Son* the following year. Between 1915 and 1916, he fulfilled his wartime service as an "interpreter, purchaser, and kitchen-boy" on the Belgian and Balkan fronts. Wounded in Macedonia, Hasenclever spent the remainder of the war in a Dresden sanatorium, completing his award-winning, anti-war version of *Antigone* (1917).

The Son was staged at the German Provincial Theatre in Prague in 1916. It not only launched the writer's career but also made an early name for the German actor Ernst Deutsch. Despite its length and high sense of melodrama, *The Son* played upon the real and growing conflict between generations. For the returning wounded and mentally-torn enlisted men, *The Son* fixed a clear blame for the world's problems on the old and powerful, with their rigid, controlling, and cowardly ways. In 1917, *The Son* won the coveted Kleist prize, thereby establishing Hasenclever as the leading Expressionist playwright.

After *Antigone*, two other major Expressionist plays followed, *Humanity* (1918) and *Beyond* (1920). During the early twenties, Hasenclever's output slowed when he became interested in Swedenborgianism. By 1924, now a Paris newspaper correspondent, he became a writer of light comedies, many of them great successes on the Berlin stage, especially *The Better Man* (1927). In 1930, Hasenclever traveled to Hollywood, where he adapted Eugene O'Neill's *Anna Christie* for Greta Garbo's first talkie. During the thirties, he traversed all of Western Europe, moving from London to Florence to the French Riviera and back again. Arrested by the Vichy police in 1939, Hasenclever committed suicide at the Milles concentration camp one year later.

Sketch of Ernst Stern in
Hasenclever's *The Son*
(Prague, 1916)

CHARACTERS:

The Son
The Tutor
The Friend
The Fraulein
The Father
Cherubim
Von Tuchmeyer
Prince Scheitel
Adrienne
Police Inspector

Time: The present (1914), during three days

Act I: The Son's room
Act II: Same, 24 hours later
Act III: An anteroom, a few hours later
Act IV: A hotel room, the next morning
Act V: The Father's consultation room, a few hours later

ACT I

SCENE ONE

(The Son's room in his parents' house. In the center wall a large window with a view onto a park, in the distance the city's silhouette: houses, a chimney. The room mirrors the moderate elegance of a respectable bourgeois home. Oak furniture, bookcases, a desk, chairs, a large map. Door stage right and left. The hour before sunset.)

THE SON: I'm twenty now and could be in the theatre or build bridges in Johannesburg. Why did I fail with the formula of the truncated cone! All teachers were sympathetic, even the director prompted me. I could have solved the task brilliantly—had I not run away at the last moment. I believe there are things which force us into pain. I could not have endured freedom. Perhaps I will never become a hero.

THE TUTOR: You have failed in your final exam. How often have I been sitting with you at this desk and we have crammed all the formulas. Did I not explain to you that the small cone has to be subtracted from the large! Answer me!

THE SON: Yes, you did tell me. I understand your pain. You are sad because this cone does exist in the world. Believe me, I'm no longer sad! I'm even lacking the fleeting gesture mocking itself under tears. You'll say I'm a weakling or a rascal. But I tell you: I was standing in my black coat in front of the blackboard—and knew very well that I held the chalk in my hand. I even knew that the small cone had to be subtracted from the larger one—yet I did not do it.

THE TUTOR: But why not! I'm asking you: why not?

THE SON: Before me someone else was examined in history: In 1800 or so the Battle of Aspern took place. And while my hand invisibly described circles on the blackboard, I saw archduchesses and long-winded boulevards. You will understand that math is destroyed in the midst of such loveliness. The dissolution of a single parenthesis would have saved me. But I preferred to despise myself in it.

THE TUTOR: We shouldn't have worked so much in recent days. Your frame of mind is understandable. You are suffering from a mental depression.

THE SON: I believe that man's soul is not quite that simple. This day is an experience. My longing for freedom was too strong. It was stronger than myself; that's why I could not fulfil it. I have felt too much and still be courageous. I have bled to death from my own self. Probably I will never have the strength to do for what I was born. Now you will realize that I could not pass the final exam: I would have perished from something.

THE TUTOR: Calm down. It isn't too bad.

THE SON: Thank you. You are good to me. You will be fired because I am an idiot.

THE TUTOR: I wish I could help you.

THE SON: My father will see to it that this won't happen.

THE TUTOR: How are you going to tell him?

THE SON: Please send him a telegram. You know his address. I am unable to do it myself. I'm not afraid of his anger but I am suffering from every human being and from every street. I am humbled by each existence which diminished my desire for it. I am revolted by the fact that a building is constructed from which the air is ruined by electric waves. How I hate all the communiqués between Emperor and soldier!

THE TUTOR: What should I telegraph to your father?

THE SON: Do not spare him. He hates me. I know he will rage. I am a coward or else I would lie that I was fired from school to make his anger rise even more. Wire him everything you want—except that you love me.

THE TUTOR: I do not understand your father . . .

THE SON: Once you yourself will be a father, you'll become like him. The father—is the son's fate. The fairytale of the fight for life is no longer valid: it is in the parents' house where the first love and the first hate originate.

THE TUTOR: But aren't you the son?

THE SON: Yes, and therefore I'm right! Nobody can understand that but me. Later on, one loses his own balance. Perhaps we shall not meet again. Listen to one bleeding advice from my heart: Whenever you will have a son, abandon him or die ahead of him. For the day is sure to come when you will be enemies—you and your son. Then God's mercy be with the one who loses.

THE TUTOR: Dear friend, all of us will go astray in this world. Why do you want to be so cruel! Go out into the street and see an animal that is frightened by thunder. Do you know how hungry girls are feeling, and have you ever met a cripple who looks for his bread at 6 o'clock in the morning? Then you will be grateful for having a father. Each one of us is wronged and each one of us does wrong. Who will throw the first stone? I was a poor fellow and my father worked to support me. I've seen how he died. And I have cried. He who has had such an experience, will no longer pass judgment.

THE SON: Who helps me when I'm sad? Do you think I can fall asleep each night when I have to go to bed? Do you think I would not know now the pain of someone not allowed out of the house on Sundays when all the maids go dancing? My father will not tolerate that anyone in the world will become my friend. I have never tasted the sweetness of even the poorest people. And why doesn't he talk with me about God? Why doesn't he talk about women? Why am I forced to read Kant secretly who does not set me on fire? And why all this mockery of everything that is worldly and beautiful? Do you think it is enough when, sometimes in the evening, he shows me the Great Bear in the sky? Smoking his cigar, he sits on the balcony below when the last car has long stopped running in the city. But I stand upstairs, fighting with all the gods and die before a woman I do not yet know. How often have I walked the stairs at night in my nightgown filled with longings like a ghost finding no rest!

THE TUTOR:If you still had a mother, you would feel well.

THE SON: My mother died at my birth. I know nothing about her. All sleep at night when I am unhappy. My mother has never appeared to me in the golden sky. She has never consoled me when I became feverish. I believe she is too young to understand this. My mother married when she was eighteen. How distant, how childish are the times into which I was born!

THE TUTOR: I do not know what to tell you. I do not want this hour to fall into the well without a drop of goodness coming over you. Perhaps your father means well! Later on you will learn how difficult it is to love someone else. Today you only know yourself. I had to go through a lot of evil in life but I do not want to make others pay for it. And because I recognize this, I will enjoy my gray hair. Dear boy, there is still so much time for hate. I feel miserable because I cannot help you. You move me so much . . . Pardon me . . . (He cries.)

THE SON: A year ago I would have cried with you, out of fright. Today I can only laugh. I am disgusted with these feelings. Do you want a glass of water?

THE TUTOR: Thank you, it's all over. I could not convince you even if I were the Prophet Isaiah. I must think about it for many days in order to believe in God again. Why is there enmity in the world?

THE SON: This smells after Salvation Army.

THE TUTOR: Goodbye. You are young. You should know that you are alive. Therefore everything you do will be good—how could it be otherwise? Now you laugh about me because I speak of love. Someday it will overcome you too and you will cry. Then think of me! Now I will send a telegram to your father. (Exits.)

SCENE TWO

THE SON: (Alone. Goes to the window, opens it. The evening sun shines.)
  Down under, beautiful to see
  Wonder nights, out of reach for me

In the black room where my youth I spent,
My bookshelves and my notebooks here:
Rise up, my magical sphere
When first to Golgotha I went.
The sun goes down. The world of all my dreams,
Where in my tennis suit I darkly stand.
I call you, roads and trees and beams
And you, the ball, held in my little hand!
In my old room I now go on my knee
And all my life tumbles into this hall:
Table, chairs and wall—oh, do not flee
And world, now take me with you on this fall!
 (*He kneels with spread-out arms.*)
In vain I knock at the bronzed door,
Separating my prison from the lust.
Music and dance I am waiting for,
A poor body, still burning in the dust.
And yet I lived, lived a life so vast
On this soil which could never last
Boundless longing was my fate—
Without the power it ever to attain.
Into the void I fling myself in pain
From which I have landed now afraid.
Up then, silken cord, let's make an end!
Never have I loved, and I am alone.
The last circle of immortal faces bend
To give me wings to a new home!
 (*He pulls a green cord from his pocket and fastens it at the window.*)
Green creature, by strange hands you're made
Why am I overwhelmed by your sight?
I am a human being too, now at the gate.
Oh, evening sun, no longer do I want to fight.
Do you have to find me at this spot!
Hand does not loosen, Earth will dwindle not.
An unknown fire makes me shiver,
In this hour around my heart an aching ring:
I am with all of you—with you I want to live!
Where, oh Death, where is thy sting—
 (*He tumbles, overwhelmed by excitement, backwards into the room.*)
Thou secret, which from me has sprung!
I do sense women, beautiful and tall,
I feel arms around to which I clung
And a sweet face my name will call.
In the threatening evening wind I hear

Unfortunate and poor ones to me so dear;
In the coffin a little child I do see sway
I have learned of so much pain and also joy.
Perhaps on this vast world there is
Still comfort and a bridge to bliss.
With twenty years I do not want to go.
I have to live. Learning is slow.
   (*He comes back to the window. The sun is setting.*)
Infinite feeling! Thou gave me a sign
The miracle to see now is my foremost task.
Concert and town—soon you will be mine!
My car approaches in the dusk.
I sit in boxes, I shall dine
With actors and the best of wine.
With a duchess in London I shall be
And a diamond pin will be given me.
A new system discover I will
How to jump by parachute from the house—
The audience should get their fill:
I shall live! Oh, gold! Oh, applause!
Thus break thou cord, instead of me thus fade—
But you, tall figures in the evening light
Make me purer and free of every hate
To be eternally alive, and with delight!
   (*He tears up the cord and throws the pieces out of the window.*)

SCENE THREE

(*The Friend enters.*)

THE FRIEND: You speak to yourself, you are very courageous.

THE SON: Today I see you for the first time.

THE FRIEND: We haven't met in a long time. I am coming from the railroad station. You are astonished?

THE SON: That I'm still here—this astonishes me much more.

THE FRIEND: I heard you failed in school. Did you want to kill yourself?

THE SON: To say it simply: yes.

THE FRIEND: Why didn't you do it?

THE SON: I stayed alive.

THE FRIEND: You owe your life to a plagiarism from *Faust*. Are you still not allowed to read Goethe? Does your father let you go to the theatre?

THE SON: No.

THE FRIEND: Why does Death meet with us so often? Today, on the train, a child was run over.

THE SON: I've seen the child. When I wanted to kill myself, I saw her. A girl, with black, curly hair, in a white dress.

THE FRIEND: It was a girl. How did you know?

THE SON: I know more than you suspect. But don't be afraid. I am not yet speaking from the beyond. I had a revelation, right here. I believe that throughout the world there exists a profound community. This I didn't know until today. I've stayed alive because once again I'm happy! When God has mercy on me, some day I shall experience love and pain. How can I explain it? There is a long road from school graduation to the supernatural.

THE FRIEND: I've rushed over to see you. I felt you would do something.

THE SON: Thus we have met in the evening en route with the express train.

THE FRIEND: Wait a moment. Let us talk about reality. My heart beats strongly. Yesterday I dreamed of you: both of us loved one woman. I had a feeling we did not know each other. We plodded along far-away snow fields before a childlike horizon. Now that I'm here, you're so close to me!

THE SON: You enter this room at the right time. It is not for nothing that you have first seen this incredible world two years earlier than me. A voice called you to help me, poor creature. Everything in me is so tense today that the sounds of the trolley cars before our house, which I detest, remind me of eternity.

THE FRIEND: Can I help you?

THE SON: Already this life has begun for me. Help me to retrieve the world to come! You saw a child die who has rescued me from death. From her little hands the power of existence has dropped on me like golden rain on the sheperd's seeds. Now that I'm alive, I want to learn much because I shall be loved. In the past I could not stand to see a street because my brain burst from all that I saw. Now I would like to go with the metal workers into their pits in order to feel there too that I am a human being.

THE FRIEND: You are drunk from being, but you do not know its poison. I perceive with terror how you have changed. Today that you begin to live, your dying begins.

THE SON: I believe in everything I saw. Why do you doubt me?

THE FRIEND: The child on the tracks is your downfall. You've tasted the blessedness of the world on your firmament. But I hate these stars, and love disgusts me for too deeply have I felt its weaknesses. All that tempted me, I have enjoyed. It was not too much that killed me but too little. I came to see you because I thought you were still pure and untouched. I wanted to warn you, listen to me! I'm spoiled in paradise and now that I am fleeing, I am alone. Why wasn't I born a cripple, then I would never have had a woman or a friend, and I would not now be here.

THE SON: We are standing across from each other, each one on his pole. But there is still a zenith to which we shall rise, you and me. Is there something I can do for you?

THE FRIEND: Return to me the fragrance of a flower in summertime while it was still forbidden to pick it for the beloved one. Return to me the longing for that trick in the circus which people love. Let me travel again, in childlike fantasy, on a rainbow from Argentina to Venice. How was I moved by the first smile of a girl sitting next to me on a church bench! And how did the little suburb carry me off to Berlin when the evening sky rose with a red tinge on the horizon! Now I walk the same boulevards where once immortality grew in me and weep that I do no longer experience anything nor can sacrifice anything.

THE SON: I look through you—you speak the truth. You have not yet reached your highest curve, due to weakness and imperfection. But only he lives who knows strongly what he is! I want to say to you: "Rise and follow me." When the world's gates will open up for me, it can only happen from beauty and greatness. Perhaps you, with your experiences, can point out to me the keys. I ask you to do it because I am so helpless.

SCENE FOUR

(*The Fraulein enters.*)

THE FRAULEIN: It's getting dark. Should I bring the lamp?
THE SON: Yes, Fraulein. When shall we have dinner?
THE FRAULEIN: In ten minutes it will be nine o'clock.
THE SON: Then bring the lamp. (*The Fraulein exits.*)

SCENE FIVE

THE FRIEND: A beautiful girl!
THE SON: Don't you know her? She is the third governess. I have to have dinner with her every night at nine. My father wants it that way.
THE FRIEND: Did you see how she entered the room? Can you imagine a woman coming to you while the world is full of other men? Aren't you a human being and don't you feel her divine steps in the dusk? You should bless your father that he lets you live with her every night—every night, oh, man! Do you know how long you will be living? Aren't you happy that so much is happening to you? She shares the dishes with you and drinks from the same pitcher. What harmony, what earth-shaking word that she has to sleep like the rest of us, prepares tea and dusts rooms while she is a god-like creature living on islands.
THE SON: I never knew what you said. How can something so beautiful be alive?
THE FRIEND: Think of Penelope!
THE SON: Since I have seen these words on cabaret programs, I no longer get

dizzy in Homer's palace.

THE FRIEND: Someday you will learn why God made all women alike—for better or worse.

THE SON: Continue to talk of this woman. I am afraid.

THE FRIEND: A wave of her hair is still lingering in this room. Why don't you love her?

THE SON: How can I?

THE FRIEND: She will open your eyes, you fool, at the closed gate. Through her the bolts will be blasted open and you might experience some of the drama of the world. Don't be afraid, she is kind. Your mother was a woman like her too. You will be her child!

THE SON: Deep sorrow fills me for what I will never be able to see or say. I only think of Siberian steppes even though sometimes I find an old man in a ditch and know that many in the snow die of hunger. I'm seized with fear that nowhere do I understand creation! I think of the moment when I walk in the spring and yet am no more than a warning sign on the sky bearing down on me. All that happens to me, happens eternally! What remains of me in this life's restless chain?

THE FRIEND: The needs of your heart, the tear in the night and the resurrection in the morning!

THE SON: Come back soon, then I will be closer to you. I want to learn of the miracle before the shadows of my solitary room will envelop me once again. I want to enter this enchanted garden even at the sacrifice of my sight. Half an hour ago I swore that I belong to joy which I do not yet know. Some time, my life will answer me, perhaps today, perhaps in a hundred days. I feel the time is not too distant.

THE FRIEND: I am confident: a good star guides you. I'll be back when you need me. Thus fly away!

THE SON: You too, my friend, in infinite emotion!

THE FRIEND: The wave still carries you forth. It has called me back. Goodbye. (*He exits.*)

SCENE SIX

(*The room gets darker. The Fraulein enters with the lamp. She sets the table and serves dinner.*)

THE SON: Fraulein, I see you have blonde hair. You are standing between the lamp and dusk.

THE FRAULEIN: (*At the window.*) The clouds are still light. In our village the cows are now coming home. How beautiful is this evening!

THE SON: (*Softly.*) And how beautiful you are!

THE FRAULEIN: (*Watching him attentively.*) Are you sad?

THE SON: Sad? Why? Because I've failed in school? No, not at all. I'm happy.

THE FRAULEIN: Then we will have dinner. (*They sit down.*)

THE SON: (*Not touching anything.*) We have been sitting so often at this table, like strangers. And we've gotten used to it.

THE FRAULEIN: Have I always been so strange to you?

THE SON: Fraulein, I've been told that you are alive and in this world. I must learn to understand much. That you have a voice and that you walk on silvery feet through the room.

THE FRAULEIN: (*Smiling.*) My, who has told you all that? You don't believe it, do you?

THE SON: (*With extreme seriousness.*) I believe everything and even more.

THE FRAULEIN: Should I prepare a sandwich for you?

THE SON: I cannot eat anything.

THE FRAULEIN: Often I have been thinking of you and feeling pity for you because you are treated so harshly. I would like to, but I'm not allowed.

THE SON: You're right. It's dark in here.

THE FRAULEIN: Don't think of it. Good times will return.

THE SON: If I were to ask you for something, would you do it?

THE FRAULEIN: What should I do for you?

THE SON: I must make love to a woman. Let me go out tonight.

THE FRAULEIN: Little boy! When did this come over you?

THE SON: Today, Fraulein. Today.

THE FRAULEIN: Hasn't your father issued strict orders not to let you go out at night?

THE SON: Fraulein, when I was seven, my father took me on a trip. How I was frightened in the tunnel—I thought of it as hell. We took a boat downstream and for a moment stood in the boiler room. Then for the first time I saw the giant fires and the black men sweating. Do you know what my father did? He gave to each of the stokers one Mark. I was so happy for the poor devils.

THE FRAULEIN: You have a good heart.

THE SON: When I grew up, I often wished my father would give me one Mark for I wanted to buy sweets. But he never did it. I don't know why. He said I would get sick from them.

THE FRAULEIN: If I had one Mark now, I would give it to you.

THE SON: What good is one Mark to me now! With it I cannot even pay the cab I want to take.

THE FRAULEIN: There are bad women. Perhaps you will return sad.

THE SON: Could I become still sadder than in the twenty years I have been waiting for the star so close-by? When will I finally hear the trumpets? Oh, Fraulein, there are hours when we leave our sphere, dreamlike, when in the summer we sit in concerts with pink ladies at the banks of the eternal river. Give me the house key!

THE FRAULEIN: (*Hands it over.*) Here, have it.

THE SON: (*Snatches it.*) So I am holding this treasured possession. (*He jumps up and staggers.*) Oh, I'm like a blind man. My eyes are not used to the light. I'm afraid I might lose it. Take it back! (*He returns the key.*)

THE FRAULEIN: You will not go out?

THE SON: (*Attentively.*) Wasn't this a sacrifice, a gift from you? If my father knew it, wouldn't you lose your job?

THE FRAULEIN: (*Smiling.*) Then help me write a letter to your father. He wants to hear each day how things are going. I don't know what to write to him. (*She takes pen and ink.*)

THE SON: By the way, I want to talk to my father. Write him to come back.

THE FRAULEIN: (*Near the lamp, writing.*) What date is today, the 20th?

THE SON: Yes, I want to talk to him. He should know it. Soon I must do something real big. I have stopped learning in that school. How much will I tell him?

THE FRAULEIN: (*Looking at him.*) Should I write all this?

THE SON: I will go to Hamburg and see the transatlantic boats. I will also keep some women. Don't you believe it, Fraulein?

THE FRAULEIN: But I cannot write this to your father!

THE SON: (*Standing behind her, pointing to the writing paper.*) Then write to him that he should come back. (*The Fraulein writes. The Son puts his hands on her shoulder, trembling.*)

THE FRAULEIN: (*Without turning around.*) What are you doing? I cannot write this way. (*The Son opens her blouse, touching her.*)

THE FRAULEIN: Oh, no—now there is a blot on the paper. (*The Son bends down lower to her.*)

THE FRAULEIN: (*Withdrawing, almost above the paper.*) No, no, if your father—

THE SON: I love you. (*She turns around, he kisses her with ardent, anxious force.*)

THE FRAULEIN: (*She gets up, turns away, then puts her hair in order. After a while.*) What's going to happen now?

THE SON: (*In great confusion.*) Something has happened. Don't be angry with me.

THE FRAULEIN: (*In a soft, kind voice.*) You were never a stranger to me. (*She takes the lamp.*) Good night! (*Exits fast.*)

SCENE SEVEN

THE SON: (*Alone. Night. August sky.*)
Since infinite stars are shining,
How differently am I devoted to each star!
They created me for living and for whining.
I'm closer to the eternal, at the bar.
Not to wild ecstasy nor painful recognition

But lead to the highest rapture me today.
So that in the most horrendous combustion
I learn in this world what I have to say.
Already do I hear the nights revealing
To the unknown spirit bliss and sorrow;
My life will overflow with feeling
Like ev'ry human, I can wait for the morrow.
For a creature in love, himself renewing,
Becomes greater in the fullness of the day.
This greatest does inspire me into doing
And thus into my life will fall a ray!
A thousand times closer let me be
That life's miracles won't me lull.
That in every birth and death I see
God is with me. This woman sure is beautiful!

ACT II

SCENE ONE

(The next day. The same room. The same hour.)

THE SON: A beautiful woman in our city has taken her own life. Lake Lucerne is being combed but her body is not found. Some maintain she has not died and is still alive. I shudder hearing this. Is she going to be resurrected from the dead? How unimportant whether her husband had a mistress! I could not fall asleep last night. I went to the park and lay down in the bushes under the sulphur-colored sky. What storm has carried this woman away into unrestrained space from her seat in the box of the theatre where she could be seen twice a week! In what darkness has she disappeared? Who has helped her in her need? Does anyone know about her tears before her rippled face submerged in the lake?

THE FRAULEIN: She has two children, a little girl.

THE SON: Therefore she cannot vanish in dust or vapor. The guardian angel lives on—you children! She will assist you during the painful hours of the day. How much of the immortal is in us! When I got up, a bird screamed over the pond: there I saw your breasts, white in the shadow of the room.

THE FRAULEIN: It was so muggy. I couldn't sleep either. For a long time I stood at the window.

THE SON: And I felt you to be sweet too and thought I was under your protection.

THE FRAULEIN: We are bad. We are sinking deeper and deeper. And your father's confidence rests in me.

THE SON: What pleasure to betray him! When yesterday I kissed you in his room—how did I enjoy this happiness. And the couch where we embraced has felt my revenge. And the dead, sneering pieces of furniture in front of which my father used to beat me, have all seen the miracle. No longer am I the despised, I'm becoming a human being.

THE FRAULEIN: Your father has helped many people in need. We must be grateful to him. Often when the nightbell rang, your father got up, fetched wine from the cellar and hurried to a dying patient. He radiates consolation in the darkness of death and poverty. He has done more good than we have.

THE SON: Yes, Fraulein, and that's why I want to talk to him. He must listen to me, he must help me—he, a doctor, who stands at the bedside of thousands of people. Will he desert his own son in his hour of despair? I will tell him everything that is in my soul. I trust that my strength is greater than his distrust has been all these years. Thus I want to stand before him: it is necessary for us to hold close together, one with the other. Let me feel your warmth before the frost of this meeting choke my heart. If I could only overcome him! Through your mouth I heard the voices of the living and of mercy. But I will try to find my father in nobility, as the God of Happiness has announced to me last night. Achilles's horses will be harnessed fiercely before my carriage! Now I have the courage to do everything for I believe in myself.

THE FRAULEIN:* Your eyes are shining—how beautiful is this fire! You're still with me, I still possess you. Yet I know that for you I am only a small footprint in the garden of high feelings. Come on, perhaps you'll have forgotten me in the morning. And today I am so much in love with you.

THE SON: Dear Fraulein, let me be with you tonight. I want to make love to you! Fulfill what innocent reverence has still shyly veiled for me. This day of waiting fate must end in purple happiness. You fires at the sky of my homeland! You blast furnaces and poplars! Let me become a man in azure light! This too I must possess in order to learn what kind of a person I am.

THE FRAULEIN: My little boy, come to me when it makes you happy. I want to be close to you! I caress your hands, and when this happens it cannot get lost. In the future you should think of me in gratitude. Don't go to any other woman. I will take care of you. And you're allowed to do with me whatever you like.

THE SON: Tell me that you love me, then I don't have to be afraid of anything. For you I could win a battle. I will do it when I face my father.

THE FRAULEIN: (*Caressing him.*) And yet how little of what you will do tonight will happen out of love. What do you know of love and sacrificial death! In you there is manliness: you will fight. I wish you would return with torn clothing and a bleeding face—then you would learn what a woman is like! But no—you should be victor! You do not love me because you love me. You must possess me. And you do not know what I do for you.

THE SON: I will not touch you if you don't want it.

THE FRAULEIN: I'm with you, nonetheless. Could I love you, yet not bring you

---

*From the Fraulein's speech to the end of this scene the two use the more intimate "Du" instead of "Sie."

a sacrifice? I know that I am condemned to shed many tears. But it has to be that way. What painful blessedness on the swaying bridge of pleasure!

THE SON: I will kill everybody who hurts you, even if he were my father.

THE FRAULEIN: How ignorant you are and how sweet! You are standing before me so strong, so bold. I must kiss you, my little, sweet hero. Thanks to God that he created such youths! Think of me whenever another woman holds you in her arms as I do. And do not kill yourself—you will soon hurt me very much. Now your star is turned towards me at its highest point—now that you have not yet loved anything and soon will have enjoyed everything. This hour will not return. Heavens may protect you from sadness.

THE SON: Tonight—swear to me that you are coming!

THE FRAULEIN: Yes, I come! There must be a human being in this world through whom your soul will pour itself out for the first time. A being who protects you and will accompany you towards the light.

THE SON: Fraulein, everything in me is heavy and dark. I see both of us standing in the clouds, midway between expectation and pain. Aren't we in my father's house which surrounds us with old age and enmity? And you speak to me in beautiful and strange words as never before. Is the riddle returning in the dark power of the dreamer? Is Aladdin's magic lamp on the nurse's knee? Oh, for that miracle which God has promised me! How can I understand it—today there is a night and tomorrow a day—shall I see the sun which sends his rays to all of us?

THE FRAULEIN: (*After a while, softly and slightly bitter.*) There are many suns and you will see them.

THE SON: What can I do for you? Should I tell my father that I'm in love with you?

THE FRAULEIN: And what is going to happen when he believes it? Will you take me with you to Hamburg?

THE SON: Yes, Fraulein.

THE FRAULEIN: I feel it, you are courageous. But who will pay for the ticket?

THE SON: Can't we walk there? Somebody will help us on the way. There must still be people, just as in the golden times, who give bread to one another, from sea to sea—I don't need my father. Just as I could die without him, I will live twice as well without him. A rustle of your dress and I won't enter this house anymore.

THE FRAULEIN: Yes, you would abduct me on shooting stars. You glow. How embarrassed you will be when the first reception clerk will ask for our name. How clumsy will you be when you shop for bread and butter in the evening. In what kind of dreamland did you live! You speak of Hamburg, and you think of Babylon and the waters of the Red Sea . . . No, don't tell your father anything. You will be going soon, but let me stay. Here I will always have something, power from you, something firm in space. If I now had to leave, how subterranean would be my steps! I want to see the day which brings you back as triumphant victor over your childhood. The lawns and the trees before your father's house—perhaps you will drive by and not enter it—will reveal to you what you have suffered. You will be happy.

THE SON: Why don't you want to come with me?

THE FRAULEIN: Because I have lost you even before you are suspecting it. Because you must leave me. Because you will live and fight.

THE SON: Then help me!

THE FRAULEIN: Today I am still able to do it. Tomorrow someone else will do it.

THE SON: Will I see you sometimes on my way? Will you appear to me, spiritually at the edge of the great boulevards?

THE FRAULEIN: The many of us who are blessed cannot get lost in someone else's heart. Remember this word when your emotions are highest! Who can say that life's vicissitudes are at an end, and where does the star rise?

THE SON: A childlike face appears before me. I brought tulips to my father at one of his birthdays. He took me to his chest—then I knew that I was alive, that I existed. A governess, one of your predecessors, once beat me up because I was singing softly in bed. Now I feel it again. Birth and existence—oh, blessedness! I shall be eternal, eternal—(*He kneels before her.*)

THE FRAULEIN: (*Holding him.*) Everything is fleeting. There is only one thing that remains: your happiness. And when I'm still holding you now in my arms firmly and when you look up to me, then I know: a message of life has been revealed to you; that's why I am here.

THE SON: I shall never leave you.

THE FRAULEIN: And when the angel will get me with his sword?

THE SON: I'm holding you. I will see you again. I will conjure you from the violets of the Acheron. Beloved woman, I would find you, tomorrow night at the cinema as unattainable queen and imaginary cocotte in a Montmartre bistro. Oh, that I have been allowed to experience this! The world becomes ever more beautiful before me! (*A car rolls by, he jumps up.*) This is my father. Come to me tonight . . . I expect you here., (*He rushes towards the window.*) A car stopping in front of the house. It's him. I recognize his step. Now may it start! With this fullness in my heart I will confront him. (*The Fraulein exits to the right. The Son returns.*)

SCENE TWO

(*The Father enters.*)

THE SON: (*Taking a step towards him.*) Good evening, Father!

THE FATHER: (*Looks at him, without reaching out for the hand, after a while.*) What do you have to tell me?

THE SON: I have not passed my exam. This worry is over.

THE FATHER: That's all you know? Did I have to return for that?

THE SON: I asked you to—because I want to talk to you, Father.

THE FATHER: Then speak up.

THE SON: I detect in your eyes the features of a scaffold. I'm afraid you will not understand me.

THE FATHER: Do you expect a gift from me because you had to pay the price for your laziness?

THE SON: I was not lazy, Father.

THE FATHER: (*Goes to the bookshelf and derisively throws some of the books down.*) Instead of reading this nonsense, it would be better to learn your vocabulary. But I know—you were never lacking excuses. It's always the fault of others. What do you do all day? You sing and recite—even in the garden and at night in bed. How long do you expect to stay in school? All of your friends are long gone. Only you are the loafer in my house.

THE SON: (*Goes to the bookshelf, puts the books back in order.*) Your anger was directed at Heinrich von Kleist. (*He touches the book fondly.*) He has done nothing to you.—What standards do you apply?

THE FATHER: Are you already a Schiller or Matkowski? Do you think I don't hear you? But these books and pictures will disappear. I shall also keep an eye on your friends. Things can't go on like this. I have not spared any money to help you. I have kept tutors to work with you. You are a disgrace to me!

THE SON: What have I done? Have I forged notes?

THE FATHER: Stop such talk. You will become aware of my harshness because you do not listen to my kindness.

THE SON: Father, I thought to stand differently before you today. Away from severity and kindness on a scale with men where the difference in age no longer counts. Please take me seriously for I know quite well what I'm saying! You have determined my future. My prospect is an honorable chair in the court building. I have to keep for you a list of my expenses—I know. And the eternal disk at this horizon will turn me until some day I will have gone to my fathers. I admit not having thought of that until today, for the period until the end of school seemed longer to me than my whole life. Now that I've failed—I began to see. I saw more than you, Father, excuse me.

THE FATHER: What language!

THE SON: Before you beat me up, please listen to me until I have finished. I remember well the time when you taught me Greek grammar with the whip. Before falling asleep in my nightgown, my body was covered with weals. I still know how in the morning you made me repeat my lessons, shortly before going to school; in fear and despair I still had to learn at home after school had already started. How often did I vomit my breakfast while running the long way to school! Even the teachers sympathized with me and no longer punished me—I've had my share of shame and worry. And now you take away my books and my friends, I'm not allowed to go to the theatre, to see people or the city. Now you take away from my life the last I still possess.

THE FATHER: He who does not work, should not eat. Be glad I haven't chased you out of the house a long time ago.

THE SON: Had you done it, I would have become more of a human being than I am now.

THE FATHER: You are still my son and I bear the responsibility for you. What you will do with your life later on, does not bother me. Today I must take care that you become a human being who can earn his living and do something.

THE SON: I know your worry, Father. You keep me away from the world because it's in your interest. But when eventually I'll bear the marks of this dull school on my face, then you give me up, cold, with a kick of your feet. Oh, for the blindness which you call responsibility! Oh, selfishness, fatherliness!

THE FATHER: You don't know what you are saying.

THE SON: Nonetheless I will try, try it now, in this hour and with all my force to come to you. What can I do that you'll believe me? I only have the tears of my childhood, and I'm afraid they won't even move you. God, give me the enthusiasm to make your heart filled with mine!

THE FATHER: Answer now: what do you want from me?

THE SON: I'm a human being, Father, a creature, not made of iron and not an eternally smooth pebble. If I could only reach you in this world! Could I get closer to you! Why this painful enmity, this fatefully wounded look? Is there a nest, an ascension to Heaven—I wanted to chain myself to you—help me! (*Falls down before him, grasping his hand.*)

THE FATHER: (*Withdrawing it.*) Get up and cut out this silliness. I do not give my hand to someone I do not respect.

THE SON: (*Getting up slowly.*) You despise me—you're entitled to it; after all I live off your money. For the first time have I broken through the filial limits with my stormy heart. Should I not have done it? What law forces me under this yoke? Are you not also a human being and am I not your equal? I was lying at your feet, wrestling with you for your blessing, and you have deserted me in my greatest pain. This is your love for me. Here my feeling ends.

THE FATHER: Do you have so little reverence for your father that you make him a fence for your guilt? Like a tramp you are on the street of feel-ings—what great things have you achieved that you dare to talk of love and hate? Are you drunk, why do you come to me? Go to bed. No more.

THE SON: Listen, Father, one more word. You should know that I suffered from hunger in your house! The governesses beat me, and yet you believed them! You have often locked me up in the attic. Often I was punished without being guilty, no one had mercy on me, Father! Yet there is joy—something golden rolling towards the firmament—why was I an outcast like a man with the plague? Why must I cry when in the circus a poor monkey drinks from a simulated cup? I know the pain of the unfree, the restless creature. That's against God! You have forbidden me to wear certain clothing and you had my hair cut off when I, out of glowing vanity, wanted it to be different than you. Should I continue to wallow in this abyss while my flesh is clinging to a thousand jags! Look at me—what have I done? Can't it be enough soon? Listen, and let me see a beacon of the merciful light. It is in your power. You have withdrawn—open yourself up to me! Give me the freedom for which I ask you hopelessly!

THE FATHER: What freedom am I to give you? I don't understand what you're talking about.

THE SON: Take me out of this school—give me to life. Be as good to me as to a sick person who perhaps has to die tomorrow. Give me some of the wine too which you get for him from the cellar! Let me drink too for I'm corroded from thirst. Father! Never have you shown for me as much affection as for the lowest creature in the hospital. Never have you embraced me when I came to say good night to you fearfully at your desk. And yet I felt and understood infinitely that I am your son. The desert of my bed where every dust grain had been counted is not so big as this word of despair. Yes, I want to reach something of you, and be it only a whimper of your eye. Even if you push me away once more: in this second my wish is greater than you.

THE FATHER: Spare your efforts, this way you are not going to catch me. What a senile, sad fool is standing before me! Is this your whole wisdom? And that's how you talk about your youth, about your education in your father's house. Aren't you ashamed of yourself? If you wanted to hurt me—now you have done it.

THE SON: No, Father, something else is separating us. Oh, what terrible conflict of nature! Can there be no bridge anymore although Earth is built between North and South Pole. Father! Blood may pour forth anew from this room! I do not want to be your enemy anymore. Accept me as a man.

THE FATHER: I do not need your advice. Nothing has happened to you for which you do not bear the guilt. What do you know of those suffering in the hospitals! You, a boy, who still has not learned to b serious and dutiful. If I were not hopeful of still being able to teach it to you, I would not deserve to be your father. I should have been stricter with you. Now I see the results.

THE SON: You don't discourage me. I will continue to come. Until you will listen to me.

THE FATHER: Haven't you understood me? What do you still want from me?

THE SON: (*Fiery.*) The utmost! Tear up the fetters between father and son— become my friend! Repose all your confidence in me so that at long last you will see who I am. Let me be what you are not. Let me enjoy what you do not. Am I not younger and more courageous than you? Then let me live! I want to be rich and blessed!

THE FATHER: (*Scornfully.*) From what book is this coming? From what journalistic brain?

THE SON: I'm the heir, Father. Your money is my money, it is no longer yours. You've worked for it, but you have also lived. It's up to you now to find out what comes after this life—enjoy your generation! What you have, belongs to me, I'm born to possess it for myself. And I'm here.

THE FATHER: Hm. And what do you intend to do with my money?

THE SON: I will enter into the enormity of the world. Who knows when I must die. Just for one brief thundershower I want to hold in my fingers the potential of my life—I shall no more attain this happiness. The greatest, yes, the noblest lightning I will use to look beyond the borders for only when I have completely exhausted reality, I shall meet with all the wonders of the spirit. That's how I want to be. That's how I want to breathe. A good star will be with me. I will not perish from any half measures.

THE FATHER: You have come a long way, indeed! You let me see all your meanness. Give thanks to God that I am your father. With what effrontery have you spoken of me and my money! How shamelessly have you spoken of my death. I have been mistaken about you—you are bad—you are not of my kind. But I'm still your friend and not your enemy, therefore I punish you for this word as you deserve it. (*Comes close to him and slaps him briefly in the face.*)

THE SON: (*After a while.*) In this room, where the heaven of my childhood still is standing, you have not spared me of the most cruel things. You have slapped me in the face before this table and these books—and yet I am more than you! Prouder do I lift my face above your house and do not blush before your weakness. You hate in me only the one you are not. I triumph! Just continue to beat me up. Clarity comes over me, no tear, no rage. How different am I now and so much bigger than you! What happened to love, what to the bonds of our blood? Even enmity no longer exists. I see before me a man who has wounded my body. Yet from his body there once came a crystal determining my life. This is the inconceivable, the dark. Fate stepped in between us. Alright. I live longer than you. (*He staggers.*)

THE FATHER: You are trembling. Sit down. Don't you feel well? Do you want something?

THE SON: (*For a moment somewhat weak in his arms.*) Oh, I have such a big load on my heart.

THE FATHER: (*In a changed voice.*) I punished you because I had to. That's past now. Come. You don't feel well.

THE SON: When once I fell from a ladder and broke an arm, you took care of me. When my childish conscience beat because I had cheated a conductor you made him gifts and thus stopped my tears. Today I came to you in greater need and you beat me. It might be better if you release me from your arms. (*He gets up.*)

THE FATHER: You did not come in need, you came in disobedience. That's why I slapped you. You know me and you know what I am asking of my son.

THE SON: How can you move a word on your lips and say: That's how it is! Don't you see constantly death in the hospital, not knowing that all is different in the world!

THE FATHER: I am a man and I have gained experience which you have not. You are still a child.

THE SON: When God allows me to live, I can start anything. Why do you want to repudiate me for that? Haven't you also played on the flowering earth and had dreams which did not come true?

THE FATHER: I have done my duty; that to me was the important thing. And you make a monster out of me without giving a thought to the fact that I was standing at your cradle. You were loved. Believe me that even now I spend many a sleepless night on your account. What will become of you? What happened to the words of your childhood, to your pure and unaffected soul? You have become stubborn and you deride advice and help. And now I should help you while you come to me bleary-eyed and evil. Am I now supposed to trust you?

THE SON: You have become a stranger to me. I have nothing more in common with you. The good which you think is so easily attained, has not reached me in your rooms. You have brought me up within the limitations of your mentality. This was your choice. But now set me free!

THE FATHER: How much has the rottenness of our times already destroyed you in that you feel so troubled. Was I not right in keeping you away from everything ugly and mean? As I see with horror, you are fired by desires. What has spoiled your heart? As a physician I have protected you from the poisons of our time because I know of their dangers. In later life you will be grateful to me for just that. But how did it happen—why did they reach you nonetheless? From what canal did this rat break into your youth? My poor boy, you're so confused. Let us forget that. (*Puts a hand on his shoulder.*)

THE SON: (*Wiggling out.*) No, Father. I love my time and do not want your sympathy. There's only one thing I ask of you: justice! Don't make me doubt you in this respect too. My life is about to come over me. The time is here to say goodbye; therefore we stand before each other. No, I'm not ashamed of longing for all that is actual and beautiful. Out into the oceans of impatience, into the liberating light! No longer the dreariness of your house and the dailiness of your person. I feel it, I'm going forwards towards a happy world. I will become its prophet.

THE FATHER: Are these your last words in the house which has fed and protected you for so many years? Who are you, smashing wantonly the noblest barrier between father and mother? Do you know what you leave behind and where you will be going? Fool that you are, who will give you food tomorrow? Who will help you in sorrow and ignorance? Am I already dead that you dare to speak to me in such a way?

THE SON: Yes, Father, for me you are dead. Your name has melted away. I do not know you any longer; you only live in the commandment. You've lost me in the snowfields of the breast. I tried to find you in the wind, in the cloud. I went on my knees before you, I loved you. You slapped my flaming face—then you tumbled into the abyss. I don't hold you. Soon you will be my only terrible enemy. I must gird for this fight: now both of us have only the will to power over our blood! One of us will be victorious!

THE FATHER: This is enough. For once, listen to me! Isn't there a breath of gratitude, some respect on your foaming lips? Don't you know who I am?

THE SON: Life has called on me to overcome you! I must accomplish it. A heaven that you do not know will help me.

THE FATHER: You are blasphemous!

THE SON: (*In a trembling voice.*) I will rather eat stones than your bread.

THE FATHER: Aren't you frightened by what you're saying?

THE SON: I'm not afraid of you. You are old, you will no longer walk all over me in jealous selfishness. Woe thee when you call your curse into the fields of this happiness—it would fall on you and your house! And when you drive me away with a thrashing—how did I once tremble before you in poor and homeless fright—I shall no longer see you, your tyrant's hand and your graying hair: only the powerfully falling light above me. Try to understand that I have floated away into the heights of another spirit. And let us part in peace.

THE FATHER: My son, there is no blessing over you . . . What will happen if I were to let you go in your blindness? Let me warn you of the sweet worms of this melody. Don't you want to accompany me on my rounds in the hospital (*scornful*): there the ruddiness of your youth bows depravedly in foam and tumor, and what rose from your mouth gaily into the air, becomes madness in the sorrowful countryside of the decaying. Thus God breaks the wings of him who ran away in spite and pride. Do not in this hour repudiate my hand; who'll know whether ever again I'll offer it to you as cordially.

THE SON: In your hands people have died whose nearness has surrounded us. But what are all these dead against me, who lives in despair?! Had I been afflicted by cancer, you would have fulfilled my every wish. For a patient who is beyond help is still allowed to use a wheelchair to ride to the coast of the blue oceans. You the living—who saves you? You call up the horror from the graves; but only he on whose head the trumpet of death has sounded, may distrust beautiful happiness! I am rising from twenty years, from twenty caskets and breathe the first golden beam—you have committed the sin against life by teaching me to recognize the worm while I stood at the highest point. Crumble to dust in the catacombs, old time, rotting world! I do not follow you. In me there is a being to whom hope has become stronger than doubt. Where shall we be? In what direction shall we go?

THE FATHER: (*To the left, locking the door.*) In this.

THE SON: What does this mean?

THE FATHER: You will not leave this room. You are sick.

THE SON: Father!

THE FATHER: Not in vain have you called on the physician in me. Your case belongs to the medical magazines, you talk feverishly. I must keep you locked up long enough until I can return you in good conscience to my house. Food and drink will be brought to you. Now go to bed.

THE SON: And what's going to happen with me later on?

THE FATHER: Here my will still dominates. You will pass your school exam. I have fired your tutor. From now on I shall determine everything. In my last will I shall provide for a guardian to carry out my intentions should I die earlier . . .

THE SON: Thus hate until the grave!

THE FATHER: You finish your studies and then take up a profession. That's the way it will be for the future. If you acquiesce in my will, it'll be to your advantage. But if you act against me, then I'll repudiate you and you'll not be my son anymore. I would rather destroy my inheritance by my own hand than give it to one who brings shame on my name. Now you are informed. And now let's go to bed.

THE SON: Goodnight, Father.

THE FATHER: (*Walks towards the door, but returns once more.*) Turn over all the money you have with you.

THE SON: (*Does it.*) Here.

THE FATHER: (*Overcome by emotion.*) I'll come tomorrow to look after you. Sleep well! (*He leaves, locking the door from the outside. The Son rests, immobile.*)

SCENE THREE

THE SON: (*Alone. A bell rings in the house. He rushes towards the door. He rattles it. It does not yield. The bell rings again. Voices are heard, a visitor is being sent away. He staggers towards a chair, sits in the middle of the room. In the window the disc of the yellow moon.*) The moon is here, just as yesterday. I live too much. Send me your angel, God! Imprisoned, in bitter need—me, a slave in the rising light. (*Looking upwards.*) You are lighted for me, tree full of candles. May I again listen to you at the room's edge, oh, what gift, oh, what gift! Why don't you come, you, my car? Do I have to suffer pain being so close to happiness? Could I only cry! Could I be born! (*In the window, in the light of the moon, the face of The Friend becomes visible.*)

THE FRIEND: Don't lose heart.

THE SON: Who are you, face of light?

THE FRIEND: The doors are locked, a servant sent me away. The route is unusual.

THE SON: It's you! You love me! Oh, God, oh God!

THE FRIEND: (*Rises in the window to half his height.*) Am I coming at the right hour?

THE SON: Can any man still be my friend, now that I'm so deserted?

THE FRIEND: Have you forgotten that Beethoven is still alive? Don't you know anymore that we have sung the chorus from the 9th Symphony? Didn't you want to embrace all people? On, my boy, it dawns. Fulfill your heart right to the moon's crust—let us stroll under the melody of joy as we once did when the lights in the concert hall went out and we were united into the night. The hour has come.

THE SON: What shall I do?

THE FRIEND: Flee!

THE SON: I am too poor, I have no money.

THE FRIEND: But in the closet there you have a tail-coat. Put it on. I will take you to a celebration. The train leaves in half an hour. Here take this mask. I'll expect you at the exit of the park. (*Gives him a black mask.*)

THE SON: It's a matter of life and death. When I'm discovered, I'm lost—my father will kill me. Is there a car available?

THE FRIEND: Many friends whom you do not know stand ready tonight to help you. They are waiting with guns behind the trees in the park.

THE SON: And whither shall we go into the night?

THE FRIEND: To life!

THE SON: How do I get out?

THE FRIEND: Leave silently through the window. We take you in our midst. Don't be afraid. (*He disappears.*)

SCENE FOUR

(*The Son rushes to the closet and, from among his clothes, takes out the tail-coat. He takes off his jacket and begins to dress. Through the window the lights of the city become visible in the distance. Lilting, almost like waltz music in coffee houses, we hear from afar and softly in the wind, the Finale from the 9th Symphony. Allegro assai vivace—alla marcia. Tenor solo and men's chorus*):

Froh wie seine Sonnen fliegen
Durch des Himmels praecht'gen Plan,
Laufet, Brüder, eure Bahn,
Freudig, wie ein Held zum Siegen.

SCENE FIVE

(*A key is turned in the lock. The door opens. The Fraulein stands on the threshold, in her hands a candle and a tablet. The Son and The Fraulein have returned to the formal "Sie."*)

THE FRAULEIN: I bring the dinner.

THE SON: Oh, it's you, Fraulein. I have completely forgotten you.

THE FRAULEIN: Your father went to bed.

THE SON: So much the better for him.

THE FRAULEIN: (*Coming closer.*) What has happened?

THE SON: You see me in a black coat so that I can step in dignity out of this house. Yonder the lanterns are already lighted! Do you see the lights on the horizon? Do you hear music, waltz and clarinet? The smell of exultant houses surrounds me. Tonight all the trains will take me into the immensely singing night.

THE FRAULEIN: Has he slapped you?

THE SON: How can you still talk of him who faint-heartedly is decaying on his bed! Look into his face tomorrow – it will pale from helpless anger and rage. This hero in the family circle: a stroke of lightning from the ether has touched him. His power was great over waifs and waiters – now it is broken. The health insurance people adore him, I laugh at him. Farewell to him!

THE FRAULEIN: Perhaps there is still light in his room. He can see you in the garden.

THE SON: His whip no longer reaches me. Below my crowd is awaiting me. Some are armed. Perhaps they share my feelings, then I will call upon them to liberate the young and noble in the world. Death to the fathers who despise us! (*For a few seconds The Friend's face reappears in the window, then vanishes again.*)

THE FRAULEIN: Don't you want to eat something? The road is long.

THE SON: No, Fraulein, in this house I will not touch anything anymore. Soon I shall enjoy nectar and ambrosia in the laps of beloved women!

THE FRAULEIN: (*In a trembling voice.*) Oh, dark and dangerous night!

THE SON: Don't be afraid. I march towards my star; I follow the law. Because the blood of the defiled slaves burns in my veins, I shall rise forcefully to a fight against all the prisons on earth. Like a criminal in the darkness, without any possessions, I leave through the fence. My house! This fire I carry away from you to pour it over people and cities. The chains are falling, I'm free! One step only, among the trees . . . Portal, how I love thee, and thee, the road, shimmering silvery to the awakening look! I'm no longer faint in heart. I know for whom I live. (*He has finished dressing himself. Stands before her.*)

THE FRAULEIN: You have forgotten the tie. I will bind it for you. (*She comes close fastening the tie.*)

THE SON: (*Bends down to her hand, formally.*) Thank you, Fraulein. Goodbye! (*He jumps through the window, disappears. The lights are stronger. Music is heard. A train rolls by.*)

SCENE SIX

THE FRAULEIN: (*Alone at the window, bending down after him. She presses a small pillow close to herself.*)

He rushes to the park as if in flight
Towards the God who has his head adorned,
For him day and night live unmourned
And twelve white eagles follow his might!
Dawn will not bring him back,
As long as the world is in his bosom mounting,
As long as women and stars
Sweet friend, may happiness never lack!
Heaven's rich hour has transported me
From the small room away to the big sea.
The wave, the night heavily on me weigh:
Where's rest, where solace, where hope's ray?
Oh, could I be somebody, and something for him do
Instead, only this little pillow I will sew
On which rest will be given him each night:
May he be guarded, without me at his side.
But when his eye in golden air will roll,
Then I wish to be close the one so dear,
Will watch eternally for the call
In darkness and unallayed tear.

(*She bends over the pillow and begins to sew, wrapped up in tears.*)

ACT III

SCENE ONE

(*A few hours later. Towards midnight. The anteroom to an auditorium. In the center a curtain is stretched, behind it, invisible to the onlooker, a lectern and the auditorium perspective. In the anteroom there are only a few pieces of furniture: easy chairs and a small table with glasses. On one wall hooks for clothing. Stage left and right small doors. The room leaves the impression as if a closed party were held before a meeting.*)

CHERUBIM: (*In tail-coat, the text of a speech in his hand, strolling through the room. Von Tuchmeyer enters, also in tails.*) Is everything ready?

TUCHMEYER: Everything. How's your speech coming along?

CHERUBIM: I'm holding it in my hands. Are the lights on in the hall? Is a glass of water on my table?

TUCHMEYER: (*Lifting the curtain a little.*) You can convince yourself: everything has been taken care of. Within twenty minutes, exactly at midnight, the chairs will be occupied. I understand many students will be coming. The hour has been well chosen. Those we want to reach will appear in large numbers. They expect the utmost from you! And who, in the middle of the night, is not burning with the desire to get revelations?

CHERUBIM: And the police?

TUCHMEYER: We are among ourselves. I have announced that we are celebrating the anniversary of our club "For the Survival of Joy." I was told if guests were to come, it is up to them. You need not be concerned.

CHERUBIM: I shall become very political and rabble rousing. Friend, my breast is full of new ideas which I will announce for the first time. I do not doubt my success! If ever, then tonight I will establish with you my "League for the Reorganization of Life." I tell you, things will be moving in an anarchistic way. That's why there should be continuous music while I talk. People should drink champagne, and those who want to dance should do so. Are we all assembled?

TUCHMEYER: (*Pulling a telegram from his pocket.*) Just now The Friend wired me that he'll be here within a few minutes. An important matter led him back. Thus we shall hear from him before the festivities get underway.

CHERUBIM: Since when do you have this news?

TUCHMEYER: For about two hours. It came from his home town. Yesterday he left here without saying goodbye. Perhaps he will bring with him new friends.

CHERUBIM: Between you and me, Tuchmeyer, haven't you noticed something in him?

TUCHMEYER: What do you mean?

CHERUBIM: I'm afraid of his shifty ways. He is not one of those who is willing to sacrifice everything for an idea.

TUCHMEYER: I have never noticed any doubts in him. On the contrary, he belongs to us wholeheartedly. How did you get that notion?

CHERUBIM: His sudden departure worries me. What may have motivated him? Did he want to pass over our celebration? Doesn't he know how important it is?

TUCHMEYER: He is one of those critical temperaments who always strive for the very opposite of themselves. He is his own contradiction, but therein lies the affirmation of his nature. Just like you I value in him something spiritual which is hidden. That's why I subordinate him unconditionally to you for you have the courage to be an exhibitionist. You are the representative ideal for our ideas, he is their counterpoint. You need each other if something is to be accomplished.

CHERUBIM: His departure is on my mind. He knows what's at stake.

TUCHMEYER: You forget his inhibitions. Before doing something, he needs to argue with himself. You live upon inspirations, he hates them. And he does not care for loud celebrations. But he is indispensable to us—the way we have grown together. Perhaps he is the strongest—the greatest he certainly is not.

CHERUBIM: Sometimes I have openly trembled before him as if he were a rival. I say that openly. But tonight, for the first time, I am totally superior to him. Whether he comes or not—I do not feel any anxiety anymore. My will is firm.

TUCHMEYER: Soon you will be standing in the hall!

CHERUBIM: Let us make good use of the time until then. I think I must talk to you. For you, the son of a privy counselor, you have lavished your inheritance on us. With you we rise and fall. My dear Tuchmeyer: to the devil with your father had he acquired something which in the long run would have benefited his son less than a good factory or mine. Therefore I keep you informed about all fluctuations to which our capital is subjected. Tonight I believe that I have achieved a satisfactory balance.

TUCHMEYER: Dear Cherubim, as long as my father lived, I sat in his office as a little clerk day after day and to me his death was a cheerful matter. Only since we became acquainted, do I know that one can live in spite of his money: that's why my belief in you is boundless. My father let me work for him and he cheated me as any little merchant in Poland. Had he not died at the right time when I detected this dirty slavery, I think I would have . . . well, etcetera. Even today I still think squeamishly of this paternal instrument with the double entry bookkeeping, of this Jewish jobber, who has spoiled my most beautiful years. Therefore I ask you: don't speak to me about balances; else I get mad!

CHERUBIM: I feel the responsibility—more than you realize. I know you are unable to redeem a note, and if you had to certify bliss with your signature, you'd rather oversleep. You are wonderful but you're unmindful of values. I don't want you to be poor some day. Your fortune finances our idea. Where would we be without you? Poor wretches without even a place to hold discussions. I have seduced you to a generosity which some day you may come to rue. No, don't blush—that's how it is. By the way, soon I will speak quite differently in the hall. Here we are only concerned with ourselves, therefore we speak under four eyes.

TUCHMEYER: To all that you tell me, I shall always answer. I would be quite unhappy if I were unable to return the dumb money, which my father has scraped together, to an idea common to people. It is only just that something which has been acquired without joy and to which so much misfortune clings, makes joy again! I'm literally burning for unsuspected sensations which, in spite of all the idiots, will materialize in this world! And if we have to accept the Ten Commandments, then one of them would be for me to extinguish the memory of my father among the living. Besides, I'm quite an egotist and would have fun doing so.

CHERUBIM: Well, then, listen to me. Just a year ago, we met accidentally—You, The Friend, the Prince and me, in a plain bar. With a few libertines, who made us pass the intervals between nights of discussion with pleasantries, we got together in a club, naming it "For the Survival of Joy." Since then we met frequently and celebrated some orgies. But I ask you now: what has happened? No dogma was proclaimed, but a couple of youths with small allowances and a few unsatisfied women have joined us—interrupt me if I am wrong. It is unnecessary for us to compete with the stars, to wage revolution in China or to make a discovery in the nervous system of frogs—all of this we are unable to do. We have the ambition not to do it. But it is important to enthuse those, who will soon be sitting in the hall, in something. It should be made clear to them that during the last twelve months none of us died. And that is much! Think of what life is like!

TUCHMEYER: Is that a contradiction to this year?

CHERUBIM: It is a contradiction. Listen to me to the end: we may have lived during those twelve months—but we do not know for what purpose. Life in itself is not enough. This question I intend to answer tonight: we live for us!

And I shall raise this part of my speech to an immense pathos; we want to make a sacrifice to death which has spared us!

TUCHMEYER: Not out of fear of the audience but out of curiosity: what is the sacrifice going to be?

CHERUBIM: By toppling the god of the weak and the deserted from his throne. In his place we raise the trombone of friendship: our heart. For we, people of today, live for the untold new! We are destined for each other. Thus let us correct the small laws of creation. Fight, deprivation and the limits of imperfect nature—let us have the courage to brutalize our ego in the world!

SCENE TWO

(*The curtain opens in the center. Prince Scheitel, in overcoat and tails, enters.*)

SCHEITEL: Good evening, gentlemen! Never mind. (*He takes off the overcoat.*)

CHERUBIM: (*Towards him.*) Prince Scheitel, it's you! You are coming at the right moment. We're discussing the possibilities for a new religion. Tonight I'll attempt a coup d'etat.

TUCHMEYER: Prince, we admire your faithfulness. You bring us the ultimate sacrifice, for you the most dangerous. How did you succeed in getting away from your father, the sovereign, for tonight? We did not expect you anymore.

SCHEITEL: Gentlemen, why all this balderdash? One learns here too. The other day I saw a play about a villain, the disguised story of my cousin the Duke. You know he had an affair with a singer, and this story was adapted for a Paris theatre. I did exactly what he did: I mixed a sleeping potion into my aide-de-camp's glass and disappeared behind a curtain. Notice that aide-de-camps always have to drink! Now I feel quite under the spell of a bad novel. Too bad that there is no woman around here. But you talk of something else. Please go on.

CHERUBIM: (*Cordially.*) Dear Prince! Right now we keep busy listing all our profits at the stock market. You could not be missing. I admit that sometimes I distrusted you slightly because of your well-cared appearance. Now I realize how right you were. Your quiet charm often threw us into the sphere of elegance. From you we received the fame of the monocle in the eye and the crown of silent salute when once you drove by, unrecognized as the prince, in a roll of drums. Your friendship was the greatest because it was indeed the most difficult.

SCHEITEL: But gentlemen, you make me blush! You are much more important and you have better chances than I have in my position. Unfortunately, luxury on the thrones has not reached as far as the mind, or else I would be the first one to come out for a republic. I have come to you because I joyfully anticipate this evening—and because I am a member of your Club for the Survival of Joy! Gentlemen, I still feel that this is a good club. Besides, I would not want to be absent on such an important occasion—even though I am only backstage.

TUCHMEYER: How did you get here?

SCHEITEL: In accordance with my rank, but on foot. When I climbed up the stairs, a couple of cars arrived and some persons already used the checkroom. These people are so nice—we shall have a great audience. Von Tuchmeyer, you must keep me company behind the curtain where we want to watch the success. I would love to sing the National Anthem; may God keep my father alive so that I may remain your friend for a long time. When he dies, I must ascend to the throne, if only on account of the newspapers. There is nothing I can do about it. In principle, I shall not take part in any coup since I have to be considerate of the brains of my descendants. You, gentlemen, are able to change the world at any time. Out of greater wisdom I have to leave it the way it is.

CHERUBIM: And we will make use of this right, Prince! Having reconciled ourselves to the idea that we are less important in this world, we want to achieve at least the highest possible development. I have the means for it and I shall apply them. Have trust in me. (*They sit down, smoking cigarettes. With oratorical emotion.*) Down in the hall I shall call everyone by his name. He may take his glass of champagne and stand next to me, and I shall say to him, you live—feel that you are happy. And then I shall assemble around me at the lectern, surrounded by women like Apollo in the Valley of Edymion, cheerfulness. You know Adrienne, with her sweet face? Think of that woman with her radiating shoulders! I will bend over her and pronounce that all men are born to happiness. And I wonder whether they will not cheer me, despite fear and confusion, and whether amongst us there is a traitor.

SCHEITEL: Bravo! Most certainly a farce in the view of statistics, but very amusing. Besides your lectern you'll find a basket with flowers. I had them placed there for you. Perhaps at that point you will throw the roses to the audience!

CHERUBIM: Yes, I am in favor of such an effect. You may hear it now: A League for Life Propaganda—therefore I must preach unscrupulous joy. Enjoy the smell of the rose without thorns. Put up tables at which one only wins and never loses! Bring women who love all of us! Long live our beautifully worldly feeling!

SCENE THREE

(*Through the door suddenly enters:*)

THE FRIEND: You are lying, Cherubim. (*All turn around, terrified. He pulls off his mask, standing before them in tails.*)

CHERUBIM: Oh, it's you!

THE FRIEND: Yes, I confess my guilt: I listened at the door. No repetition is necessary. I heard everything. And I declare war on you!

CHERUBIM: What does this mean?

THE FRIEND: This means: in ten minutes the hall will be crowded but you will not give a speech tonight.

CHERUBIM: Are you mad? I must talk. Whence this tone?

THE FRIEND: You will find out. Of course, I cannot prevent you from talking, but then I will speak after you.

CHERUBIM: (*Pale.*) What are you going to talk about?

THE FRIEND: About truth, my dear. You have been very diligent, one must say. Except, I'm afraid, this time your tricks will fail you.

CHERUBIM: My tricks. . . ?

THE FRIEND: And the roses, my friend. Watch out they are not transformed into rotten eggs which are going to land on your head. (*They all surround him.*)

CHERUBIM: Say, what has brought about your change within twenty-four hours?

THE FRIEND: It seems you're all tense. The hour needs brevity. Cherubim! This beautiful name you have given to yourself. Until now I did not think much to pronounce this name in its full sound. Now I am revolted. I cannot look into your eyes anymore. How did you dare to use this name of the angel! And indeed: do you intend to continue preaching to these infatuated people intoxication and drunkenness? Doesn't anything in you revolt against the lie? Deceived admiration which we paid to your curly head! You who proclaim God on earth—how shallow is your empire!

CHERUBIM: (*Jumping back with all signs of horror.*) A leper is among us!

THE FRIEND: (*In great seriousness.*) No, but one who has begun to recognize the thorns. What are you enjoying? What have you accomplished? Have you done in abundance something good or bad which has opened your eyes? Did you cry when, after a wasted night, news of a catastrophe appeared in the newspaper? Have you killed one of your enemies? And even when you felt the impotence of all that is earthly—was that of any help to you? What good is this gesture, this loud-mouthed baroque? I am revolted. You intended to fly off in cheerfulness and you are only deeper in morass. And you call this a new program?

TUCHMEYER: Don't listen to him. He is mad!

THE FRIEND: Herr von Tuchmeyer! It's true: you have sacrificed your inheritance to the idea of joy—but what if that idea was a fallacy? Who proves to you the correctness of an action? Your money and your soul are in this club—what would you say if you live for only a ridiculous thing? Yes, you childish minds: this proof is not difficult to produce in view of such heroes! If one has reached the end of his wisdom, the antithesis usually sets in. With one word: why are you still alive? Your aim has been achieved. Why don't you disappear? (*Nobody answers him.*) Your silence speaks loudly. Why didn't those questions cross your minds? What have you really pondered? Defend yourself! Is there an error in my presentation? Now, you monuments of nothing, go into your house of cards.

CHERUBIM: I only want to say one thing against you, dearest friend: how painful it would be if you too were away from us, in the fields beyond this laughing world!

THE FRIEND: Does that say anything against me? Is it at all necessary to live? And does it justify your masquerade? I am here to prevent that others, who feel bad, share your joy. To possess joy is to kill. I will eradicate that bacillus! Therefore don't be cheerful about me. It is still too early.

TUCHMEYER: What madness to talk against the world because you are alive! A trap for your mind which we have so much admired. You have stumbled miserably. A penitent always seems funny. Go into a monastery or, if the part of a clown is more appropriate to you, join an American circus.

THE FRIEND: Dear sir, for a year now I have, together with you, become frail— that's why I do neither the one nor the other. But as you will understand, I have the desire to liberate myself from you—you would do the same thing if you were in my place. Therefore let me speak!

CHERUBIM: In short: what do you want?

THE FRIEND: To convince those over there that there is no use.

CHERUBIM: (*Rushing towards him.*) You will not do that!

THE FRIEND: Step back! Is this your face? Now you reveal yourself to me: I thought your will is so firm! Why, then, don't you dare to fight? Let both of us talk, one after the other—or did you secretly already give in? Then have the courage to confess it and leave quietly. Why all this noise?

CHERUBIM: Traitor! Out with you! (*He and Tuchmeyer push him against the door.*)

SCHEITEL: (*Seizing them by the arm.*) Gentlemen, stop this! Let me say a word too. Are we here in parliament? Let everybody do what he wants. I have nothing at all against rebels and anti-monarchists. And I say it openly: I put myself on the side of the rebels—I feel they are right! He asked: why? His questioning impresses me. Can you give him an answer?

CHERUBIM: (*Drying his front.*) My God, yes—but not today! This paradoxical fluff—where everything is at stake.

SCHEITEL: Forget about the stakes. He who is stronger will be victorious. I don't believe in either of you. You want something—then battle for it! I can't help it, but there he is right. I consider it irrelevant to actions of any kind. But when it happens, it should be done honestly. You, Cherubim, don't impress me any longer as a man certain of himself.

CHERUBIM: Prince, I haven't worked for nothing. I cannot fight because I am conditioned to all registers of enthusiasm. If something goes wrong now, everything will tumble . . .

SCHEITEL: Let it tumble! One thing tumbles after the other! You do not have to husband your mental gifts: be glad about that. Nothing is yet lost—or did you seriously believe in yourself? Just before you have talked of your relevance. Then you have lied! You have subjected yourself to the eternally new—do it now!

CHERUBIM: (*In despair.*) No, I don't. And I don't want to. I cannot.

THE FRIEND: (*Coming closer.*) Cherubim, for the last time this blasphemous name and then into the nameless tent. Something bigger than you has entered here—fall into line. You've had your share of the pink star, do not any longer attach a false glitter to the urn. You have wasted all your heart and for that we loved you. That you erred was unimportant: you have lived, you have not achieved the heights. Nonetheless (*tries to grasp his hand*) thank you!

CHERUBIM: (*Pushes him away.*) I don't want your gratitude. I still live! I take up the fight. (*He straightens up.*) Where are my friends? Let's see whether they all desert me. (*He looks around.*)

TUCHMEYER: (*Walking towards him.*) I stay with you.

THE FRIEND: Fine. You want me to pull the mask off your face in front of all. I shall not spare you. Fight to the end. If you fall, you will be trampled upon—and fall you will. (*The musicians in the hall begin to tune their instruments. Light and the noise of those who have already arrived.*) Do you hear the music? Say—are you not afraid? Watch out—I'll talk against everything —and against you. Your women and your curl will be of no avail. I know the purposes of roses and champagne! When I talk, there'll be no fooling around. I shall prove the emptiness of your arguments—I know all your ins and outs! I will bring the howitzers of doubt into play: just watch out that not all of your joys will burst like air bubbles in view of such salute. My son, the hour of judgment approaches; I too am armed with fire. (*Rousing audience in the hall.*) Are you listening! Are you listening! Already you are pale. Not an earthquake, just a little word will destroy your heaven. I'll search out the demons from all corners and let them waltz around. I'll make a death's head out of your face. I'll uncover you just as an accountant uncovers graft. They'll stone you, my friend!

(*Cherubim, trembling, grabs a bottle of champagne and drinks.*)

THE FRIEND: You drink? Courage! You might stammer. You don't want to be spared—fine, I'm wicked enough to call the police. I'll have you arrested for incitement to lewdness! Then you may ponder for a while all your nonsense. Why should you not bear the consequences of what you are teaching? Better people than you have died on the cross.

SCHEITEL: Gracious goodness, one does not talk like that of my state. Please, that's no fun. If the police are really coming, I could not help you, I'm not yet of age. What are your thoughts?

THE FRIEND: In that case you disappear through the emergency exit.

TUCHMEYER: (*With cold composure.*) As long as I am here, nothing is going to happen.

THE FRIEND: Herr von Tuchmeyer, I know you have money. Others have it too. That does not make you worse than others — but beware of blunders. By the way, you will always come out alright; just don't make others comrades of your subaltern feelings. You may waste your money without qualms, some day it will roll again on your shoulders. But what good is this world of Monte Carlos and operettas to us? Aren't we older at every well and does not a new darkness surround us? Are we alive only to use this word continuously in barracks? To hell with such jokes! I hate all people who while dying still see the green in the mirrors of the trees. All those who have not felt aversion, despair and the penetrating risk in running away quietly, should be hanged. It must be recognized that we approach eternity through danger. What can we make of the cock's crow of luck! Learn to despise yourself! God punishes him who has too much enjoyment.

TUCHMEYER: Haven't you exchanged with us enthusiastically vows of friendship? Why do you leave us? You commit perjury. I am ashamed of you.

THE FRIEND: Dear Tuchmeyer, forget about the crusade. You may still be blessed with champagne and embraces. We cannot do so any longer. Permit us to think about it. We do not always stay at the age of twenty, and there are hardly any geniuses here (*he turns towards the Prince*) with the exception of you, Majesty. I say it for the last time: I am rotten and I have the courage to admit it publicly today. Whoever may talk before or after me: I shall prove the opposite. And if you don't believe me, come closer: my heart does not beat, I have barely more than 80 beats of the pulse per minute. (*He opens his jacket slightly. Renewed applause from the hall, then quiet. The overture begins.*) I hear the overture already. A good arrangement. (*To Cherubim.*) Prepare your wrists. Things get started.

CHERUBIM: (*Breathing heavily across the table.*) Let's agree on a compromise. I will not speak. But you won't speak either.

THE FRIEND: Nothing. No compromise. One of us will speak.

CHERUBIM: That means you want a scandal . . .

THE FRIEND: I leave you a way out: a third person will speak.

CHERUBIM: Who is this third one?

THE FRIEND: You agree? Decide for yourself!

CHERUBIM: My beautiful, my brilliant work. . .

TUCHMEYER: Don't do it. I'll stand by you.

CHERUBIM: (*As if awakened by this voice, stares at him.*) I yield. I save your money!

THE FRIEND: Now I get to the bottom, old chap! You secure for yourself the capital. Good luck! We don't need it. You have not spared yourself this final effect. You a fighter in God's hand! Now, Iscariot and Company, speak up again: may God grant you faithfulness, and comfort your widow.

TUCHMEYER: Stop it; I am still here! Who is the traitor around here? You, Cherubim, have cowardly deserted your greatness. And you, who have you become all of a sudden? Now the threads have been torn—I hesitate too—in whom should I believe? Was my money and, worse, was my belief in vain? Does my dead father thus avenge himself? Is this a way to bankruptcy? (*The overture ends. Loud applause. The noise from the hall increases.*) The first number is over. Fast now! Things must go on. I start to become my own stage director. We cannot very well stop in the middle of the program . . . after the first number. (*In despair to the Prince*) Prince, say something! Now comes the main thing. When nothing happens, the people will kill us . . . You are silent too? There is no emergency exit here. Doesn't anybody give a sign???

THE FRIEND: (*Raising one arm.*) Now all of you be quiet—not a single word. Not one word, do you understand me? I give you the sign. (*Goes to a door, opens it, calling.*) Come on, now!

SCENE FOUR

(*The Son, wearing a black mask and tails, enters.*)

THE FRIEND: (*Guides The Son, who does not see, hypnotically, without even touching him with his fingers.*) Breathe! There are human beings here! The ride is over. No more the fearful confinement on the train. Nobody pursues you. Here you will live. (*He lifts The Son's mask for a moment, looking into his visionary face.*) Raise your face! Earth rises—here there are no guards to beat you up. (*He leads him in front of the curtain, close to the hall.*) Do you hear them there? They wait for you. Talk to them. Evoke the pains of your childhood! Tell them what you have suffered! Call for their help, call on them for a fight! (*Soft music from the hall, as at the end of Act II from the Ninth Symphony.*) What do you see?

THE SON: (*Under the spell, remote and lost.*) What brilliance! What brilliance! Eye, you're shining! Here it is beautiful. Here the star is greeting me.

THE FRIEND: Whom do you see?

THE SON: (*With groping arms.*) When we had a celebration, I was allowed as a child to appear before the ladies during the dessert. Now I stand anew among ice cream and fruits, under the brilliant chandelier. Ladies and gentlemen—I know you—an awkward boy says hello to you. (*He bows slowly.*) I have seen their traces at night! Oh, that I am allowed to be with them. I come from the lightless ether, one of the poorest, yet I am here. That I can partake of such a miracle!

THE FRIEND: (*Pulls open the curtain and pushes The Son onto the lectern in the hall.*) Now talk to them. No longer a dead man—you are free!

SCENE FIVE

(*Roaring noise in the hall, the music stops. Briefly, the lighted hall with many people is seen. A long sound of expectation, surprise and astonishment is heard, then quiet.*)

THE FRIEND: (*Muted.*) Stand next to the curtain, Tuchmeyer, and listen! (*He rushes forward as if he were directing invisibly, and from behind the curtain, a choir.*) Let us all take part in this act. Now everything depends on . . . (*The voice of the speaker is heard but the word cannot be made out. In the anteroom there is an air of great excitability.*) There stands a man who in twenty years has suffered more than we have enjoyed in one year. That's why God has sent him . . . (*Unrest in the hall.*) What's the matter?

TUCHMEYER: He pulls off his mask. His eyes cannot see anything yet. He speaks of his childhood. Many cannot understand him . . . Now he talks louder. A few get up and come closer.

THE FRIEND: (*Clenching his hands.*) Does he move his hands?

TUCHMEYER: No – yes – now.

THE FRIEND: (*Opening his arms.*) . . . does he stretch them out like this?

TUCHMEYER: He is mad. He says that he takes upon himself the torment of the childhood of all of us.

THE FRIEND: He speaks the truth! Go on, what does he say?

TUCHMEYER: Now he has jumped down from the lectern. He stands among the people. He says: we all have suffered from our fathers – in basements and attics – he speaks about despair and suicide.

THE FRIEND: (*Bending forward, all his muscles tense.*) May the spirit assist him! (*He moves his hands and the features of his face with magic force.*) Do you listen! Tell it to them! (*A terrible will works within him to force the speaker under his thoughts.*)

TUCHMEYER: There will be a disaster. He says: the fathers who torture us should all be brought to justice! The audience is delirious . . . (*Tremendous tumult in the hall.*)

CHERUBIM AND SCHEITEL: (*Left and right at the curtain.*) All in revolt! They close in on him. The chairs are moving, the tables . .

CHERUBIM: (*Screaming hysterically.*) Bravo! Marvelous!

THE FRIEND: (*In front.*) Quiet! (*He draws a gun from his pocket.*) I'll kill him if he loses!

TUCHMEYER: (*At the curtain.*) There – now –

THE FRIEND: (*His back towards the hall, without turning.*) What?

TUCHMEYER: He tears off his clothing. He bares his chest. He shows the weals from his father's beatings – the scars! Now he is surrounded by so many that no longer can he be seen. Now – they grasp his hands – they hail him –

THE FRIEND: (*Triumphant.*) Now he is victor! Now he has achieved it! (*He puts his gun in a pocket, turning around. In the hall roaring applause and cheering.*)

TUCHMEYER: They carry him on their shoulders. The students carry him!

THE FRIEND: What does he say?

TUCHMEYER: He calls for a fight against all fathers—he preaches liberty—"We must help ourselves, for nobody helps us." They kiss his hands—what a tumult! They carry him on their shoulders out of the hall! (*More cheering.*)

THE FRIEND: He has established The League of the Young Against the World! Everybody should add his name to the list!

TUCHMEYER: (*Tearing his notebook in two.*) All should register. My father does not live anymore. Today he died a second time. (*He throws pages on the table.*)

CHERUBIM: Death to the dead! My father does not send me money anymore. (*In a loud voice.*) I sign up!

THE FRIEND: (*To Scheitel.*) And what does Your Majesty think? (*He holds a list close to him.*)

SCHEITEL: Give it to me!

THE FRIEND: This is called revolution, Brother Prince!

SCHEITEL: (*Ecstatically jumps on a table, putting up his arms similar to the beacon of the Statue of Liberty.*) Gentlemen, we are a generation. We will never be as young as we are now. There are many idiots—but, oh hell, we live longer! (*Standing on the table he intones the Marseillaise. The others join in, also some voices from the hall.*)

ALL:

Aux armes, citoyens!
Formez vos bataillons!
Marchons! Marchons!

ACT IV

SCENE ONE

(*The next morning. A hotel room in the style of a chambre garnie, but without bed. Breakfast is served on the table. Adrienne makes her hair in front of a mirror. The Son, slack in his tail-coat.*)

THE SON: Now that you comb your hair, it occurs to me that you must have made love to many men before me.

ADRIENNE: Why?

THE SON: I am tortured by a strange vanity.

ADRIENNE: (*Continues combing.*) I love you.

THE SON: But you have taken money from me!

ADRIENNE: And you? Are you living off the air? Haven't you also taken money for your speech last night? We all must eat.

THE SON: That's true. I took the money. I have performed for it an act from my childhood.

ADRIENNE: It's no one's concern with whom I will sleep tomorrow. I am a woman and cannot do anything else.

THE SON: I have been lifted unto shoulders. I must reflect about it, then it becomes clear to me. I am in another world.

ADRIENNE: You have made revolution yesterday? Don't you remember? Perhaps there are already reports in the paper.

THE SON: What happened eight hours ago is already history for me. Yesterday I still crammed history.

ADRIENNE: (*Wistfully.*) There you can see how revolutions come about!

THE SON: (*Smiling.*) No, you are wrong. I am not that clever. I am not an actor. I was genuine.

ADRIENNE: You don't know anymore what you did?

THE SON: I remember, we took a car driving towards the outskirts. I saw you only fleetingly. You seemed very beautiful to me. My God, I have completely forgotten to thank the students. They carried me around in the rain for about half an hour. Somebody pressed money into my hand.

ADRIENNE: Is it much?

THE SON: It'll be enough.

ADRIENNE: You come from a distinguished family. It is obvious from your underwear.

THE SON: How does this occur to you?

ADRIENNE: My boy. You are inexperienced in love and don't know anything about the most beautiful games. You still need an education. A man of your station must have it.

THE SON: I thought this comes by itself.

ADRIENNE: Men are not that intelligent. Some day you will want to marry. You might be taken in badly, your wife will deceive you because you do not know anything.

THE SON: I did not know that. What is to be done?

ADRIENNE: Do you want to learn from me? I'll teach you everything there is to know. And you'll become very clever.

THE SON: My father did not even teach me what to do after making love. This at least would have been his duty.

ADRIENNE: Fathers are ashamed before their sons. It's always been like that. Why aren't the sons sent to us? They are sent to universities.

THE SON: How much disgust and misfortune could be prevented if only a father were moral!

ADRIENNE: Instead we are being pursued by the moral squad!

THE SON: I understand. You begin to play a part. One has to demand from one's father to lead us with a free heart to the whore . . . A new goal for our League. I will mention it in my next speech. (*He runs around excitedly.*)

ADRIENNE: (*Finishing her hair.*) In the meantime, let's have breakfast. (*They sit down.*) Have you never before had breakfast with a lady after the first night?

THE SON: Never. Why?

ADRIENNE: You are awkward. All have buttoned my blouse. You don't know the simplest rule of etiquette.

THE SON: I am a beginner in love: this I realize fearfully. But the art is great, and a young man must know about it before doing advanced math. I accept your proposal. Teach me! I admire you: you know so much more than I do. When last night we went up the stairs, passing by the rude waiters—I was so anxious. We have been wandering through the miracles of life—from all the rooms of this ill-reputed hotel streams poured forth, dark and subconscious ones . . .

ADRIENNE: Pass me the butter!

THE SON: Yes, and how you took the overcoat and threw it on the bed—I shall not forget it. So naturally, so clearly. Now I know how to ask for a candle which is missing.

ADRIENNE: Next time you shouldn't be so uneasy.

THE SON: For the first time I saw somebody disrobe. And to savor this slowly! How beautiful is a money deal. We are all among ourselves.

ADRIENNE: Did you like me?

THE SON: First blue, then pink; the black of the stockings? I liked the laces very much.

ADRIENNE: And me?

THE SON: I do not remember how you looked.

ADRIENNE: (*With great composure, taking another slice of bread.*) You don't love me yet.

THE SON: Seriously—don't be mad at me. I was disappointed. How prosaic is a body and quite different from what one imagines. Adrienne, you lived for me when you left the car and entered the corridor. How you know everything in a strange house! You are a heroine! Without you I would have crushed to the earth in shame! In faded velvet at the bannister—I think it is just as charming to walk across gold fields and into Malaysian joints. I have not noticed any longer something terrestrial in your feet!

ADRIENNE: Some men love my feet only. I have to dance naked for them on the carpet!

THE SON: Whither does this word lead to? What a magic circle! In the panopticum there once was a lady with blue tattoes—there are many things one knows nevertheless.

ADRIENNE: Why haven't you slept?

THE SON: I was not tired. I loved you so much in the dawn, resting on the same bed with you when you no longer felt anything for me. I believe that only then did I love you completely.

ADRIENNE: (*With quiet superiority.*) You can't do it yet. But you will learn it.

THE SON: I am eager to learn this art. What fears are rising to take what is being offered to you! One has to overcome them.

ADRIENNE: I have lost my gloves. Give me a new pair!

THE SON: (*Putting a gold coin on the table.*) I don't know the price of gloves.

ADRIENNE: That's too much. I'll bring you some of it back. (*Putting on her hat.*)

THE SON: Where are you going?

ADRIENNE: Home, to change.

THE SON: When will you be coming back?

ADRIENNE: Should I fetch you?

THE SON: I shall be waiting for you.

ADRIENNE: Do you have some small change for the trolley?

THE SON: (*Gives it to her.*) Do you have any siblings?

ADRIENNE: Let's not talk about this. My sisters are decent girls.

THE SON: It's strange to think of that.

ADRIENNE: Why do you want to know?

THE SON: I am looking for someone equivalent to my weakness. You are too superior to me.

ADRIENNE: I'm not losing my balance that fast!

THE SON: I hate everybody who knows about my condition. I can understand a man killing a woman who sees through him.

ADRIENNE: But Bubi! Who talks about such things at your age!

THE SON: You are awakening my slumbering talents. Since I know you, I see certain things in myself clearer. The delight at your sex stimulates thinking. You always find a way to yourself.

ADRIENNE: (*Confidently.*) Tonight there is dancing at the Piccadilly. I'll introduce you! Afterwards we go to a bar. (*She now wears hat and overcoat.*)

THE SON: (*Watching her slim figure.*) "Toréador, en garde . . ."

ADRIENNE: Goodbye, Bubi!

THE SON: (*Kisses her hand gentlemanlike.*) Goodbye, Madame! (*She exits, waving to him.*)

SCENE TWO

(*Lighting a cigarette, The Son walks with long steps through the room. He deposits the ashes on a plate. The Friend enters.*)

THE FRIEND: Good morning.

THE SON: You are here already?

THE FRIEND: You don't seem happy to see me?

THE SON: (*Embarrassed.*) Oh, yes—what's the time?

THE FRIEND: It's 11 o'clock. You have just had breakfast? At home you usually do not get up at such a late hour.

THE SON: I need a new suit. How do I get one?

THE FRIEND: Listen, I just saw sweet Adrienne leave.

THE SON: I love her.

THE FRIEND: No, you're wrong.

THE SON: She will teach me.

THE FRIEND: I didn't mean that. What will she teach you? You may just as well jump that grade—you are preparing for better things. To take seriously a woman of her kind is not quite worthy of you. You will get into a conflict with the doctors. I advise against it.

THE SON: It tickles me to experience a new danger. I'm really mad about her.

THE FRIEND: Soon you'll have enough of her.

THE SON: In what area?

THE FRIEND: Do you forget that your father may pick you up any moment now. You are not yet of age, my son.

THE SON: Now that I enjoy life for the first time, back into slavery? Never.

THE FRIEND: Don't call that trivial situation life. A dull night with a woman— and you are not even disappointed? You were never as shallow as with this woman. Each one of your mad words last night was greater. I have come to meet a prophet and find a little fugitive who is in love. You play a satire on yourself! Your Fraulein in your father's house was tremendous. But this whore, what a stupid dummy!

THE SON: In my life she is at least as important as you are.

THE FRIEND: Let's be serious. If you could see your little feelings under a magnifying glass, you would be astonished to find how it's crawling with lice.

THE SON: But I don't want to see it. I tell you, she will pick me up here and that's it.

THE FRIEND: Then be happy. (*He takes his hat.*)

THE SON: Where to?

THE FRIEND: I leave you to the whore. I feel sorry for you.

THE SON: Are you mad? Is that a way to leave the room?

THE FRIEND: No, my boy. It's either—or. Pimps are born every day.

THE SON: After so many stations I finally want to do something completely.

THE FRIEND: You have this opportunity.

THE SON: And how?

THE FRIEND: When is the rendezvous?

THE SON: In half an hour.

THE FRIEND: Then we can talk for twenty minutes. Let's sit down. (*They sit across from each other.*) You admire that girl? She may be trained and quite efficient in her field, I admit. That's much. But haven't you done something a few hours ago? Man, you were standing in a European hall—think of that! What fame rests upon your shoulders? Do you think it is that easy to shake off responsibility? Then you deserve to be hanged. He who tosses an idea into the world and does not see it through, should die in the fires of hell. There is only one thing I recognize unconditionally as having a right to exist—the action. And how do you now stand here? They saw you from out front, Prometheus, and now they see your behind—nightingale and simpleminded fellow! Somebody should hold up your trousers.

THE SON: What are we talking about? Of your action, not of mine. You bear the responsibility for me—I was under your spell, I know. Why didn't you say all this yourself? Above all, answer this!

THE FRIEND: They know me, unfortunately. Too often have I shared their need. I'm no orator. The flame is denied to me; in the end I would only talk against myself. But you own their souls. I don't know why, but you do. It's the greatest power—and you don't use it. That's enough to drive me mad. First I get you out of your cage and for two hours you are the embodiment of the force of my ideas. But already you betray me and hide behind the instincts of the mob.

THE SON: When today in the dawn I made peace with myself, I also recognized this strange stage play. I had to ask myself who I am. The suspicion grew that your help was not quite so impartial. I don't complain about my role, but—

THE FRIEND: I will admit that my will dominated you. I abused you from the very beginning. Even during the speech I dictated to you, without your knowledge, words and gestures. Your hatred of me is quite understandable.

THE SON: (*Getting up.*) Hm.

THE FRIEND: (*Pushing him down.*) Just a moment. Now the talking is up to me. When I saw you then, in the hour of suicide, bleeding from your fight, it suddenly became quite clear to me: here was the man whom I needed. For I saw with the greatest excitement that you possessed what we all were lacking—youth and the glow of hatred. Only people like this can become reformers. You were the only one, then, the vital one, the caller: it is God's will. Thus I resolved to put you on a pedestal from which you cannot fall down.

THE SON: Are you certain of this?

THE FRIEND: Yes. An indestructible, unspent force drives you to the front. Perhaps it should not have happened. But since it did happen, you can no longer back out.

THE SON: And what shall I do?

THE FRIEND: Destroy the tyranny of the family, this medieval furuncle, this witches' sabbath and torture chamber filled with sulphur! Do away with the laws, restore freedom, man's greatest treasure.

THE SON: At this point of the axis of the earth I am glowing again.

THE FRIEND: Then ponder that the fight against the father is the same as the revenge against the princes one hundred years ago. Today we are right! Then crowned heads oppressed and enslaved their subjects, stole their money and imprisoned their spirits. Today we are singing the Marseillaise! Every father may still let his son go hungry and enslaved without being punished, and prevent him from doing great things. It is only the same old song against injustice and cruelty. They stand on the privileges of the state and of nature. Away with both of them! For one hundred years now tyranny has disappeared—let us help a new nature to grow! They still have the power which those once had. They can still call the police against the disobedient son.

THE SON: An army be summoned! We too have to conquer the castles of the robber knights.

THE FRIEND: And to destroy until the last generation. We will preach against the fourth commandment. And the theses against idolatry must be nailed once more at the Castle Church in Wittenberg! We need a constitution and protection from beatings which force us to respect our torturers. I will formulate the program for I can prove its correctness. You'll lead the army.

THE SON: But who is going to help us? Until we have reached the 21st year we are subject to the whip and the madness of the paternal ghost.

THE FRIEND: Is it the first time that something is being done for freedom? Long live the flags and scaffolds of the revolution! When the old is dead, new laws are made. We will shout until we are heard in parliament under the golden dome. We risk our blood for something great. And this idea, this fire, powerful on each day in the world, will not be extinguished by superior power or deceit. We must be victorious because we are stronger.

THE SON: Aren't we alone—the two of us in this room? From what places will there be an echo?

THE FRIEND: From all where there are young people. Haven't you spoken last night? Didn't you hear the voice of the one a thousandfold? Be convinced: the hour has struck! And it demands the sacrifice.

THE SON: What can I do? I am only a poor devil who has been banished.

THE FRIEND: You have made a beginning—finish the work. Now do the utmost. Take up the holy duty!

THE SON: What great thing have I accomplished that you put all your cards on me?

THE FRIEND: The fate of millions lies in your hands. What you saw last night is only a small part of the powerful nation of sons ready for your action. The spark is ignited—toss it into the powder keg! Now a tremendous, unprecedented fall must occur which will make the whole world revolt. Yesterday your speech went out—today you must do it!

THE SON: Then tell me, as once before at a turn of my life, what I should do.

THE FRIEND: (*Taking a gun from his pocket.*) Do you know this black instrument? It harbors death. A quick clutch—and life is snuffed out. Look carefully: with this piece of metal I would have destroyed you last night, but you were victorious. You have overcome death: that makes you immortal in life. Look at it, it is loaded. I give it to you. Take it.

THE SON: Against whom?

THE FRIEND: Soon you'll be a captive.

THE SON: No!

THE FRIEND: Yes, the bloodhounds are on your tracks.

THE SON: No!! No!!

THE FRIEND: Your father knows where you are. He called the police.

THE SON: Who—has done this?

THE FRIEND: You want to know: me.

THE SON: You. . . !

THE FRIEND: (*With great composure.*) I told your father where you are.

THE SON: (*Grasps the gun and aims.*) Betrayal! Pay with your life! (*He fires, the gun fails to go off.*)

THE FRIEND: (*Unchanged.*) You didn't wind it up. I knew you would shoot at me. But it's still too early. I am not the right target. You must pull the gun apart—this way—now the bullet is in the barrel. (*He does it and gives the gun back to The Son.*) Now you may shoot.

THE SON: (*Dropping the gun.*) Forgive me. (*He puts the gun in his pocket.*) I'll keep your gift.

THE FRIEND: And now that the last cliff has been navigated—how useless would a murder be at this very moment—I will tell you why I did it. I know of the temptation to go to bed with fame and women. But I need not be afraid—I see you're still burning. That is good. But everybody has to put himself to the test, if only on account of the weakhearted and ignorant. In a campaign both have to be considered. (*He looks at his watch.*) In not more than ten minutes, figuring the speed of the police, you'll be led off in chains before your father. You stand before him, the chains off, eye to eye. And he will pronounce your verdict: forced labor. What will you be doing then? (*He stands quite close in front of him.*)

THE SON: (*Stepping back.*) What end of the world have we reached? . . . Can thinking still go on? . . . I feel dizzy . . .

THE FRIEND: (*Following him.*) What will you do? Where are you going?

THE SON: (*Pressed towards the wall.*) You are terrible. There is nothing left here. (*Screaming.*) Patricide!

THE FRIEND: (*Stepping back.*) God be with you.

THE SON: (*Plunging forward, grasping his arm.*) I can't do it! I can't do it! (*In unspeakable fright.*) Let go of me! (*He falls down before him.*) I beg you!

THE FRIEND: (*Unyielding.*) Man! Once the grandiose idea has taken hold of you, you can no longer escape it. You are in its grip, for better or worse. You have no more rest. Go forward and carry it out!

THE SON: (*After quite a while.*) How can I end a life—me who hardly was born. Superhuman courage is necessary even to destroy the smallest animal. Once I choked a dog to death and was unable to sleep for a few nights. I am too weak. Don't make a murderer of me! The Erinnyes are already within me now.

THE FRIEND: Is cowardice victorious? And you wanted to go into battle!

THE SON: Save me from a terrible nightmare.

THE FRIEND: And yet just before you have aimed the gun at me in cold blood! How can this be reconciled? Why does not my shadow pursue you? Did I do more to you than your father? Answer, why could you do it in my case?

THE SON: How well was this effect achieved! I understand—behind me the trap was closed. Woe upon you for you won't save me. I hate you boundlessly . . . Now I feel: I could do it.

THE FRIEND: Who cares about us and a dead man. Hundreds of thousands will live!

THE SON: There are noble fathers!

THE FRIEND: We do not fight for the exception—we fight for the deed!

THE SON: Why do I have to achieve it in horror?

THE FRIEND: Because no one but you is given the power.

THE SON: (*Rising proudly.*) Whatever I'm doing, I will not do it for power's sake. What do I care! I want to suffer to the end for my own poor generation. I alone had to suffer the great injustice. I shall do it! With you I have nothing any longer in common.

THE FRIEND: You gave your word. (*Quiet sets in.*) A few more minutes and you'll be freed from my presence. Shall we meet again? Perhaps not. One of us could make the great jump—perhaps it won't be you. I mean the full distance. (*The Son does not answer.*) I could appear to you in a seance. But I don't care for that. Rather would I decay monistically. While on shifting grounds still next to each other, we should make things clear to ourselves.

THE SON: (*Absent-minded.*) To disappear from the golden star . . . once again into the night . . . who will now help me in my need?

THE FRIEND: (*In a firm voice.*) For the first, the most important time: you will help yourself. Here in death your life begins. You stand in midst of the greatest fate. What you have lived for so far were confinement and night chapels or so it seemed to you. One does not live with his signboards. Prove, my boy, that you are not lost!

THE SON: (*Quietly and meekly.*) I am so much afraid of death.

THE FRIEND: Haven't you died before? How come I surprised you at it?

THE SON: Then I didn't know the world. Then I was rich. Then I could die.

THE FRIEND: Be courageous. Today you are better.

THE SON: And when I stood in the hall—you forget?

THE FRIEND: Only now will you totally become yourself. I take my leave. You have overtaken me. There is nothing anymore I could give you.

THE SON: I'm going to my death. Do you know what that means?

THE FRIEND: Him or you. He must die who has not achieved his life . . . He who hates life in another person should not be afraid of his own death. No dog is defeated without a fight! With us it is best that we are seeking out dangers, that we are not born without them. Thus save your generation—our whole generation: the best we possess. Even though bad and transient, we must get there some day.

THE SON: And the one against all! Is there space in the old world?

THE FRIEND: Down with all profiteers! Give no quarters—none was given to you! Don't shudder: it is God's will that laws change.

THE SON: Let's wait for the police. These few seconds are a trial by ordeal. I am ready to go. The hangmen will find me courageous. No, I shall not submit. If no one enters here to chain me, I shall flee, and no harm will come to him. But if it happens (*raising a finger*) I swear! And I will provoke the most awful duel. But I want to see the crime that a father hands over his son to the police. When that occurs, nature has been dehumanized. Then someone else may guide my hand!

THE FRIEND: Think of that oath!

THE SON: The cloud is billowing in the sky. I could pray: keep the evil away from me!

THE FRIEND: You need no Christ on the cross. Kill what has killed you!

THE SON: (*In tears.*) I am weak like the small sacrificial animal. Yet I have strength.

THE FRIEND: (*In profound emotion.*) Doubt and temptation are given to us just as the infinite to make us time and again founder on our own will, yet attain the highest. Believe me for I know all the pitfalls, and I say it trembling: we only live in order to be even more glorious. Happiness and torture and madness are not in vain—so let us go to work, Brother, between the shadows, so that Death will not reach us until the very end. There is only little space left between us—the bridge of the common stream is already arching. Hither you now go. I'll call your name with respect; soon many will do so.

THE SON: Is there absolution for what I am doing?

THE FRIEND: It is in the belief of people whose saviour you will become.

THE SON: And if it fails? When I am fooled by ghosts? When hope will founder?

THE FRIEND: Then we would not be standing here. Our little being is the grain of great fulfillment. You only live out the fate of your birth. What once moved your soul—today you'll finish it.

THE SON: I feel as I had lived a long time ago.

THE FRIEND: Then live anew! Live in order to understand your being's endless chain! Don't have doubts any longer. A beacon illuminates our poor fate. Brother before death: once more we are allowed to be together.

THE SON: (*In great emotion.*) Give me your hand!

THE FRIEND: Is there anything I can do for you?

THE SON: Here, take the money. I received it yesterday. (*He hands it over.*) I left my father's house poor and I intend to return that way. Believe in me! (*They stand opposite each other, highly determined.*)

SCENE THREE

(*A knock at the door.*)

THE SON: (*In a clear voice.*) Come in!

INSPECTOR: Who of you gentlemen is the son of the doctor?

THE SON: It's me.

INSPECTOR: (*Approaches him.*) Please follow me.

THE SON: Your identification?

INSPECTOR: (*Showing his badge.*) Here.

THE SON: (*Polite.*) Thank you. May I ask you one question to clarify things for me: has my father sent you?

INSPECTOR: We have been asked to take you to him.

THE SON: Alright. (*The Son and The Friend look at each other.*)

INSPECTOR: (*One step closer.*) Since you are under suspicion that you might flee, I have to tie your hands.

THE SON: Then you take away a criminal?

INSPECTOR: (*With a shrug of his shoulders, apologizing.*) I'm sorry . . .

THE SON: (*Stretching out his hands.*) I do not object. (*He is tied, The Son and the Inspector exit.*)

SCENE FOUR

THE FRIEND: (*Alone, opens the window.*) They push him into the wagon. In chains! Now, on to the guillotine, hangmen! It's your heads which will roll! (*He steps forward.*) He will do it. Triumph! Here my strength is at an end. (*He sinks into a chair.*) I think it's now my turn. (*He looks at himself as a photographer would.*) Is this the correct posture? Please smile! Who photographs the moment of disintegration? (*He pulls out a flask.*) Nothing more than this sensation on earth—that's little. One should not think of one's end. (*He opens the flask, smelling.*) Damn it! Curiosity is great. Is it true that one dies out of interest? Would it be possible to write down the memoirs of this second? But fame is sad and art no longer attractive. No, rather this way. And even when he commits the deed, what will have happened? He lives and will hate me even more. What have I talked him into? I will disappear and give the lie to myself. To say yes to life is permitted only to a scoundrel who knows already in advance how he will end. It's time now. Monologues before death are frequent. I lived to my own satisfaction. I swear: the madness will not reach me here! I am faster than the ghosts. (*He pours the liquid in a glass and reflects.*) Beautiful things occur to me. Ghost manufacturers could enrich themselves from my death. Devil, why am I still talking? I am afraid to trot all by myself into the yonder!!! (*He jumps up, trembling, and listens.*) What's that: steps on the stairway? That's most certainly sweet Adrienne! Heaven gave her a job: she should serve me destruction in a drop of champagne . . . (*He leaves to meet her.*)

ACT V

SCENE ONE

(*A few hours later. The Father's consultation room. A long room: in the central wall a door left and right, on the side walls one door each. To the left The Father's desk with books and telephone, in front of an easy chair. Before the center wall glass cabinets with medical instruments, to the right an examining table. On the right side wall a bookcase, a smaller table with chairs. On one wall a reproduction of Rembrandt's "Anatomy.")*

THE FATHER: Thank you, Inspector. Did my son resist?

INSPECTOR: The young man was rather quiet. We had expected to find a madman. Instead we encountered two gentlemen talking. There was no reason to use force. Nevertheless, according to your wishes, we tied his hands. The trip over here was also absolutely without incident. Perhaps, sir, the measures taken were a little too harsh. Often called to judge men, I have always used coercion only with regret. Perhaps it will be possible to lead the young man on the right path with kindness. I am convinced he is not a bad man. There are much worse ones around!

THE FATHER: Inspector, I have watched him for twenty years. I am his father; furthermore, I am a physician. I ought to know.

INSPECTOR: Sorry, sir, I did not want in any way . . .

THE FATHER: Quite the contrary: I am asking you for your opinion. You are certainly an experienced man but you look at things from your perspective. I believe I am not mistaken. I have pondered long before making a decision. Kindness is no longer possible! Only the utmost severity can change him to the better. This boy is depraved to the very bottom of his character. He wants to evade my will—that cannot be allowed to happen under any circumstances. You haven't heard his speeches! Today's youth is battling all authority and decency. Be glad you don't have a son like him.

INSPECTOR: Sir, I do have sons. And I love them! I could not call a curse on their heads. I know the terrible tragedy only too well! We have to deal with criminals and animals. Before pushing my own blood into this abyss, I rather would not want to live anymore. Even in the case of youthful criminals reprimands and probation are possible under the law. What terrible things has your son committed? Did he rob, forge, murder? These are the creatures we deal with: this is the company you will drive him to. May I ask your advance forgiveness for a candid word: you stigmatize him for the rest of his life. You stamp him with the mark of the court. He has undertaken a little fling against your will . . .

THE FATHER: (*Laughs scornfully.*) A little fling!!

INSPECTOR: You have the right on your side and you will punish him. But does that justify humiliation? I'm afraid the use of chains cannot be undone—a misfortune may happen!

THE FATHER: He has refused to obey: it is not for the first time. If he—who is my son—leaves my house disgracefully, what else can I do but make him feel my power! Otherwise I am the dishonored one. What will people think of me? How will I be looked at? If no other means will help, I must use this ultimate one. I owe this to my sense of duty—towards myself as well as towards himself. I still believe I can change him to the better. He is young—this may serve as a warning for his life. Inspector, to me you are a stranger. Nevertheless, I have told you more than anybody else. Please have confidence in me. In this hour I feel heavily burdened. I only want the best, according to my conscience. But this I cannot let pass! You are a father yourself. What would you do in my place?

INSPECTOR: A being whom I have fathered cannot be depraved. That to me is the ultimate law! We are aging. Why should our son not be young?

THE FATHER: Inspector, I have been a member of a students' club. I have fought for my honor with the sword. I am still bearing the traces. (*He points to a scar on his face.*) I have to keep my house pure. I cannot allow insults from a child to go unpunished. Besides, to me the responsibility of an educator weighs too heavily to be compared to that of a twenty-year-old boy.

INSPECTOR: I am afraid we talk at cross-purposes. I too have fought in my youth. But the number of semesters and student duels doesn't seem to me to be a valid yardstick. Our sons require that we help them. Sir, we got to do that. Whether they are better or worse than we are is a matter of time, not a matter of the heart.

THE FATHER: I am shaken—I also apologize for an open word in a serious hour. How can a father, an official talk like that! Our young people get worse and more depraved from day to day. That is a well-known fact! And we should not check such decay in adolescents? I consider it my holiest duty to fight aberrations and I shall do it as long as I breathe. In what kind of world are we living! Here read in the paper how far we have come! (*He takes the paper, points out a story.*) Yesterday a stranger preached against fathers in a secret meeting. That can only be a madman!! But thousands listen to such poison and suck it up voraciously. Why doesn't the police take action? These bums are a danger to the state. All seducers belong under lock and key; they are the scum of the earth.

INSPECTOR: (*With a look at the paper.*) This meeting was known to the police. It is a club of young people. It stands under the protection of a highly placed personality.

THE FATHER: Well, well, then we shall soon have anarchy!

INSPECTOR: I can set your mind to rest about this lecture. It was directed only against immoral fathers.

THE FATHER: (*Scornfully.*) Against the immoral! And the government supports such activities? All the more it is our duty to protect ourselves against betrayal in our own families. No, Inspector, the utmost harshness, the utmost harshness!

INSPECTOR: We are the people of the courts. How much perdition do we see! Believe me, I don't want to hang an innocent, least of all my own son. And if he does me wrong a thousand times, I am still his father. We fathers have to win our sons first before knowing what they are.

THE FATHER: You seem to see a son as something quite peculiar.

INSPECTOR: (*Modestly.*) I look at him as a creature given to me and whom I have to serve.

THE FATHER: (*Getting up.*) Inspector, I thank you. I too know my duty as a father, but in a different sense. I do not wish any disappointments on you! Even in this case I shall try to talk kindly to my son—as long as this is possible. I cannot say anything more. Please bring him in now!

INSPECTOR: I shall untie your son. He will find his way to you by himself. (*He bows and leaves. The Father sits down on the chair at the left.*)

SCENE TWO

(*The Son enters slowly through the center door. He is still in the tail-coat and remains at the door, in a watchful posture.*)

THE FATHER: (*Gets up and walks towards him.*) Here you are. (*He stretches out his hand.*) Don't you want to give me your hand?

THE SON: No, Father.

THE FATHER: We have to talk to each other. Sit down. (*He walks to his desk, looking at him.*) You don't look well—do you want anything to eat?

THE SON: I am not hungry.

THE FATHER: Do you first want to change clothes and go to your room?

THE SON: No, thank you.

THE FATHER: (*Sits in easy chair, back of the desk.*) Well, then sit down. Let us talk. (*The Son sits down, opposite him, at smaller table.*)

THE FATHER: Last night you secretly left your room; you have been forbidden to do so.

THE SON: You have called the police. You had me brought here in chains.

THE FATHER: I wish to get an answer to my question: where have you been during the night?

THE SON: Under the guise of education you have committed a crime against me. This will be revenged.

THE FATHER: (*Jumps up, but controls himself.*) I warn you!

THE SON: I am not here to beg you for something in yesterday's tone. I have found you to be small-minded and inferior, I am here to demand an explanation, and also atonement: an eye for an eye. You will not hear from me a single superfluous word. Today I shall play the sober part in which you did not succeed yesterday. Keep all your little emotions aside. Do you want to examine me about my mental state—you are welcome to do so. I am not indulging in fantasies. Should I lie down on this table? (*He turns towards the examining table.*)

THE FATHER: (*Pulls from behind the desk a whip and bends it over his knees as if he wanted to examine it.*) Go on!

THE SON: (*Upon the gesture with the whip dips his hand in his pocket and leaves it there.*) You may have your merits in auscultating lesser individuals. But beware of touching the whip! (*He lifts, without The Father noticing it, the gun halfway from his pocket.*) I have my own certificate. I am completely sane and know exactly what I am doing.

THE FATHER: (*Subconsciously intimidated, lets the whip drop momentarily; at the same time the gun disappears in The Son's pocket.*) You were found in a hotel of ill repute this morning—what do you have to say?

THE SON: It's the truth. I was there.

THE FATHER: (*Astonished.*) You don't deny it?

THE SON: Not at all. Why should I?

THE FATHER: (*Taking notes on a sheet of paper, as in an examination.*) What did you do there?

THE SON: I slept there with a woman.

THE FATHER: (*Rising rigidly.*) You have . . . enough . . . get out of here!

THE SON: (*Without moving.*) Our talk is not yet finished. As I told you already: it concerns you.

THE FATHER: I tell you: get out of here!

THE SON: (*Also rising.*) You allow that I absent myself?

THE FATHER: Everything else you'll hear in your room.

THE SON: (*Walks to the center door, locks it.*) Then I must compel you to listen to me. (*He takes the key, stretches out his arm in a threatening gesture.*) Sit down or there will be a catastrophe. You don't want it any other way—you'll get it. (*He walks towards The Father who raises the whip as if he wanted to use it, but in a sudden spell of dizziness he falls backwards into the easy chair.*) For the last and bloodiest time I am asking you here and now: will you let me leave your house peacefully? You have tortured me long enough. But your power over the defenseless child is now at an end. Before you there stands someone determined to go all the way. Choose! (*He waits for an answer. It does not come. He goes back to his table, sits down again.*) Let's go on talking.

THE FATHER: (*Comes to from his absent-mindedness.*) My hair has turned white.

THE SON: What do I care about your hair—think of yesterday's words you have spoken. We are men. At least I consider myself one.

THE FATHER: What is it that you still want here?

THE SON: My right. And this time I intend to succeed to the very end.

THE FATHER: Give thanks to your creator that in this hour I am too old. Otherwise . . . But the last word has not yet been said. Speak up! I will not bear the reproach on my deathbed that I was the first one . . . Finish speaking! I want to get a clear picture of you before tearing up the bond which still ties me to you.

THE SON: Father, you won't have to tear up anything. Whichever way you may be on your deathbed—you don't move me any longer. Just leave me to the furies and take care that you can die peacefully! Therefore listen and believe me what I say to you: set me free! I stand before you in terrible seriousness.

THE FATHER: I laugh at your seriousness. An insane man stands before me.

THE SON: Father, let us forget all this. But end this posture. Your life is at stake!! Everything be undone, torture and revenge and deceit. Cross me out in your heart as a son. And now, let me go . . .

THE FATHER: (*Scornfully.*) Not yet, my son.

THE SON: Well, then—when I fled from your power many, who were hidden in the garden, went with me, armed with guns.

THE FATHER: (*Attentively.*) What does that mean?

THE SON: And in the same night, one hour later, I have talked to them, against you, the tyrants, the fathers—you, who have contempt for everything that's great—yes, turn pale. I am no longer given unto your hands. Your intellect is too small for an idea, thus yield to the deed! We are not insane, we are people and we are alive. We live doubly because you want to kill us. You will not take one step out of this room without being beaten, spit upon and crushed by the thousands I have called. Thus we take our revenge on you and your power, and none of the gods will desert us. (*As The Father wants to answer:*) Yes, I have begun the revolution in the midst of the torture chamber in which I stand—and soon my name will be in the headlines. Now a nation of sons is fighting when you will long be decayed to dust. Here, read in your newspaper. (*He throws a paper at him.*) Are you trembling? Is this your true face? Yes, it was me! I have spoken!

THE FATHER: You are lying! You are lying!

THE SON: Here is the mask of the unknown. (*He pulls it out and swings it through the air.*) Do you still have doubts? It is me!!! Now I want to see your end—in your own room . . .

THE FATHER: (*Shaking over the table.*) Say that you are lying, or else I forget myself.

THE SON: (*Erect.*) Will you set me free? I don't want your money. I'll give it to the poor. You can disinherit me. The only thing I want is my life! I still have much to do in the world. I will not bleed to death from these few seconds.

THE FATHER: I am your father no longer.

THE SON: You never were. Father—who knows it today? Where was I born? I was a stepchild only. Should I ever have a son, I will make amends for the evils I suffered. Oh, wonderful, great light, could I experience to be a sweet child's protector!

THE FATHER: (*In all his harshness before him.*) Your wish will be granted. You don't have a father anymore. I have offered you his hand—you have turned it down with contempt. The curse may come over you. I repudiate you. But because you have brought shame over me last night, I also extinguish you. In my hour of death I will think of my word: I have forgotten that you are my son. Today you see me for the last time. Don't dare to ever enter my house again. I will have you driven out by dogs. Here I take the whip and throw it at your feet. You don't deserve that my hand still touches you. (*He throws it down.*) Now you may go.

THE SON: Father . . .

THE FATHER: Do not pronounce this word!

THE SON: Will you set me free?

THE FATHER: Free? (*He laughs shrilly.*) One more year you are still under my power. At least one more year I can protect humanity from you. There are institutions existing for such a purpose. Now leave my room and don't ever return!

THE SON: (*With iron calm.*) The room is locked. No one is leaving. (*The Father gets up, walks slowly, awkwardly to the side door on the left. The Son speaks in a frightful voice.*) Stop! Not another step! (*The Father for a moment almost paralyzed by the voice, sits down at the desk. The Son pulls unnoticed the gun from his pocket.*)

THE FATHER: Help against madness . . . (*He grabs the telephone receiver. The Son lifts the gun high up.*) Please police headquarters.

THE SON: Look here. (*He aims at him and says in a clear voice.*) One more word and you are no longer alive!

(*The Father makes an involuntary motion to protect himself. He raises his arm. The telephone receiver falls down. The raised arm sinks down. They look each other in the eye. The gun remains aimed at The Father's chest. Then The Father's body begins to twitch, the eyes roll and become rigid. He is briefly convulsed, then he slowly slumps over the chair to the floor. A stroke has ended his life. The Son with unchanged face notices The Father's fall. His arm sinks down, the gun comes down with a thud. Then he himself sinks automatically, as if his consciousness were interrupted, into a chair near the table.)*

SCENE THREE

(Through the right side door The Fraulein enters. She sees The Father, rushes towards him but realizes he is dead. Then she recognizes The Son in the chair and slowly moves towards him.)

THE FRAULEIN:
 Now you are here again—and at your feet
 The home is blended with the wonderland.
 Is there no voice near you to greet!
 Now be welcome by a mother's hand!
 And your brow, after such heavy fight,
 I will carefully dry to the last bead.
 I do not ask, I know the suffering knight.
 He will no longer hate you: he is dead.
THE SON:
 Do you still know the boy who left you here?
 Don't ever believe that to you I've return'd.
 Where is the man to overcome such fear?
THE FRAULEIN:
 Poor friend, all your bridges are now burn'd.
THE SON:
 No, Fraulein, wherever this may lead,
 From the horizon no longer comes the pull.
 I know that only sacrifice precedes deed;
 My heart is bleak, once it was all too full,
 Much have I done, but I'm no more of use,
 Gone is the passion once so great.
 Much is fulfilled—yet far I'm from profuse:
 The cloud moved on. The force remained.
 When over the dead I step once more here
 Into life—then I am away and far.
 In ecstasy I cannot disappear,
 Thus I may vanish towards a new star.
 What in my mind now seems quite sore,
 Soon I'll see quite bright and clear.
 If I shall kindle fires more and more,
 I will not be there: I shall be here!
   (The Fraulein kneels before him, as he did, before her, in Act II.)
 I see the heaven over you now shine

The one I have seen in my very first night.
Could I now on your bosom whine
My tear would appear in a diff'rent light.
And could today the words I say—
Birth and existence—in your lap once both—
Your love would no longer make us sway.
I am too poor. The Earth has let me go.
  (*Slowly both get up.*)
Into pain and lovelessness, into the fate
Of what I recognize, my body drives away.
If I'm surrounded by emptiness and hate:
My mind is fully creative on this day.
With me for what is vital to unite
I have not shunned Death's eternal might.
Now man's greatest power to proclaim
Towards freedom, is my heart's new aim!

(*They clasp their hands together, then exit towards different sides. The Father's body, in the center of the room, remains.*)

END

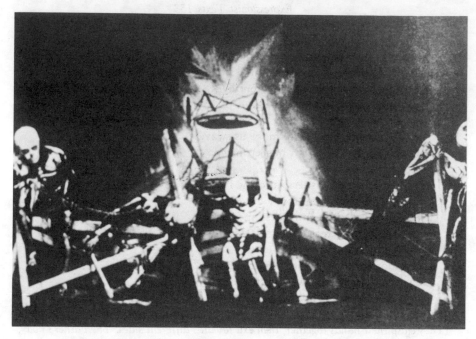

Karl-Heinz Martin's production of Toller's *The Transfiguration*
(Berlin, 1919)

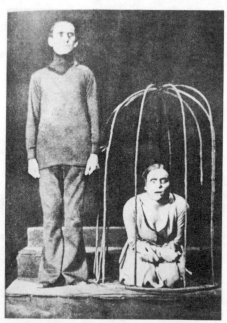

Jürgen Fehling's production
of *Man and the Masses*
(Berlin, 1921)

The Transfiguration

[1919]

Ernst Toller

Translation by Edward Crankshaw

Among the German Expressionist playwrights, Ernst Toller (1893-1939) had the most intensely dramatic life and career. Born to a wealthy Jewish family in the eastern part of Imperial Germany, he suffered from an acute complex based on his parents' religion and means. Two years after his father's death, the eighteen-year-old Toller studied in France, matriculating from the University of Grenoble. In 1914, he secretly crossed into Germany in order to volunteer for frontline military duty. His insistence on exposure to fighting in areas of combat soon gave way to a militant pacifism. In 1916, Toller was hospitalized, and a new education and rejuvenation took place. He became a radical Socialist.

By 1918, Toller was leading a strike of the munition workers in Munich. Within one year, he found himself President of the Workers and Soldiers Council in Bavaria, at the head of a potentially violent revolution. Searching for new and humane ways to foment a brotherly union with the counter-revolutionary reaction, Toller was despised and ridiculed by many of his comrade-in-arms. His Bavarian Soviet republic was also defeated, and in 1919 Toller was sentenced to five years in prison for the crime of treason.

During Toller's convalescence in 1917, he began work on an autobiographical drama called *Transfiguration*. It told the story of a Jewish artist, like himself, who attempts to demonstrate his love for his German fatherland by volunteering for the front, only to discover the unheroic madness of mechanized warfare. Toller handed out dialogue from *Transfiguration* at the Munich barricades and read sections of it at strike meetings. An overtly political Expressionist play, *Transfiguration* was completed in prison. Performed at Die Tribüne, a small left-wing theatre in Berlin in 1919, *Transfiguration* electrified its audience. Toller's blending of proletarian activism within a scaled-down but forceful Expressionist text—in addition to Fritz Kortner's masterful performance—made *Transfiguration* one of the most exciting productions of the period.

Curiously, Toller himself never saw *Transfiguration* although the Bavarian Minister of Justice had offered him a pardon at the time. As a matter of principle, he remained in jail for the entire five-year sentence. Both the solitude and the publicity proved helpful to his career; nine plays and mass spectacles as well as several books of poetry were produced during those years. *Man and the Masses* (1920), staged in 1921 by the Berlin director Jürgen Fehling, was especially successful and considered by many critics to be the last significant Expressionist production.

When Toller finished his prison term in 1924, German politics and the public's taste in drama had changed markedly. He continued to publish essays, travel accounts, autobiographical books, poems, and plays but few had the impact of his prison work. Except for Erwin Piscator's production of the semi-documentary *Hoopla! We Live!* (1927), Toller's plays were largely ignored. In 1933, he fled Germany for exile in Switzerland and Great Britain. Working for various anti-fascist causes, especially for aid to Republican Spain, Toller spent his last years in Hollywood and New York. But the victory of Franco in Spain and the unexpected collapse of the anti-Axis partners around Hitler's Germany brought Toller into a state of deep despair. In April 1939 at his New York apartment, he committed suicide.

CHARACTERS:

Friedrich	Old Gentleman, an anti-pacifist
People	Professor
Friedrich's Sister	Priest
His Mother	Agitator
His Uncle	Student
His Friend	Girl Student
Gabriele, the Friend's sister	Man with the Turned-Up Collar
First Soldier	Sick Man
Second Soldier	Woman
Wounded Soldiers	Death as the Enemy of the Spirit
Madman	In the Guise of a Soldier, a
Corporal	Professor, a Judge, a Night
Hospital Nurse	Visitor
Doctor	Soldiers
Officer	Cripples
Beggar-Woman	Nurses
Her Husband	Hospital Orderlies
Chairman	Skeletons
	Prisoners

The scenes "Troop-train," "No-man's Land," "The Wounded Soldiers," "The Lodger," "Death and Resurrection," and "Mountaineers," are on the borderline between reality and unreality, to be thought of as scenes watched distantly in a dream.

The action takes place in Europe before the beginning of regeneration.

ALARUM

Shatter the cup, the blinding crystal cup,
Its magic spills
As thick as pollen from the blackened hearts
Of blood-red tulips.

We wandered in a twilight world of wonder,
Touching with gentle hands the legends there;
Building great dream cathedrals
Of sunshine and faith,
While roses fell around us . . .

Sudden a screaming discord: Murder!

Heavy with dreams and blind we stood,
With horror ringing in our ears.
Mankind cried out.

We saw vulgarity run mad;
Our feet were set on quicksands of despair.
A man cried out.

A man, a brother,
Molded by suffering and joy,
A mad illusion and disdain;
A man, temple of the will,
Of rapturous joy and holy sorrow.
We heard the fierce and urgent cry:
The way!
The way!

O poet, lead us.

PROLOGUE
(Which can also be regarded as an Epilogue)

(Night in a vast military cemetery. The graves, which are arranged in companies, are each marked by a simple grey cross of iron. Some of the crosses are decorated with a rose, others with a flaming heart, others with a little wreath of wild flowers. Apart from this they are all alike. Only the name and regiment is inscribed on the crosses of the private soldiers; but at the side of every Company are the officers' graves marked by larger crosses decorated with flaming suns and each bearing the date of birth and civil occupation of the dead man. The skeleton figure of Death-By-Peace enters wearing a top-hat and carrying a brightly colored silk handkerchief. With him is the skeleton figure of Death-By-War wearing a steel helmet and carrying in his hand a human thigh-bone—his Field Marshal's baton. His breast is covered with orders.)

DEATH-BY-WAR: Well, here we are, old friend.
  If only I had known you had trouble with your lungs
  . . . However, believe me when I say I'm sorry . . .
  I should hate to think
  You regretted coming.
  Well, here we are . . .
  Everything nice and tidy
  And in order.
  There they are, buried by Companies;
  Subalterns, N.C.O.'s and Privates
  Just as in life—all quite correct.
  Our gallant heroes!
  The names are really quite superfluous.
  But there they are—pure piety:
  Numbers would have been enough.
  And over there are the officers . . .
  If you'd care to see who they were—
  In civil life, I mean.
  If you care to glance at them?
DEATH-BY-PEACE: Hm, hm, hm, hm!
  Magnificent, my friend.
  Magnificent!—I really mean it.
  You make me quite envious.

DEATH-BY-WAR: You flatter me, dear friend.
   I must confess
   I thought your skepticism foolish;
   I am familiar too with civil life.
   But now I'm only too glad
   To know you are convinced.
   And now with your permission
   We'll have them up on parade.
DEATH-BY-PEACE: Oh, certainly.
DEATH-BY-WAR: In Companies,
   Forward
   March!
   (*From the graves the skeletons of dead soldiers and men arise wearing steel helmets.
   They stand stiffly at attention by their graves.*)
   Shoulder arms!
   (*The skeletons snatch up their crosses and shoulder them; the officers hold theirs as
   though they were swords.*)
   Attention!
   Officers
   Take command!
   (*The officers hurry to the right, ranging themselves as Company leaders.*)
   Dress by the right!
   Eyes front! Quick march!
DEATH-BY-PEACE: Congratulations, sir! My heartiest congratulations!
   Really, you know, it would be terrible
   If I tried anything like this!
   Thousands and thousands
   Of women and children,
   And a few old, halting graybeards
   For officers,
   Leaning on their umbrellas.
   Yes, I must admit you have me beaten.
   There is a certain order
   In your life;
   Mine is pure chaos.
DEATH-BY-WAR: Really, my friend, you flatter me.
   Practice and discipline — that's all.
   You should apply it too. . . .
   In Companies, right wheel!
   Halt!
   Attention!
   Stand at ease!
   Senior officer forward!

(*A Colonel salutes and steps shakily forward.*)
Very good.
Lay down your arms!
(*They put back their crosses.*)
Attention!
Company,
Roll heads!
Colonel,
You will take charge.
(*The Soliders, hands on hips, roll their skulls, supervised by the Company Commanders with the Colonel as Commander-in-Chief.*)

DEATH-BY-PEACE: You really thought of this yourself, my friend?
Your own idea?

DEATH-BY-WAR: How do you mean?

DEATH-BY-PEACE: All this business—
Did it originate entirely in your own skull?
That's all I mean . . .

DEATH-BY-WAR: I see. Well, well—
It's not so simple as it sounds . . .
How shall I put it?
I'm sure you'll understand . . .

DEATH-BY-PEACE: Yes, I see, I see.
But wait a moment.

DEATH-BY-WAR: Attention!
Company, dismiss!
Back to your grrraves!
(*The men return to their graves.*)
Thank you, gentlemen . . .
Criticism can wait until next time.
(*The Officers return to their graves. There is silence. Then suddenly Death-By-Peace bursts out laughing.*)
You surprise me, sir!
Did anything go wrong?
Was anything overlooked?
(*Death-By-Peace continues to guffaw, fanning himself with his bandana.*)
Explain yourself, sir!
Your laughter is insulting!

DEATH-BY-PEACE: Your humbug is insulting!
I was right to doubt your word—
I'm nothing but a fool to let myself
Be humbugged into admiration.
I called my kingdom chaos . . .
I did myself injustice.

I am the leveller
In whose eyes all are equal.
There are differences, of course —
The rich are sometimes tactless . . .
Still, such discipline as yours
Is foreign to our world.
You play at being victor,
You who yourself are vanquished —
Vanquished by war, my friend,
Conquered, and compelled
To die by numbers!
Officers, N.C.O.'s, military discipline —
A regular barracks!
You should have been a Sergeant Major!
Death subservient to a lot of Colonels —
Whatever next!
My friend, your bluff is called!
You'll be the general laughing stock
Unless you clear off quicly
While you can!
DEATH-BY-WAR: Infamous! Intolerable!
I refuse to argue!
DEATH-BY-PEACE: Just one small paradox
To bring this little interview
To a successful close . . .
You are a modern Death —
A product of the times,
Comparable to the futile living of today
Where everything is rotten under tinsel.
Goodbye, you petty, miserable Death,
Goodbye, you snobbish little hypocrite,
Propped up with military phrases.
Goodbye, and give my compliments
To your lords and masters,
The men of war!
Haha! Haha! Hahahaa!
(He goes off shaking with laughter.)
DEATH-BY-WAR: (Stands dazed; then tears up a tuft of grass and wipes the sweat
from his skull.)
Goddamn his eyes!
It seems to me
I'm just about played out!

FIRST STATION

SCENE ONE

(An ugly room in a townhouse with the furniture barely perceptible in the dusk of evening. Standing in the windows of the houses across the street are Christmas trees lit up by candles. Friedrich leans against the windowsill.)

FRIEDRICH: They are lighting the candles. Candles of love. Mysteries reveal themselves, love reveals itself in the light of candles . . . while I, a Jew, outcast, struggle between one shore and the next, far from the old and farther from the new. A nasty hybrid. Wasn't there a sudden stirring of sympathy in the room when she said, come and see me? Many thanks, Fraulein—your humble servant—you may be sure I shall be punctual. Artificial smile to order! Tragicomic puppet. . . . No—I'll no longer drag around my weariness. What are they to me—my people? Their blood is in my veins, but what is that to me? It is to you over there I belong—to you. A simple creature, ready to prove himself. There must be an end to all this compromise and self-division! An end to all this proud defense of what I really scorn! I must be brave. *(His Mother enters.)*

MOTHER: Back at last, Friedrich? Where have you been all day?

FRIEDRICH: Wandering, Mother. Wandering—as usual. Don't look at me like that, Mother . . . I've told you—wandering. Like him, Ahasuerus, the Wandering Jew whose shadow crawls through fettered streets, who hides in dark and pestilential cellars, who gathers rotten swedes in the frozen fields at night . . . Yes, it is him I seek; my great brother, Ahasuerus, the eternal wanderer, the homeless one . . .

MOTHER: You blaspheme against your name, Friedrich. You are not homeless.

FRIEDRICH: Then where is my home, Mother? They have homes, over there; homes of their own to which they belong. Over there they are at one with themselves and their homes . . . free from the weariness of life, the sickness which corrodes and poisons thought and feeling . . . They can laugh, over there, and live with joy in their hearts. They have their own land in which they are rooted, for which they can live and die.

MOTHER: You are feverish, Friedrich.

FRIEDRICH: Yes, I am feverish, Mother! Won't you give me a sedative? If only you were feverish as I am! Now you are sad, Mother. Now you grieve because I have never been a good son—the good son who always smiles so lovingly upon his mother . . . like the good sons of all your friends. Oh, they are so touching, those tastefully composed family pictures from well-bred homes!

MOTHER: I refuse to talk to you, Friedrich. You are restless and full of foolish thoughts; and it's all because you are out of work. I don't want to hinder you in your ambition. Go on with your sculpture if you must. But first make some provision for your future. Take up some steady job to earn the money for your sculpture. I may say your uncle Richard agrees with me in all this.

FRIEDRICH: So Uncle Richard agrees! Well, well, well! And didn't he cite the case of Strindberg, who spent the last ten years of his life "a ruined man"? . . . Didn't he say how he regretted having missed a chance of immortality through Strindberg? Missed his opportunity to become a "figure in literary history," as he puts it so beautifully? Yes, if only he had given Strindberg a little money when he asked! If only he had done that, this righteous citizen! But if ever he met a second Strindberg he would soon decide he was nothing but a decadent dilettante and leave him to starve, calming his own agitated conscience by increased speculation on the Stock Exchange. Good, kind, business man.

MOTHER: Your father was also a good, kind business man, remember.

FRIEDRICH: I know, Mother, I know! Yes, he was kind and good, too. He left you to work and run the house while he went off on shooting parties . . . good, kind father! He would talk to me about living respectably, about the solid virtues. And when I wanted to get away—to get away from here—he forced me to stay. . . . He was my jailer!

MOTHER: Friedrich! I will not allow you to speak like that of your father. Believe me, Friedrich, your words hurt nobody but yourself. . . . However, you are upset today, and I have no desire to upset you further. . . . We will talk about it later when you are calmer. . . . Meanwhile I have just one thing to ask you, a tiny favor—just to please your old mother. Friedrich, I beg you to attend Divine Worship. People would be so . . .

FRIEDRICH: People! Why not be honest and call it Public Service, not Divine? What is your God but a cruel and narrow judge, judging all men by cut and dried laws? Judging always by the same dead laws? Divine Service—homage to bigotry! It's revolting! Are you any more free when you leave your House of God? No, no. . . . And the narrowness of this noble House of God is suffocating, I tell you, suffocating!

MOTHER: When your father died he left us very badly off. I scraped and saved to keep you, to send you to school, to make life easier for you than it had been for us. I slaved to make things easy for you in every conceivable way. You must understand: I am your mother, you are my child. Everything I had was for my children. Nothing, nothing for myself.

FRIEDRICH: True, Mother, true. I could weep even to think of it. But am I ungrateful, am I quite a brute to you? No, I am not that, Mother. You care for my material needs; you tried to make it easier for me to earn money now . . . yes, you have laid the foundations of my material future. But what have you done for my *soul*? You taught me to hate all who don't belong to our race. Why?

MOTHER: They do not like us. They only tolerate us. They despise us.

FRIEDRICH: Oh no, oh no! They are full of kindness, gentleness and love; all-embracing love. Look! See the candles they have lit over there—candles radiating love and kindness. . . . I called you mother because you bore me, but can I still call you mother when you leave my naked soul exposed, as foolish mothers leave their babes naked to the cold? (*His Mother goes out silently.*) Now a bond is snapped. . . . Or was it really broken all those years ago? . . . It had to break. . . . Mother . . . (*Silence.*) No, it's no use. . . . Now they are giving out the presents. The children are singing now. When did I ever sing here in my childhood—really sing? (*His Friend enters.*)

FRIEND: Good evening, Friedrich! Gabriele asked me to come, and anyway I intended . . .

FRIEDRICH: Tell her I cannot come. I'm feverish, ill.

FRIEND: I don't like to leave you alone.

FRIEDRICH: No? Very kind, I'm sure. Thank you, thank you. . . . However, sit down—over there. Would you like to do a little bargain? A good table knife for a box of drawing tools? The compasses are admittedly a little faulty, but you'd hardly notice it. I've arranged them in the box so that they look all right.

FRIEND: Friedrich, why must you torment yourself like this, and me too? (*Friedrich embraces his Friend and begins to sob.*) There, you poor fellow.

FRIEDRICH: I am not poor; and I don't want your sympathy. I don't need it. Nor your sister's either. I'll release her from the humiliation of being seen out with me. I've women enough over there in the narrow streets . . . I've enough money for that. But I don't need you. I am strong enough by myself. I need nobody, neither them nor you.

FRIEND: In that case I had better go. But you can always count on me.

FRIEDRICH: Count on you? Ask you for help? Never! . . .

FRIEND: No, I did not mean it like that. But before I go I had better tell you what I came for. . . . Special late night final—fighting has begun in the Colonies. They want volunteers. I wish I could go myself, but my people won't allow me to.

FRIEDRICH: (*As though suddenly awakened.*) Won't allow you?—And you let the matter rest there? You can't be serious. . . . They want volunteers. . . .

Forgive me if I behaved like a brute just now. Forgive me if I spoke roughly. . . . Volunteers wanted. Release, release from stifling, barren, narrowness! Oh, but the struggle will unite us all! The greatness of the times will make us all great. . . . The resurrection of the spirit. . . . All pettiness forgotten, all childish limitations swept away. . . . Once more shall the spirit shine forth in its eternal beauty. . . . As for me—as for me, this is a Heaven-sent gift. . . . Volunteers wanted! Was I half-hearted? I feel myself strong! Strong to embrace my duty. Now I can prove that I belong to you! Now I can prove I'm no outsider! . . . Where can I enlist? At the town hall? (*Friend nods.*) I am so happy, so happy. Apologize to Gabriele for me. I have found my country at last. Tell her that joy has come to me—joy on the evening of love. You see the Christmas trees over there? A tree in every window. . . . Tell Gabriele that I thank her from my heart; and greet her for me. She will understand why I do not come myself; she will understand and be glad. (*Rushing out.*) Now I can prove myself, prove myself! (*Darkness.*)

SCENE TWO

(*Compartment of a traveling troop-train. Badly burning oil lamps shed a meagre, flickering light on the sleeping Soldiers huddled close together. With them one silent soldier [with Friedrich's features] and another with a skull for a head: both shadowy figures.*)

FIRST SOLDIER: How long must we rattle through the night.
  Lurching, lurching in the grinding of machinery,
  Tortured machinery?
SECOND SOLDIER: Time without end and space without end,
  Days, weeks, nobody can tell.
  Would that I lay sleeping in my mother's womb.
THIRD SOLDIER: Would that an earthquake had swallowed up the house
  When my mother lay in my father's arms.
FOURTH SOLDIER: Would that a fiery ball from Heaven
  Had struck down the man who lured
  My mother to the wood.
FIFTH SOLDIER: Words, foolish words! Year after year
  The bitter coffin holds us here enclosed;
  Year after year the flesh falls away,
  Human flesh stinking and decayed.
SIXTH SOLDIER: Aimlessly we wander, like frightened children
  Driven by a senseless tyranny,
  Murdering, hungering, creatures of violence—
  Children, frightened children,
  Overtaken by a long dark night.

SEVENTH SOLDIER: If only I could pray. Kind and sweet words
  Which my mother so tenderly taught me,
  Babbled now with careless lips and cruel . . .
FIRST SOLDIER: Endlessly we journey.
SECOND SOLDIER: Endlessly the engine roars and groans.
THIRD SOLDIER: Endlessly we marry, endlessly we breed;
  And evil springs eternally from lust.
FOURTH SOLDIER: Stars spring from the womb of Time
  And Time eternally is ravaged and gives birth.
FIFTH SOLDIER: Endlessly rotting.
SIXTH SOLDIER: Endlessly children in fear of the father.
SEVENTH SOLDIER: Sacrificed by mothers, shivering, cold.
ALL: Endlessly journeying,
  Endlessly . . .

SECOND STATION

SCENE THREE

(An hour before sunset. A water-hole in the desert.)

FIRST SOLDIER: Dusk is falling, but the heat is as thick as a blanket. Is the boss asleep?

SECOND SOLDIER: Why shouldn't he sleep? Tent pitched, mosquito-net put up, while he stood watching with his hands in his pockets—now he's sleeping.

FIRST SOLDIER: They can sing if they want to. I've had enough for today.

WOUNDED MAN: Water!

FIRST SOLDIER: Give him water! (Friedrich gives him water.)

WOUNDED MAN: Take the corpses away. Everwhere I go there's corpses.—You want to saw my leg off? It hurts all right.—But I wanted to be a dancing master, one, two three . . . one, two, three—that's how a waltz goes.

FRIEDRICH: Try to sleep, chum!

WOUNDED MAN: But take the corpses away. I don't want to teach them to dance . . . they . . . are . . . tormenting . . . me . . . I suppose I'd better though . . . Won't anyone strike up? . . . (Sings.) One . . . two, three, one . . . two, three—that's how a waltz goes.

FRIEDRICH: Try to sleep. Give me your hand. I won't hurt you. I'll put a cool wet cloth on your forehead. Dreams will come and ask you to dance, garlanded dreams—they'll dance with you over the heather, and away to your home.

WOUNDED MAN: (Sings.) One . . . two, three, . . . one . . . two, three . . .

FRIEDRICH: Oh God!

FIRST SOLDIER: Why bring Him into it? He's all right for the officers, bringing true religion to the heathen with fire and murder. I am the Redeemer, rejoice in Me! Only let them blow your brains out and you'll find eternal bliss!

FRIEDRICH: It must be; it must be!

SECOND SOLDIER: What must be? Fire and murder? Or hospitals and madhouses?

FRIEDRICH: For our country's sake!

FIRST SOLDIER: Country? I don't know so much about country. All I know are toffs flinging money about and workers sweating to save it.

FRIEDRICH: But how could you live without a country? I'd go mad with all this horror if I couldn't grit my teeth and say "It's all for my country."

SECOND SOLDIER: You're a funny one to talk like that.

FRIEDRICH: Why any funnier than you?

FIRST SOLDIER: And you a foreigner? Ha, ha!

FRIEDRICH: I'm not a foreigner. I'm one of you.

SECOND SOLDIER: If you fought with us a thousand times you'd still be a foreigner.

FIRST SOLDIER: (*Calmly.*) There's a curse on you. You're a man without country.

WOUNDED MAN: A man . . . with . . . out . . . a . . . coun . . . try . . . one . . . two . . . three . . . that's . . . how . . . a waltz goes . . .

FRIEDRICH: Haven't I proved myself, on duty here and at home, in raids and on guard?—haven't I proved that I'm one of you?—Have I ever panicked and run away? Have I ever skulked in shell-holes?

SECOND SOLDIER: You're still a foreigner.

FRIEDRICH: Then I'll have to fight for my country in spite of you. For who can rob me of it? I carry it in my heart.

FIRST SOLDIER: (*Genially.*) You'll have to get used to the idea, chum. If it comes to that none of us has got a country. We're just like a lot of whores. (*The two Soldiers lie down and sleep.*)

FRIEDRICH: The outraged earth trembles under me; the trees are withered; the wilderness crawls nearer—where shall I go? I entered a house and it burned to ashes over me. (*Laughing aloud.*) Ha, how the rafters crackled in the blaze! (*The Lunatic during this last speech has crept up to Friedrich.*)

LUNATIC: Little brother . . .

FRIEDRICH: Who's that?

LUNATIC: Little brother . . .

FRIEDRICH: What do you want?

LUNATIC: Don't be afraid.

FRIEDRICH: Where have you come from?

LUNATIC: The sandstorm drove me here.

FRIEDRICH: You live over there?

LUNATIC: Live? I died over there. . . . Aye, there are many dying over there. . . . They're running, running . . .

FRIEDRICH: From the sandstorm?

LUNATIC: I'm thirsty.

FRIEDRICH: Here, drink this.

LUNATIC: I can drink my own blood, I don't need yours . . . fool . . . idiot . . . blockhead . . . little brother . . .

FRIEDRICH: You're bleeding!

LUNATIC: Don't worry about that. I can drink blood.

SECOND SOLDIER: What's all that row?

FRIEDRICH: I think — (*Second Soldier notices the Lunatic.*)

SECOND SOLDIER: He's ill, that fellow! (*Lunatic begins to babble.*)

FIRST SOLDIER: Mad, is he? He'll have strayed from the camp along the line.

LUNATIC: (*Begins to weep.*) Home . . . I want to go home . . .

SECOND SOLDIER: Take him to the Red Cross station.

FRIEDRICH: Oh God!

FIRST SOLDIER: I am the Redeemer, rejoice in Me. I'll take him over to the Red Cross. The Red means that the blood will be washed away.

FRIEDRICH: It must be so. It is for our country's sake! (*Corporal enters.*)

CORPORAL: Another man wanted. Patrol to get information about the enemy reserves. One of you must come back, so we're sending five to make sure. Any volunteers?

FRIEDRICH: I'll go. I'll go, and damn you all! (*Darkness.*)

SCENE FOUR

(*No-man's land. Dark clouds sweep across the face of the moon. To right and left are barbed-wire entanglements in which hang skeletons white with quicklime. The earth is torn up with craters and shellholes.*)

FIRST SKELETON: I feel so lonely.
  The others all lie sleeping round.
  Still, I feel the cold no longer,
  The deadly cold which racked me through
  While I hung dying here
  Caught between friend and foe.
  The quicklime did its work,
  The bloody shreds of skin and flesh
  Soon fell away.
  Aha! Now I can clap my hands!

(*The Second Skeleton, caught in the opposite wire entanglement, moves.*)

SECOND SKELETON: There, they've started up again,
  The blighters. I have to dodge
  Their blasted bullets all the time.
  Still, I don't feel hungry any more —
  Who's that? A cold and bony hand . . .
  Let go, I tell you,
  Let me go!

Ah, I forgot . . .
It is my own right hand
Clutching with rigid fingers
At myself . . .
FIRST SKELETON: Don't look so down, old man!
I've learnt to do a nigger dance
And rattle my loose joints.
Today we're no more friends and enemies,
Today we're no more black and white,
Now we're all alike.
The worms soon ate our colored skins,
And now we are all alike.
Gentlemen . . . let's dance.

(*The Skeletons between the wire entanglements shake of the earth from their bones.*)

SKELETONS: Now we are all alike.
Gentlemen . . . let's dance!
FIRST SKELETON: The colored ribbons on our chests
Have long ago decayed.
Our names were in the newspapers
All bordered round with black.
Aha—let's dance!
SECOND SKELETON: You over there! You without legs!
Pick up your shins and rattle them,
Clap time for us while we dance!
ALL: (*Laugh.*) You over there! You without legs!
Pick up your shins and rattle them,
Clap time for us while we dance!

(*The legless Skeletons pick up their shin-bones and rattle them together. The others dance.*)

FIRST SKELETON: Haha, what have we here?
You over there—why don't you dance?
ALL: Gentlemen . . . let's dance!
SKELETON: (*Half-hidden.*) I'm so ashamed!
SECOND SKELETON: Ashamed?
Really gentlemen . . . shame! (*He covers his nakedness with his hands.*)
I think we all were—once. (*All cover their nakedness hastily.*)
FIRST SKELETON: The wilderness drove shame away forever.
Who us knows shame today?
Fools! Idiots!
Aren't we all naked here?

Behind our naked bones
Yawns emptiness.
SKELETON: (*Half-hidden.*) Not emptiness . . .
FIRST SKELETON: What?
SECOND SKELETON: Good God . . .
ALL: Hihi! Hoho!
    Hihi! Hoho!
FIRST SKELETON: My good sir, are you not well?
    Good sir, we wish to dance!
ALL: To dance! Dance!
SKELETON: (*Half-hidden.*) I'm not a man.
SECOND SKELETON: What then?
SKELETON: (*Half-hidden.*) A . . . girl . . .
FIRST SKELETON: Gentlemen! Cover yourselves!
SKELETON: (*Half-hidden.*) Just thirteen years old . . .
    Why do you look at me like that?
FIRST SKELETON: Young woman, regard me as your protector!
SKELETON: (*Half-hidden.*) Then I need not be afraid?
    I mean, there were so many.
FIRST SKELETON: So many when?
SKELETON: (*Half-hidden.*) That evening.
    Even today I don't know why they did it.
    Did it really have to be like that, sir?
    One had hardly gone away
    Before the next got into bed with me.
SECOND SKELETON: And then?
SKELETON: (*Half-hidden.*) And then . . . I died of it.
FIRST SKELETON: She died of it!
    A charming phrase!
    A lovely phrase!
    She died of it!
    Gentlemen, you are trembling
    And your hands . . . hoho . . .
    Your hands are still . . . (*All lower their hands.*)
    There's no shame here, my child!
    How should there be? . . . Would you know
    Us from yourself?
    Now we are all alike.
    Into the middle with you, then,
    If I may make so bold!
    You have been outraged?
    Good; so have we all!
    It's nothing but a waste of breath

To talk about it now.
There! You're a clever girl!
Stand here, please, in the middle.

(They all join hands and form a circle, dancing vigorously round and round the skeleton of the girl.)

THIRD STATION

SCENE FIVE

(*Dawn. A Field Hospital, a simple, white-washed room. Over the bed is a crucifix.*)

DOCTOR: He's still sleeping.

SISTER: He's done nothing but groan and throw himself about for the last three nights. He fancies he's wandering through the desert. Cries for water. Cries he must reach the mountains, the rocky peaks; but the desert stretches endlessly before him and he can't escape.

DOCTOR: Quinine, double doses of quinine. A case of nervous shock, those others would think. Think! Think! We don't think, we diagnose. It's nothing of the kind. Quite a different matter altogether. . . . Chronic debility of the digestive organs—three spoonfuls of castor oil and two aspirins night and morning . . . uninteresting little case, quite uninteresting. Where is the new one? Was he given castor oil when they brought him in? No? Really, sister, that's most annoying. Inexcusable too. I can't put up with any neglect of duty here. Matter of principle! Principle!

SISTER: Shall I tell him when he wakes up?

DOCTOR: Of course, of course. A little upset's all to the good. Stimulates the muscles of the rectum. (*Both go off.*)

FRIEDRICH: (*Delirious.*) Where are you all? . . . Oh, the desert sandstorm . . . like a stinging, gritty fog . . . no rest . . . on . . . on . . . I don't know you—who are you? . . . Ahasuerus . . . cursed one! . . . Back, back! No holes for you here . . . I won't go with you . . . no, (*shouting*) no! (*Waking up.*) Water! (*Red Cross Nurse enters.*)

NURSE: There, drink this.

FRIEDRICH: Are you the Mother of God?

NURSE: You must lie quite still.

FRIEDRICH: You bear the cross . . . the cross upon your arm . . . My God, is this where they wash away the blood?

NURSE: We are going to heal you here.

FRIEDRICH: Yes, heal. Your hands are gentle and cool on my forehead. Look— see how hard mine are.

NURSE: Work has stained and roughened them.

FRIEDRICH: You wear the cross of love, you dispense love . . .

NURSE: To all who lie here, to black as well as white. ·

FRIEDRICH: Only to us? That's not enough, nurse—why not to all the others too . . . to all . . .

NURSE: They are fighting against us.

FRIEDRICH: Yes, I know . . . It has to be . . . How long have I been here?

NURSE: Three days now. You're quite a hero, you know!

FRIEDRICH: Did they take me prisoner?

NURSE: You were found lashed to a tree; the sole survivor.

FRIEDRICH: Not to a cross . . . the sole survivor . . .

NURSE: Do you feel strong enough to see the Colonel? He has your decoration. (*Friedrich is silent.*)

COLONEL: Congratulations, young fellow! Your gallantry under the most horrible tortures was simply superb, and your country recognizes your devotion. I have been elected to present you with the cross for valor. You were a stranger among us, but now you have become one of us.

FRIEDRICH: The cross? And now I am one of you?

COLONEL: Now you are one of us . . . (*Noise outside.*) What's that?

NURSE: (*Joyfully.*) A great victory, God has granted us a great victory! Ten thousand killed!

COLONEL: You see, my friend . . . Victory is in the air, and you are one of the victors. (*Friedrich is left alone.*)

FRIEDRICH: The jubilation in their faces! Ten thousand dead! Ten thousand have died that I may find a country. Why don't you laugh? Is that liberation? Is this a time of greatness? Are these the people of greatness? (*Staring rigidly before him.*) Now I am one of you. (*Darkness.*)

SCENE SIX

(*Part of an immense room made oppressive by the lowness of the ceiling. Rows of beds in which lie wounded soldiers, all in gray shirts. Hospital Orderlies appear.*)

ORDERLIES: Everything nice and tidy,
Everything in order.
Beds in a nice neat row,
All alike and tidy.
Well, we've done our duty.
The doctor when he comes will find
Nothing at all to grumble at.
We're ready for him now.

(Professor enters with his class of Students. He wears a well-cut black morning coat. Instead of a head he has a skull, and his eye-sockets gleam through gold-rimmed spectacles.)

PROFESSOR: Yes, gentlemen,
    We can face all horrors here.
    We might indeed call our work positive,
    The negative being the munition works.
    In other words we deal in synthesis;
    The armament men are merely analysts.
    Haha!
    Chemists and engineers can quietly make new weapons
    And manufacture unconceived-of gases;
    Their services to war are greatly valued.
    But we, my friends, are not content
    To do the rescue work that's proper to the doctor.
    While we are here, before we go the rounds,
    Let me just demonstrate the last of our achievements,
    Entirely due, I must admit, to my own labors.
    Just show the seven new cases on the screen.

(Orderlies put up a square white screen. One of them beckons and seven naked Cripples march forward like clockwork figures. They are all truncated. None of them has arms or legs. Instead they jerk along with black, artificial legs, parading before the screen in single file.)

ORDERLY: Halt!
    (The men obey. In the silence the clicking of their artificial limbs is audible.)
    Left turn!

(They obey. Suddenly a dark lantern flashes out, and the expressions of the seven cripples, illuminated by the dazzling white beam, are seen to be all alike and stereotyped.)

PROFESSOR: Best view from here, gentelemen.
    These are the men, for whom our glorious work
    Has brought regeneration and rebirth.
    Three months ago they were mere passive stumps!
    Today they stand before you—men!
    Did you observe the pleasing willingness
    With which they carried out my orders?
    To say nothing of the exquisite precision
    Of their synthetic movements.
    So: here they are, my friends,
    Restored in life and limb;
    Men, citizens, useful members

Of society, waiting each to fill his place.
But there is more than meets the eye,
You have not guessed my masterpiece—
How should you?—Come closer, gentlemen!
These men, these stumps that were,
Can now enjoy the great prerogative of man.
By delicate and subtle mechanism
I have restored their procreative powers.
No longer impotent, once more they can
Enjoy the pleasures of the marriage bed!
(One of the Students [with the features of Friedrich] falls into a faint. Orderlies
hurry to revive him with water.)

PROFESSOR: (Smiling sympathetically.)
Poor young man, to faint in work like this!
How would he fare upon the field of battle?

(The Student covers his face with his hands and goes out, his walk involuntarily
reproducing the mechanical walk of the Cripples. The electric light is extinguished.
The Professor, the Students, the Cripples and the Orderlies all turn pale. A Blind
Soldier gets out of his bed.)

BLIND SOLDIER: Tell me, brothers, is it evening?
Is it night?
Night-time is soothing;
Night has cool, soft hands
To stroke my empty eyelids
Quietly.
Day is cruel to me,
The sun is scorching like a bitter fire,
It burns into my skin with pitiless breath.

ARMLESS SOLDIER: Will no one hear me?
I've been calling for so long.
Will no one help me?
Just a little necessary service . . .
Please help me, quickly, someone . . .
It is so horrible to have to lie
In one's own dung.

SPINAL PATIENT: You'd make a fuss if you'd been hit like me.
I'm used to it by now.
I hardly know today
Whether I am a man still or a living lavatory.
My bowels are blown to bits;
My heart's the only living thing about me . . .

Will no one here blow out my heart as well
And make a job of it?
I wallow in my filth, and fill myself and you
With loathing.
I curse my heart that keeps on beating.
My soul is long, long dead with loathing.
Only my heart beats on unpitying.
When I came to, the doctor said to me:
The bullet grazed your spine,
But we have saved you.
If that man knew what lay in store for me
He was a devil.
The only kindness he could do for me
Would be to drug me into sleep and death.
And if he did not know what lay in store for me
The madhouse is the only place for him.

FOURTH SOLIDER: (*Whose body is subject to ceaseless, horrible convulsions.*)
The madhouse . . . yes
That's just the thing . . . But no!
I know a better thing than that . . .
A dugout,
Shut him in a dugout
And blow the lot to bits . . .
Slowly—not too fast . . .
Direct hit!
When the smoke had cleared
I looked around . . no good;
Now way out at all . . . buried
. . . Buried . . . Alive . . .
I went mad . . . I clawed the head-boards
With my nails . . .
I swallowed earth;
My mouth was full of earth.
Digging, digging upwards . . .
Eating my way to air, to light . . .
I ate earth then;
I never knew it tasted good . . .
And then I fell asleep.
I woke up and was here . .
Was it all that earth
That makes me tremble so?
Did I return to earth too soon?
And am I paying for it now?

Or is Earth having her revenge
For my escape?
FIFTH SOLDIER: (*Poisoned by gas.*) My breath's a ruddy sparrow
That pipes and whistles . . .
My lung's a nest of sparrows . . .
But sparrows fly away,
Fly South in winter-time.
ALL: Each has his song;
We ought to form a male-voice choir.

(*A Priest enters [with Friedrich's features], a crucifix in his uplifted hands, which he holds out to the Wounded Soldiers.*)

PRIEST: I bring the Savior,
Oh sad-faced sufferers.
He knows your misery and pain,
All ye who are oppressed, oh come to Him.
He offers healing, love.
ALL: Why does all-powerful God
Permit our suffering?
You say He knows
Our pain and suffering;
Then He is evil
To let it be.
PRIEST: Blasphemy!
ALL: You dare to call it blasphemy?
He it is who utters blasphemy,
And we who are blasphemed.
He, who asks us to believe
That He is with us in our suffering!
You dare call us blasphemers?
Then look, look, look at us!

(*The Wounded Soldiers raise themselves in their beds. The Priest slowly raises his head, and as he looks at them his eyes widen with horror. Slowly his upraised hands break the crucifix in two. He sinks to his knees.*)

PRIEST: How dared I ever
Think myself a priest,
With fine-spun sophistries
Proclaim myself God's chosen one?
Black horror seizes me
To think of those who solemnly ordained us.

I see the blasphemy
Of empty priesthood,
And I would cry aloud:
Free yourselves, free yourselves from all false priests!
Oh Christ, how are your teachings mocked!
There is no healing,
I see no light
To light this endless night;
Nowhere a guiding hand.
Prepare for your salvation . . .
How could I, myself in need of consolation,
In bitterer need than you,
Dole comfort out to you?
I can no more;
Now I walk with you, and your head . . .
ALL: Good luck,
    You enviable one!

(The Nurses enter in a long procession.)

THE NURSES: We bring you medicines,
    Poor suffering ones;
    Drinks to assuage your thirst,
    Cooling cloths
    To ease your burning pain,
    Soothing tablets
    To lull you into sleep.
THE WOUNDED SOLDIERS: What use is sleep to us?
    Tomorrow only brings another day . . .
    Oh, bring us drugs to lull us
    Deep, deep, into an endless night,
    That we may wake no more!
THE NURSES: You ask too much, poor suffering ones.
    Healing we bring,
    But death we may not bring.
WOUNDED SOLDIERS: Too late, too late.
    Your mending and your patching
    Does us no good.
    Why did you not prevent this horror?
    Why start your botching now?
    If you had taken thought before
    You could be dancing now
    With strong and joyful men!

THE NURSES: You wrong us.
THE WOUNDED SOLDIERS: Look closely at us, look,
  And say again
  We wrong you,
  You know not what you are, dear nurses.
  Array yourselves in mourning;
  Cover your faces, bow your heads;
  Forget your Christian charity,
  Or call it wretched, barren, botching.

(*The Nurses raise their heads, shape their lips to a shattering cry, collapse. Darkness. Then suddenly the lantern flashes out again. The seven Cripples are still standing before the screen, watching them the Professor, the Students and the Orderlies.*)

PROFESSOR: It really is a splendid bit of luck
  That we have all these cases here to study.
  Tomorrow we will make a comprehensive
  Round of all the wards.
  Meanwhile, let me repeat
  My words of introduction.
  We can face all horrors here.
  We might indeed call our work positive,
  The negative being the munitions works.
  In other words we deal in synthesis;
  The armament men are merely analysts.
  Haha!

FOURTH STATION

SCENE SEVEN

(*Early morning. A studio. Friedrich is working at a more than lifesize statue of a naked man, heavily muscular, with clenched, uplifted fists. There is brutality in the pose.*)

FRIEDRICH: (*Working.*) The stone resists my efforts; my hand upon the chisel cannot bring it to life. The chisel chips marble, dead marble; am I powerless to breathe life into it? If so I'll do no more. I will not be content to carve a mere memorial to life. . . . Life intense must stream from my creation . . . to wake men from their sleep . . to fire them to fight for their country until death . . . to hurl defiance . . . Defiance against whom? . . . The enemy, of course. . . . But who decides that there shall be an enemy? Is it some spiritual power within us that forces us to fight? . . . Or is the enemy selected arbitrarily? . . . There's a contradiction there. . . . Why can I not succeed? . . . The problem is so great. Am I too small to symbolize it? Too puny to pierce that brazen armor? (*The Friend enters.*)

FRIEND: I was so anxious I had to come—but I see you are working. My mind is full of foolish thoughts, but I won't disturb you. I will go.

FRIEDRICH: My dear fellow, you won't disturb me in the least.

FRIEND: I see your great work will soon be finished. You've certainly labored long and earnestly at it.

FRIEDRICH: A year. But what's a year for the completion of a worthy symbol of our triumphant Fatherland?

FRIEND: Do you still doubt?

FRIEDRICH: That your country is now mine as well? No . . . Only . . .

FRIEND: Only?

FRIEDRICH: I sometimes wonder if there is not something higher still. And yet I don't really want to know. For if I knew there would be no escaping my destiny, I should become Ahasuerus, the Wandering Jew.

FRIEND: And Gabriele? Would she let you wander? Would you not find fulfillment at her side?

FRIEDRICH: The struggle takes no account of women; perhaps not even of us ourselves.

FRIEND: Gabriele would be unhappy.

FRIEDRICH: Gabriele is strong.

FRIEND: Yes, she is strong.

FRIEDRICH: We come together, proudly, joyfully.

FRIEND: You are so strong!

FRIEDRICH: So strong!

FRIEND: Farewell! (*The Friend goes. Friedrich works. The doorbell rings and Friedrich goes to the door.*)

FRIEDRICH: Beloved! (*Gabriele enters. She tries to smile.*) You look sad, my beloved. If I believed in good fairies I should wish that one would change my clumsy hands to butterflies, to brush away the sadness from your brow like pollen from dark flowers. I should wish to be with you among the sand dunes where the children play; I should wish to climb high mountains with you, to wander with you on the farthest slopes. To wander with you in the darkness through dreaming towns, to overcome you in the poppy fields and kiss you there with gladness in our hearts. . . . You are silent, dearest. You do not smile. . . .

GABRIELE: The tears are welling in my heart . . . but they are frozen, and cannot reach my eyes. (*Friedrich sits quietly beside her, and takes her hand.*) I am going to leave you.

FRIEDRICH: (*As though he had known what she would say.*) You are going to leave me. (*Then, as though suddenly awakened.*) . . . You . . . are going to . . . leave me? . . .

GABRIELE: I must.

FRIEDRICH: For my sake?

GABRIELE: For your sake.

FRIEDRICH: Do you love me?

GABRIELE: I love you as a woman loves a man whom she would have sweep her like a tempest, whom she would have as the father of her child.

FRIEDRICH: And yet? . . .

GABRIELE: When my father said he would disown me forever if I married you it was as though I were caught in a sudden blizzard; the icy snowflakes burnt me. I came to you smiling. But my father would cast me out from my country forever—never to see it again, never again to tread its soil. It is my childhood's memory, it is the blood that feeds my heart. I have fought against its influence for many days and many nights. And today at last I saw clearly: I can never give it up.

FRIEDRICH: And I thought you were strong!

GABRIELE: Perhaps it is because I am strong.

FRIEDRICH: But I shall stay . . . I too have roots, I too have a country of my own, to which I am bound with my heart's blood, to which I have sacrificed

my heart's blood; your country, my country. The whole great Fatherland.
You are weak, Gabriele, weak.

GABRIELE: Perhaps . . . Farewell! (*She goes.*)

FRIEDRICH: Farewell, you who are strong. And now the dusk has fallen round
me, dusk eternal. Day has slipped into the far golden sea. Night dreams in
cloven gorges where the black moths flutter, a night that will never lift
again. Oh Gabriele! If you'd betrayed me—robbed me of my faith! . . .
(*Sunbeams fall on the statue.*) So you would remind me? The triumph of the
Fatherland. I believe in that, I will believe in that; I will believe in it and symbolize it forever. If it costs me my life I will do it. (*He sets to work again. A
hurdy-gurdy starts up in the courtyard below. He goes to the window, returns and
renews his labors. The bell rings. Friedrich opens the door. A Woman enters, a war
cripple, miserable and emaciated.*)

WOMAN: Alms for the poor, alms for the poor. (*Friedrich, about to offer her money, stops and considers.*)

FRIEDRICH: Are you a war cripple?

WOMAN: (*Weeping.*) Must I tell you? (*She shows him her ulcerated hands.*)

FRIEDRICH: Poor soul.

WOMAN: They surrounded me, they sidled up to me like jackals. . . . What
should they know? Driven out to fight like cattle. What do cattle know of
morals? What can they know? And one among them was diseased and corrupted, and infected me. How can I tell you whether he was bad or not?
They called him a hero. They were all heroes. Wretched cattle in a
slaughterhouse.

FRIEDRICH: It had to be, poor woman, for our country's sake.

WOMAN: For our country's sake? Our country? For the sake of a small handful
of rich men who feast and debauch and gamble with the products of our
labor. Ah, how I hate them! Brutes, devils! I know them well; I was one of
them myself. God reward you for your labors, they say! But what sort of
God is it that lets us rot away in misery? That mocks us with his "blessed are
the poor, for theirs is the kingdom of Heaven." The God of love and pity
and charity bazaars! When I slink by their lighted halls and see them revel-
ing within, I think I see their God crowned among them, scattering confetti.
We are brutes . . . just brutes . . . forever brutes. (*The Woman collapses on a
chair, sobbing.*)

FRIEDRICH: (*After a pause.*) Was your husband at the front?

WOMAN: Yes, out there in the colonies. My bonny husband.

FRIEDRICH: Won't you bring him in?

WOMAN: Shall I? I tell you, you'll have a shock. It will put you off your work.
He's not a pleasant sight, my husband. The disease eats deeper year by year.
Still, if you really want to see him, sir. . . . He was the one that brought me
to disease. (*The Woman goes out, and returns leading her Husband with his
hurdy-gurdy. His face is a mass of sores.*) Say good day to the gentleman.

HUSBAND: (*Stammering.*) God . . . be . . . with you. (*Friedrich looks at him steadily, then begins to tremble.*)

FRIEDRICH: Is it really you, my friend? My poor, poor friend!

HUSBAND: (*Fearfully.*) God . . . be . . . with you.

FRIEDRICH: You need not be afraid, poor fellow. It is I, Friedrich, Friedrich—we served in the same company, we marched across the endless, glowering desert together, we suffered thirst and hunger together. Don't you remember the fellow who volunteered to go on that tricky reconnaisance? We two, we together. We drew lots for the job, and I drew the longest straw. Now do you remember, my poor friend? (*Husband begins to cry miserably.*)

WOMAN: It's no good sir. It's no good talking to him. He remembers nothing now, nor ever will.—He cries because he thinks he ought to cry. He can just think that much, but no more. The doctor said he'd soon have to help him out of life. Well, sir, now you've had your entertainment—can we go, sir? (*The Woman leads out her Husband, who is still miserably weeping.*)

FRIEDRICH: Madness, madness. Where? Where to go? Ahasuerus, where are you? I follow you, Ahasuerus; joyfully I follow you. Anything, anything to escape! A million shattered arms are stretched towards me. The agonizing cries of a million mothers echo in my ears. Where? Where? The unborn childrn whimper. The madmen cry. Oh, holy weeping! Speech defiled! Mankind defiled! . . . For our country's sake! Oh, God . . . can it really be? Can a country really ask this much of us? Or has our country sold its soul, sold it to the State? Sold it in a dirty business speculation? Perhaps the State is a pimp, and our country a whore to be sold for any brutal lust—blessed by that procuress, the Church! Can a Fatherland that asks so much really be divine? Can it be worth the sacrifice of a single soul? No, no, no! A thousand times no! Rather wander without rest, without hope, wander with you, Ahasuerus. (*He throws himself upon the statue.*) I shatter you to fragments, victory of the Fatherland! (*He seizes a hammer and shatters the statue, then sinks down, an inanimate heap. After a time he rises again.*) Now I must wander through the wilderness, without rest, without hope . . . I cannot, I am filled with loathing. Gabriele leaves her lover for a little plot of land . . . And I betray my Fatherland, the Fatherland in which I believed, to which I pledged myself, to which I dedicated my life-work—I betray my Fatherland for the sake of two poor, miserable beggars . . . No, not betray. I cannot go that way, I will not. It leads through nights of rain and storm, through plague-stricken streets; it loses itself in the wilderness. Farewell, Gabriele! (*He goes to the bureau and takes up a revolver. Through the open door his Sister enters and regards him and the broken statue.*) You come too late.

SISTER: I come in time.

FRIEDRICH: My path is blocked.

SISTER: Your path leads upward.

FRIEDRICH: Back to my mother?

SISTER: To her, yes; but higher still.

FRIEDRICH: Back to my Fatherland?

SISTER: To your land, yes; but higher still.

FRIEDRICH: I can see no higher; I am dazzled.

SISTER: I will shield your eyes; then you will see. Your path leads to God.

FRIEDRICH: Haha! To God! God crowned among the revelers, scattering confetti!

SISTER: To God, who is spirit, love and strength;
To God who dwells in the heart of humanity.
Your path will lead you to humanity . . .

FRIEDRICH: To humanity . . .
I am not worthy.

SISTER: Soon like a mask you will cast aside
So much that now seems worthy in your eyes.
Who knows what in the end will prove
Your real worthiness?
He who desires to join humanity
Must find it first within himself.
The path I bid you follow
Sinks to the depths and climbs the heights,
Leads you darkly through the underworld,
The underworld called criminal by fools.
But you are both accused and judge.

(*Friedrich buries his face in his hands, then rises, staggers, stretches out his arms.*)

FRIEDRICH: Sunlight streams through me,
Freedom and sunlight.
My eyes have seen the path
And I will follow it.
Alone, and yet with you;
Alone and yet with all the world,
In the knowledge of humanity.

FIFTH STATION

SCENE EIGHT

(*Bedroom of a city tenement. In the two beds, the Woman, the Children, the Lodger [with Friedrich's features].*)

THE LODGER: (*To the Daughter.*) I can't bear it.
    We sleep with moans on every side, and cries.
    I can't bear it any more.
    Come, and I'll hold you to me
    And turn you inside out.
    Like a soft woolly cap.
DAUGHTER: Stay here . . . I won't leave you
    She's groaned like this at night
    Ever since we had the news
    That he'd been crushed to death at work.
    Then, of course, the eleventh child
    Which she was carrying at the time
    She brought out dead.
    A bit of luck that was.
    I should have had to wash the kid myself.
    No one will have her as a waitress now
    Because she'll sing and dance
    Like someone mad
    In the middle of her work,
    And offer prayers and hymns . . .
    She's always at the bottle now.
    Who is there now to keep the kids?
    . . . There's only me.
    And that means overtime at the works.
    Stay here, and I'll do everything you ask.
LODGER: All right; I'll stay.
    I think she keeps me here

Moaning and crying in the night—
Doesn't she mind you being a whore?
DAUGHTER: She used to nod her head
When the other lodger beat me . . .
Does that make you cross with me?
LODGER: Cross with you, fool?
What else could you have done?
If he forced you?
It's only her that gets on my nerves.
Suddenly when you're in my arms
She shrieks or groans.
DAUGHTER: I almost envy the children.
They sleep all day from hunger
And all night from dirt and weariness.
They'd really have been better off
Brought up in an orphanage.
LODGER: That's not right . . .
DAUGHTER: No, no—I only thought of it.
LODGER: She nods when a blackguard beats her daughter
And shrieks and groans
When her daughter hugs me to her.
What was that you said . . . the orphanage . . .
The orphanage . . . The orphanage . . .

(*Darkness descends on the room.*)

LODGER: (*Dreaming.*) The orphanage . . . the orphanage . . .
(*Silence. Lodger, dreaming.*)
Now she will shriek no more,
Groan no more . . .
Now are you content?
Now you are in the orphanage . . .
The orphanage . . .

(*The Night Visitor enters, his death's head thickly veiled.*)

THE NIGHT VISITOR: Lodger, get up.
It's time for work.
LODGER: All right, I'm coming.
THE NIGHT VISITOR: Make haste.
LODGER: Where are you taking me?
THE NIGHT VISITOR: Don't ask me where, just come.
You are in good hands.

(Phosphorescence flickers round the Night Visitor and the Lodger, who stands there in his workman's blouse. The Night Visitor takes his arm.)
Can you see the house?
LODGER: There, over there, I see it glimmering.
It's funny—are you taking me
The proper way?
THE NIGHT VISITOR: I am taking you the right way—
The narrow way!
The only way!
LODGER: That's not the factory.
THE NIGHT VISITOR: Use your eyes, look, look!
What is it then?
LODGER: It looks like a prison . . .
Look at the shining roof—
It's thick with gold!
THE NIGHT VISITOR: Right! Right!
What do you see now?
LODGER: High walls with iron spikes.
And in the walls
Holes barred with steel.
THE NIGHT VISITOR: Right, right!
LODGER: No, that's not the factory
That's a prison!
Let go—Let me go to work!
THE NIGHT VISITOR: *(Grips him firmly.)* I'll take you to your work,
The only work you and your like are fit for.
Take off your spectacles of everyday
And learn to see things as they really are!
You thought this was a prison?
Well, look, look!
We are here.
Look at the name above the gates!
You're trembling—let me read it for you:
You see I've not betrayed you:
The great factory!

(Darkness. Then for a few moments the roar of machinery, the pounding of pistons, the whirring of wheels and the hissing of molten metal and steam.)

SCENE NINE

(Death and Resurrection. The ground floor of a prison [the great factory]. In the corridors are triple-bolted cell doors. The spiral stairways leading to the upper floors have

rectangular openings to allow the whole prison to be overlooked. On the cement floor, at the bottom of the staircase, a Prisoner lies [with Friedrich's features], his head flung back, his arms flung out as though he were crucified. Judges in black coats hurry by: their heads are skulls.)

JUDGES: (Fiercely.) Get at the facts of the case! The facts of the case! (Prisoner cries out shrilly.)
WARDER: It wasn't my fault;
  I was just taking him downstairs.
  Like you said,
  To see his wife, — you gave permission.

(Warder and Chief Warder hurry over to the Prisoner, bend over him and raise his head.)

CHIEF WARDER: He is still breathing.
WARDER: I knew he was a godless man,
  I always knew it.
  He wished another dead;
  He murdered him in all his dreams.
  And now he's killed himself;
  Broken the Church's holiest command
  Twice over.
CHIEF WARDER: He meant to kill himself, so who are we to stop him?
JUDGES: (Scornfully.) Get at the facts of the case! The facts of the case!

(Prisoner cries out accusingly.)

WARDER: So help me God . . .
  It wasn't like a human voice at all!
CHIEF WARDER: It was the devil himself!

(Prisoner shrieks in accusation, and the doors of the cells burst open. In the open doorways stand the Prisoners, their arms limp and swinging loosely. They raise their eyes in rapture.)

PRISONER: (First softly, then with increasing resonance.) Horror lies within these prison walls—
  Unplumbed, unfathomed; a bottomless morass,
  An endless swamp,
  A silent swamp.
  In the long, empty twilight hours
  White maggots crawled out from the iron bars.

I did my best to ward them off, I struggled . . .
It was no use.
Gray maggots gnawed into my flesh.
PRISONERS: Hear us! In suffering we are united.
Behind these prison walls damp horror lies concealed,
Unplumbed, unfathomed; bottomless morass.
PRISONER: Once I saw red flowers;
I stretched my hand to grasp them,
Found it was my heart.
And as I held it dumbly in my hand
It was devoured by maggots, gray and blind.
I ate with them.
PRISONERS: Hear us! In suffering we are united.
Once we saw red flowers.
How sweet they seemed, red flowers;
The were our hearts.
And as we held them dumbly
They were devoured by maggots, gray and blind.
We ate with them.
PRISONER: I looked down through the shaft;
I saw them land there, I saw firm land.
CHIEF WARDER: And there your wife was waiting.
PRISONER: And there my wife was waiting . . .
WARDER: You broke the Church's holiest command—
Repent before you die!
PRISONER: What do you know about it, brother?
It is so far beyond all good and evil,
Repentance, heavenly recompense.
I heard a voice; it said:—
All, all deluded;
He was not nailed upon the Cross by men,
He crucified Himself.
PRISONERS: We too know that . . .
We knew it long ago.
He crucified Himself.
CHIEF WARDER: Think for a moment of your wife.
It's I who have to break the news to her,
A nice job too!
After all, I suppose my job
Is looking after people.
PRISONER: I'm thinking of my wife.
I'm thinking of my child as well,
Which she is bearing towards the light

In a body racked with pain.
My child . . .
Sum total of my guilt,
My guilt which never dies.
Ourselves we go
Slowly and painfully upon our way
And send out little children
To crucifixion.

(A pregnant Woman rushes in through a door in the background, cries out, and throws herself down by the Prisoner.)

WOMAN: Oh, why have you done this?
   I was waiting for you . . .
PRISONER: The pain goes deep.
   Someone is always waiting for us—
   But we burn the last bridges,
   And night comes down and blots out every path
   Which leads to you.
   Further we roam . . .
   Knowing you are waiting . . .
   And further still, and further . . .
   Mocking we wander further . . .
   Even though we ourselves are waiting.
WOMAN: The child . . .
   Does your child mean so little?
PRISONER: It means so much . . .
   Yet it was guilt towards my child
   That cast me into the abyss, blasted,
   Blasted since the day
   When man first rose against his kind
   And, hating, murdered man.
   To children we
   Are gods and saviors . . .
   Helplessly we watch
   The long road to the Cross.
WARDER: Blasphemer!
   Holy Mother of God forgive him!
PRISONER: Impotent, impotent too, like all the rest,
   With her lying offers of pardon.
   She mourns for her son unceasingly;
   In this alone
   Is she innocent and pure.

WOMAN: What is there now for me in life . . .
    I can only kill myself,
    Myself and my child . . .
    What else is there for me?
    What else?
PRISONER: What else?
    Come close and I'll tell you.
    Perhaps through crucifixion only
    Liberation comes;
    Perhaps the powers of light
    Spring only from His blood.
    Perhaps through crucifixion only
    Can redemption come,
    The way to light and freedom.
PRISONERS: Brother, you light the way.
    Through crucifixion only
    Shall we liberate ourselves.
    Through crucifixion only
    Shall we find redemption,
    And the way to light and freedom.
PRISONER: Woman . . . Mother . . . (*He dies.*)
CHIEF WARDER: Come. He is redeemed.
WARDER: Burdened as he was with sin . . .
PRISONERS: From sin he has released himself,
    Too weak to find redemption . . .
WOMAN: (*Crying out.*) Husband! . . . (*She wrings her hands in lamentation.*)
CHIEF WARDER: Come.
WOMAN: I cannot come . . .
    My child . . .
    My child . . .

(*There is silence interrupted by soft music. Then the Prisoners leave their cells, forming a semicircle round the Woman. The sun shines on them all.*)

PRISONER: (*A Woman.*) A child.
    How many, many years have passed
    Since last we heard the laughter of a child . . .
    How many, many years have passed
    Since last we played with children. . . .

(*The Prisoners stand looking at the Woman full of awe. She holds the child out to them, her face distorted with pain, yet transfigured. The prison roof gives place to the limitless sky. Darkness.*)

SCENE TEN

(*The stage is hidden by thick mist. A country road is visible. The Wanderer [with Friedrich's features] appears.*)

THE WANDERER: I feel today as though
   This were a new awakening.
   As though the grave had split asunder
   And shown the sky again.
   The earth-chained vessel breaks.
   Judge is now prisoner,
   And prisoner judge;
   And both stretch out their hands,
   Casting aside their triumphs and their shames
   Like crowns of thorns.
   The morning breaks.
   The mist dissolves.
   I know my work.
   I know it now.

SCENE ELEVEN

(*A large meeting room decorated with colored paper flowers, and with sentimental paintings of war on the walls.*)

CHAIRMAN: I call upon our gallant old friend. (*An Old Man, an anti-pacifist, mounts the dais.*)

OLD MAN: Ah yes, those were indeed the days! The days when our victorious comrades swept conquering forward while the enemy ran before us like a lot of sheep; the days when a great cry ran through the land—"My Country!" (*Friedrich enters.*) Those were indeed the days! The great days! Magnificent days! Now you're whimpering for bread. What's the significance of a loaf of bread? If you want work, get it! And what does it matter whether you feed on potatoes or roast meat? (*The crowd murmurs.*) Have you so soon forgotten the great deeds that were done in the name of our Fatherland, the blood that our heroes shed?

A CRY: Are we any the less heroes because we happen to be still alive? (*The Old Man leaves the dais.*)

CHAIRMAN: I call upon the Professor.

PROFESSOR: (*On the dais.*) As the chosen representative of that Science which is proud to be the servant of our State today, of that Science which is ultimate truth and final knowledge—as the chosen representative of Science, I should like to pick a bone with the honorable gentleman who preceded me. The cause of your distress is not bread, nor the lack of it; neither bread nor science nor culture. Go, gentlemen, and study the laws of causality, try to grasp the law of association in regard to all phenomena . . . The Science in whose ranks I have the honor to serve is inspired by a holy devotion. It is here to help our glorious State, to account for it as a complete ethical organism. (*Threatening murmurs from the crowd. The Professor leaves the platform.*)

CHAIRMAN: I call upon his Reverence.

PRIEST: Brothers in Christ, heed my words. As our Savior once said to His disciples, "I am not come to bring you peace, but a sword," so I am come to bring you not soothing rhetoric but iron truth. In time of war did I not preach and say unto you: "Annihilate the enemy, choke him with poison gas and shatter him with bombs, destroy him ruthlessly with submarine and blockade. All that you do finds favor in the eyes of God!" For the Lord of Hosts was with you, and an angel strode before you and withered the ranks of the enemy. . . . Think of those bygone days of glory and forget your petty cares. Think on Him who died for you upon the Cross.

CROWD: Away with the clergy!

Down with the rich!

We are hungry, hungry, hungry!

CHAIRMAN: (*Striking a bell.*) I call upon the Agitator.

AGITATOR: You are right, brothers! What do the old fire-eaters mean to us? Or the professors? Or the priests? Christ has become the rich man's God. We don't need Him any more, you and I. What we need is bread. What we need is money. We've got to fight against stupidity, we've got to set up reason in its place—and by we I mean you, the people. But first let's have a look at what these fellows have just been saying: "State" is a new name for Fatherland; that's what they said, and it's a lie. That's a conception that has nothing but a few thousand square miles of earth as its foundation. A few languages, one of which is permitted while the others are suppressed. And any amount of notices saying "Forbidden." They'd like to say, "Permitted the rich, forbidden the poor." That's what they'd say if they had the courage. And then there's taxes: let the rich down lightly and pile it on the poor. That's their motto. When the rich find they haven't castles enough and want new villas on the Riviera they say damn it all, we'd bettter have a war. Sit down at that phone at once and set a few dozen lies going so that someone will have to declare war on somebody. Start up a society to care for the wounded—a few more or less don't matter—and get a few war memorials designed while you're about it . . . Now for the Church and the Priests —shall we have a word about them too?

CROWD: Down with the clergy!

AGITATOR: I thought as much. Well, and what then? What but exalt the healthy reason, as typified in you, the people? That means bread and decency and work and our rights. And what must we do? Simply overthrow stupidity. That's what we've got to do. Break up the mansions of the rich! Oh, I can see you at it! All your pent-up energy released, fighting gloriously at last. Holding aloft the flag of freedom! Women embracing you with feverish arms! Masses surging! Shots ringing out! I'll write you pamphlets to guide you and verses to inspire you, verses which shall themselves be bloody deeds! My words shall go with you like the martial blare of trumpets! Blood flows! The blood of freedom! March! March!

CROWD: Yes, this time we'll march!

    We're really hungry!

    This time we'll really fight!

    Bread! Bread! Bread!

CHAIRMAN: (*Violently ringing his bell.*) Here is someone called Friedrich who wishes to address you. (*Friedrich presses through the crowd and mounts the dais.*)

FRIEDRICH: Gently, brothers, gently! I know you need bread. I know poverty is eating at your bodies. I know your misery, your wretched, stinking hovels. I know oppression and the look in the eyes of the outcast. I know, too, of your hatred. But in spite of all that I beg you to restrain yourselves, for I love you.

CROWD: Let's listen to him.

    He's right.

    He loves us.

FRIEDRICH: I understand your deep disgust of men who bring dishonor to the name of God. I understand it indeed. But let me warn you against the words of him who called on you to march on the rich, against the glittering half-truths of his words! His reasoning did not go very deep. Can't you see the man for what he is? This opportunist agitator? Yesterday his talk was all of individualism, today he cries: "God is the people!" And tomorrow he will cry: "God is the Machine!" Therefore the people are machines. Nonetheless he will delight in the swinging pistons and the whirling wheels, the smashing hammers. For him the people are the masses: he knows nothing of the people as men and women. Have no faith in him, for he has no faith in humanity. It is better for you to suffer want than to follow the precepts of this man without faith.

PEOPLE: He asks us to suffer want!

    Down with him!

    Down with him!

    We must march! March!

    We are hungry!

    Hear him out first!

    Just hear him out!

FRIEDRICH: I am not speaking now of material want, my friends. It is not right that you should suffer hunger. I wish you bodily comfort and spiritual want.

I wish you this in the name of the love that unites us all. You must no longer starve. You must be rich, you must find your life's fulfillment. I will fight side by side with you against poverty and misery . . . but wait one day longer, wait until midday. Come to the marketplace and let me speak with you there. (*Excited uproar.*)

A WORKMAN: Well, we've gone hungry so long now that one more day can't make much difference.

PEOPLE: Yes, we will wait!
No, no more waiting! March!
We are hungry!
Hungry!
Let us wait!
Wait!
Let us wait!

(*The crowd goes out. A few young people remain behind. A Student approaches Friedrich.*)

STUDENT: What is the good of learning when the spirit is denied? What is the good of reason when we must suffer in its name? You must be our leader.

FRIEDRICH: We must advance together, side by side. (*A Girl Student approaches Friedrich.*)

THE GIRL: In the name of love, be our leader. Once more humanity must be vitalized by love. We will bear no more children until love encircles us with radiant hands. Lead us!

FRIEDRICH: Now down the arches of the years I see
The great cathedral of mankind arise;
Through doors flung wide
The youth of every nation marches singing
Towards a crystal shrine.
Dreams dazzle me—
No misery, no war, no hatred left on earth,
And mothers garlanding bright girls and boys
For games of joy and dances of increase.
Stride on, oh youth, stride on, oh fruitful youth,
Fruitful eternally amidst a barren world;
Within your breast
You bear the life divine.

(*The young people, hand in hand, leave the room in twos and threes. The room is now half in darkness. As Friedrich turns to go the Girl suddenly appears out of the darkness.*)

THE GIRL: My lips are parted with desire. My heart is consumed with glowing passion. . . . I will serve you, I alone. . . . Leave the others. . . . They only understand force—and even if your force is for the good. . . . I must serve you.

FRIEDRICH: Serve the spirit, serve your God.

THE GIRL: I shudder before Him; He is coldness and death.

FRIEDRICH: Say rather passionate warmth!

THE GIRL: I shrink before Him. But you . . . you I love . . . To you I offer myself; embrace me. Take me . . . my burning breast. . . . My womb cries out for you . . . I ache for your embrace. . . . Give me a child. . . .

FRIEDRICH: I do not want your breast nor your embrace. Has the whole world rights over my body. (*With bowed head the Girl goes slowly out.*) Wretched woman! Unredeemed. (*A Man with a turned-up coat collar rushes into the room.*)

THE MAN: I hate you.

FRIEDRICH: I call you brother.

THE MAN: I hate you. I know you; don't think I've not recognized you. I've seen you in my room on lonely nights. Why don't you turn monk? Leave us in peace! What do you want with the mob? You desecrate God!

FRIEDRICH: I celebrate Him.

THE MAN: (*Hurrying away.*) I hate you!

FRIEDRICH: Brother, you betray yourself.

SIXTH STATION

SCENE TWELVE

(*A precipitous rock-face leading to a narrow ledge. Two men are climbing the rock.*)

SECOND CLIMBER: (*With the Friend's features.*) Stop, stop!
  I shall fall,
  I am giddy.
FIRST CLIMBER: (*With Friedrich's features.*) Come, pull yourself together;
  It is not far now.
SECOND CLIMBER: The ledge is narrow;
  We shall slip and fall
  Down, down into the abyss.
FIRST CLIMBER: Perhaps, but courage! Courage!
  The ledge to which we climb
  Rewards all danger with stupendous height,
  With air brighter than light, clearer than fire.
SECOND CLIMBER: In the name of friendship, stop!
  An icy coldness sweeps down from above.
FIRST CLIMBER: It is the glacier,
  Dazzling and remote.
SECOND CLIMBER: The silence there
  Oppresses heart and mind.
FIRST CLIMBER: You're hearing ghosts.
  Fasten the rope about you.
SECOND CLIMBER: I would have thanked you once
  For freeing me from lowly tyrannies.
  But now you lead me on
  From terror to worse terror.
FIRST CLIMBER: Not everyone released
  Is really free.
SECOND CLIMBER: Up there no one will hear you.
FIRST CLIMBER: The mighty walls of rock rejoice to hear

The sound of shouting voices,
And echo them in joyful repetition.
SECOND CLIMBER: I'll go no further . . .
FIRST CLIMBER: Then I must go alone.
SECOND CLIMBER: You'll leave me here,
Your old companion?
FIRST CLIMBER: It is not I who leave you.
SECOND CLIMBER: In the name of friendship, stay!
FIRST CLIMBER: In the name of friendship
(*He climbs rapidly higher.*)
I must go!
SECOND CLIMBER: Can you still hear me call?
Think of the days when we were young together!
FIRST CLIMBER: Your voice is like the scree
That breaks away and plunges
Loosely down the mountain-side.
Youth advances with me.
How easily youth climbs!
SECOND CLIMBER: You go too far —
Take care, take care;
I am afraid for you.
FIRST CLIMBER: Myself I cannot leave
So I leave you. (*Almost at the summit.*) . . .
Farewell!

(*Darkness.*)

SCENE THIRTEEN

(*Square in front of the Church. Friedrich enters and leans against the archway of the door.*)

FRIEDRICH: The sunlight warms the roofs and strokes the blinded windows of the narrow attics. My breast expands. (*His Mother comes across the square dressed in mourning.*) Mother!
MOTHER: (*Scarcely glancing up.*) All these years you've never come, till I began to believe I carried you once more beneath my heart.
FRIEDRICH: I bring you all my love; let me hold you gently in my arms and kiss your tired and wrinkled face.
MOTHER: You are dead for me! You left your family and estranged your people.
FRIEDRICH: I am nearer to them now than ever I was before.
MOTHER: You belong to the others.
FRIEDRICH: To the others, yes, but to you as well.

MOTHER: Nobody can belong to us and to the others. We are a proud people.

FRIEDRICH: Mother! Don't you feel the earth as a single mighty womb quivering in travail? Think of the torture you suffered in bearing me—thus is the world convulsed today . . . a lacerated bleeding womb, bearing all humanity anew.

MOTHER: I am too old, my life is nearly done. I don't understand you.

FRIEDRICH: (*Covers his face with his hands.*) Mother! (*His Mother goes. His Uncle enters.*) Dear Uncle!

UNCLE: What does this mean? What do you want?—I warn you not to count on me. I refuse to acknowledge you.

FRIEDRICH: I don't want money, Uncle; but I do want you to acknowledge me.

UNCLE: Wait a minute, wait a minute! Do you mean to tell me that you've earned enough to keep yourself? No, your coat is shabby; you can't hide that from me.

FRIEDRICH: You delude yourself, Uncle.

UNCLE: Delude myself? Well, if I do it's only because you force me to. You brought my business to the verge of ruin. "His nephew's an enemy of our people"—that's what they all said. You brought misfortune to your whole family.

FRIEDRICH: If I did it was only because there was no escaping it.

UNCLE: Your presence is distasteful. You are really impossible.

FRIEDRICH: Uncle, I struggle with you because I must. But it is not against you that I am fighting; it is against the dark walls and barriers built up round the real you.

UNCLE: I knew it, you traitor! You even dare attack your own flesh and blood!

FRIEDRICH: I did that long ago, Uncle. (*The Uncle walks out. The Doctor enters.*) Good morning, doctor—remember me still?

DOCTOR: Ah . . . you . . . Oh yes, very ordinary case—debility of the rectum. How is it now? All right now? Digestion good?

FRIEDRICH: Tell me, doctor; do you believe in humanity?

DOCTOR: What a damn-fool question! Believe in humanity! I believe that most people have a good digestion, and those who have not should be given a dose of castor oil—one tablespoonful for adults, one teaspoonful for children. Stupid question. Really quite simple-minded. A man who can ask that wants looking into . . . Stand still . . . Say Ah . . . Close your eyes . . . Highly developed psychosis.

FRIEDRICH: Your medicines will never make people healthy.

DOCTOR: You must come and see me at once. Today. I have just bought a nice sanitorium. A water-cure might do the trick even now. But come at once, and don't count on anything. Typical everyday case. Report this afternoon. Room seventeen. (*He hurries off. A Sick Man with restless eyes shuffles in.*)

SICK MAN: Well, I must say you really seem to believe in it.

FRIEDRICH: In what?

SICK MAN: In yourself, and in humanity generally.

FRIEDRICH: I believe in humanity, certainly.

SICK MAN: He he! . . . And in love as well.

FRIEDRICH: I cannot live without love.

SICK MAN: And all that for the sake of . . .

FRIEDRICH: Liberating humanity.

SICK MAN: I see—you are not interested in building public lavatories, then? A pity—a great pity. Let me tell you something, my dear sir. For a long time I myself tried to redeem the world with love . . . But it's no good. The only thing to do is to build new lavatories. The one's we are used to are always too dark, and hidden away. . . . I know what you're thinking—what on earth is behind all this? I'll tell you—simply to teach humanity that the only infallible panacea for all its ills is universal suicide. It's no good trying to cure them with love—I've tried it and I know. . . . It's no good trying to cure them with love—I've tried it and I know. . . . So now I'm building lavatories.

FRIEDRICH: Have you put your plans before the doctors?

SICK MAN: Oh yes, I've been to see them about it several times already. But they didn't want my plans—said they'd thought of it themselves already.

FRIEDRICH: And you would really like all men to kill themselves?

SICK MAN: Yes!

FRIEDRICH: Why don't you go about preaching war, then?

SICK MAN: Oh no, they mustn't do it that way. They must kill themselves voluntarily. . . . Well, what about it? I advise you to think it over very carefully. The building of lavatories with an eye to self-annihilation.

FRIEDRICH: Poor fellow!

SICK MAN: You pity me! *You* . . . pity . . . me . . .

FRIEDRICH: You are sick, corrupted with disease.

SICK MAN: (*As though suddenly awakened.*) I can't believe in love! I can't, I tell you . . . only whores . . . only whores . . . No one has ever loved me. (*Shaking his head he hurries off.*)

FRIEDRICH: I must seek him out—today. . . . I'll ask my mother to look after him . . . no . . . that girl who came to me. (*A Woman who has entered during the foregoing scene moves nearer with studied provocation.*)

WOMAN: What do you think you're doing? . . . Can't you see that love and goodness are eternally separated by a hopeless gulf? That love crouches ready to spring like a rabid dog licking lascivious lips? That love and goodness glare into each other's eyes like deadly enemies? . . . Ha ha! . . . You're on the wrong track this time, my young friend! Don't answer me. Your answer is nonsense. Your goodness is nonsense. . . . Love lashes the body. . . . Let me tear at your breast with my teeth until the blood flows, red blood over white teeth; let me kiss your thighs. . . . Your goodness! . . . You are a fool, a miserable, wretched fool. You and your goodness—you suffocate me!

FRIEDRICH: And you? Who are you?

WOMAN: Woman! (*She goes. Friedrich leans silently against the doorway of the Church. His Sister enters.*)

SISTER: There was a light in your eyes, Friedrich.

FRIEDRICH: Dear friend.

SISTER: What will you do, Friedrich? How shall you symbolize humanity's victory this time?

FRIEDRICH: No special symbol is needed for that, no proof. Humanity can see victory in its heart, can see it in all my work.

SISTER: And you will stay here?

FRIEDRICH: I shall stay here, and yet still be going further on my way. Through pestilential streets and fields of poppies, over sunlit, snowy mountain peaks and through the barren wilderness—knowing all the time that I am not uprooted, knowing that I am rooted in myself.

SISTER: One must die and be born again to find one's roots.

FRIEDRICH: But that knowledge is only a beginning.

SISTER: And whither does it point?

FRIEDRICH: Towards humanity.

SISTER: And beyond humanity?

FRIEDRICH: Beyond. . . ? I can't think of that yet. I feel as though I'm dwelling in limitless space. It is glorious to know that one may be anchored and yet still wander.

SISTER: Goodbye, Friedrich. I shall watch your journeyings. (*She goes. People stream out of the Church and others join them in the square from all the side streets.*)

CROWD: That's him, the one that's going to speak—
He said we must wait until midday.
Now he will have to speak,
Since we have waited.

FRIEDRICH: Brothers, sisters; there is not a single one of you of whom I have ever heard, yet I know you all.

You, my child, go every day to school; you go in fear. In the schoolroom the day is overcast and dark, yet outside the sun is shining. The teacher sits at his desk like one of those evil spirits in the fairy-tales you read in secret. He glares at you and scolds you because you haven't done your homework. And yet your heart is full of strange experiences. You would gladly talk to him about them, but he talks you down and accuses you of not having learnt the Scriptures and of not being a good Christian.

And you, slim and delicate in your maidenhood; you too I know . . . Only a few weeks ago you left school with joy in your heart; it seemed that youth and freedom beckoned you with heavenly bells . . . push a single lever backwards and forwards, backwards and forwards. Always the same lever. And your breath becomes heavy in the stifling atmosphere, and your eyes fill with tears when you think of the sunlight grimed by the dusty windows, of freedom and youth and flowers.

And I know you too, woman, careworn and worked to the bone; I know how you live in your wretched garret with your hungry, shivering children; how at evening you open the door to your husband with a spirit dulled and body tired to death.

And you, husband, I know you too; how you are filled with horror at the very prospect of returning home to that room with its evil smell, its squalid misery, its festering disease. I know how you hate those who gorge themselves at your expense and then sneer at you if you go to the inn to drink yourself insensible; insensible, that you may think no more and see no more.

And you, young girl, —I know of your nights of hot desire.

And you, young man, —I know of your restless seeking after God.

And you, rich man, for ever heaping gold on gold, despising everyone —yourself and others too.

And you, woman, a tree heavy-laden with rare fruit which no one comes to pluck, so that you break and wither in your superfluity.

And you, soldier, pinched in your colored coat which drains all joy from life. I know your astonished eyes when you see before you the figure of striding youth.

How could the artist symbolize this youth?

Because he exists, he really is.

And so it is with all of you.

Distorted images of true humanity!

Gasping for breath, joyless, embittered—

All because you have buried alive the spirit . . .

Mighty engines thunder day and night,

A million spades are ceaselessly at work

Piling still more rubble on the spirit's grave.

Your hearts are dry and withered. The hearts of your fellow-men you regard as convenient bell-pulls which you can tug at when you feel inclined. You throw glittering gold pieces at their feet and say they are spring-awakened birds flying rejoicing through the air. You pave your streets with gold pieces and tell yourselves that you are treading rich green fields enamelled with wild flowers.

Your lips shape barren laws, iron prison houses gnawed with rust.

Your hands raise walls around you, and you say, beyond them is your jungle.

You sow hatred in the hearts of your children, for you know no more of love.

You have carved the figure of Christ in wood and nailed it to a wooden cross, because you yourselves refuse to go the way of crucifixion which alone can bring redemption.

You build castles and prisons and set men to rule over men, men who serve neither God nor humanity but a phantom, an evil phantom.

For the mothers and their children you raise cruel and subtle pillories — for you well understand the art of torture.

You mothers who bear children, and from indifference or false pride sacrifice them to frivolous lies and illusions — you are no longer mothers.

You are all of you, all of you, no longer men and women; you are distorted images of your real selves.

And yet you could still be men and women, still be human, if only you had faith in yourselves and in humanity, if only you would grant the spirit its fulfillment.

You could stride erect where today you creep along crooked and bent.

Your eyes could be filled with the light of joy, while today you are half-blind.

You could go forward with winged feet, while today wherever you go you trail after you iron chains.

Oh, if only you were men and women — men and women unqualified — free men and women!

(During this long speech there has been ever-increasing disturbance among the crowd. Some have kneeled down. Others, weeping, bury their heads in their hands. Some lie broken on the ground. These now rise again in gladness; others open wide their arms to heaven. A Youth rushes forward.)

YOUTH: To think that we ever forgot! We are men, men and women!

SEVERAL WOMEN AND GIRLS: *(Half-aloud.)* We are men and women!

ALL: We are men and women! *(Softly, as though smiling to themselves.)* We are men and women! *(There is a silence.)*

FRIEDRICH: Now, brothers, now I bid you march! March now in the light of day! Go to your rulers and proclaim to them with the organ tones of a million voices that their power is but illusion. Go to the soldiers and tell them to beat their swords into ploughshares. Go to the rich and show them your heart, your heart that was once buried alive beneath their rubbish. Yet be kind to them, for they too are poor, poor and straying. But the castles — these you must destroy; destroy them laughing, the false castles of illusion. Now march! March forward in the light of day.

Brothers, stretch out your tortured hands,
With cries of radiant, ringing joy!
Stride freely through our liberated land
With cries of Revolution, Revolution!

(All the people are now standing with outstretched hands. Then they join hands and march away.)

ALL: Brothers, stretch out your tortured hands
  With cries of radiant, ringing joy!
  Stride freely through our liberated land
  With cries of Revolution, Revolution!

                    END

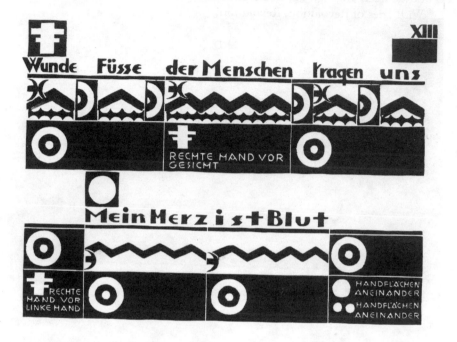

Schreyer's original performance score of *Crucifixion* (1920)
top line indicates verbal text, the second vocal intonation,
the third scenic movement
top section—*The Mistress (double cross):* Wounded feet of men carry us
bottom section—*The Mother (white circle):* My heart is blood

Crucifixion

[1920]

Lothar Schreyer

Translation by Mel Gordon

Without intending to do so, Lothar Schreyer (1886-1966) bridged Expressionism's abstractionist beginnings from the Vassily Kandinsky's Blaue Reiter movement (1911) to Oskar Schlemmer's Bauhaus Theatre Workshop (1923). Indefatigable, Schreyer, through his manifesto-like writings, productions, and artworks, pioneered Kandinsky's notion of *Geist* performance during the early postwar period. Although the Berlin theatre critics and his audiences were mostly indifferent to Schreyer's creations, his impact on the second wave of Modern German Dance in the middle twenties was considerable.

Born in a town outside Dresden, Schreyer studied art history and law at the universities of Heidelberg, Berlin, and Leipzig. His interests slowly changed to poetry and theatre, and by 1914 Herwarth Walden had published a few of his poems in the journal, *Der Sturm*. Released from wartime service in 1916, Schreyer was appointed an editor of *Der Sturm*, which he immediately transformed from an art and literary monthly into a cultural apparatus. A "Sturm-circle," a "Sturm-school," and even a series of "Sturm-evenings" soon appeared. Following the Futurists' experiments in "sound artistry," Schreyer and his friends created over one hundred sensational, if sometimes incomprehensible, Sturm-evenings.

Like the Symbolists and Kandinsky before him, Schreyer attempted to structure all the theatrical elements into new spiritual and dynamic patterns. Certain sounds, colors, and movements, Schreyer believed, could "touch the strings of the spectator's soul." Schreyer's Expressionism was based on the production of feelings and emotions in the audience, not the performers. In October 1918, the first Sturmbühne performance took place with a production of August Stramm's *Sancta Susanna*. The brightly-colored and abstract cardboard costumes as well as the performers' "secret speech and limb-exercises" baffled the critics. There was nothing "human" in Schreyer's Expressionism, only a kind of mechanized and muted hysteria.

Schreyer retreated to his native Hamburg, where he formed a new *Geist* theatre, the Kampfbühne. Between 1919 and 1920, he directed seven plays there, including two which he wrote. Little is known about the critical response to any of the productions. One Schreyer play, *Crucifixion* (1920), however, was published in a special, oversize book format which contained elaborate colored markings and symbols that clearly notated the sound and movement requirements of each of the three performers. At the invitation of Max Reinhardt, Schreyer returned to Berlin, where he staged his esoteric play *Man* (1920). Again the Berlin audiences were confused, their "soul-strings" too difficult to touch. Finally, calling his productions "living art," Schreyer's work was better received in Dresden.

In the summer of 1921, Walter Gropius, the founder of the Bauhaus, offered Schreyer a teaching post, which he quickly accepted. At the Bauhaus, Schreyer continued to mount *Geist* performances but their mystical and religious qualities offended his more functional-minded colleagues. In 1923, one of his students, Oskar Schlemmer, took over the Theatre Workshop. Abandoning the theatre completely, Schreyer taught art and art history in various cities. After a conversion to Catholicism in 1933, he turned his full attention to research of ancient and medieval Christian art. Schreyer remained in Hamburg until his death in 1966.

THE MOTHER: I suffer.

THE MISTRESS: Cross crucifies us.

THE MAN: Wounded feet of men carry us.

THE MOTHER: My heart is blood.

THE MISTRESS:

  Never do I flower.

  Root-protected I grow.

THE MAN:

  World circles round us.

  Ring of stars irradiates round the world.

THE MOTHER: My heart blazes at night.

THE MAN:

  We wander, dream-wander.

  Awake-wander, far.

THE MISTRESS:

  Dust is in wounds.

  Lonely eyes pierce me.

THE MOTHER:

  Search, ask.

  Nothing.

  We imagine nothing.

THE MISTRESS:

  I want to overthrow with arm-in-arm.

  Flee before me, feet.

  No one heals the wounds.

THE MAN:

  In the ocean depths drips the blood.

  In the earth's depths beats the heart.

THE MOTHER: My child is born.

THE MISTRESS:

  Men take root in my breast.

People cast me aside.

THE MOTHER: My child sleeps in my womb.

THE MISTRESS: Man groans in the thigh-dance.

THE MOTHER:
  My child goes away from me.
  And plays far away from me
  And departs.

THE MAN:
  Young men watch a bride.
  Boys pray to moonflowers on
  star-vines, illuminating the world.

THE MOTHER:
  In my dead child lives a strange person.
  My son returns home and lies.
  My son.

THE MISTRESS: I love.

THE MOTHER:
  I give away my son.
  Without farewell, my son departs.

THE MISTRESS: I am.

THE MAN:
  We perform all tasks.
  Flames break at midnight.
  Watch, watch.
  Human wounds burst.
  Monstrous.
  Greatly-fixed around.
  Abyss darkening, destroying us.
  Watch, watch.
  Finger in the wound.
  Kisses in the wound.
  Whips in the wound.
  Moon turns pale.

THE MOTHER:
  World warns, my child.
  World howls.
  Men raise hands.
  Men raise feet.
  Brains star.
  Hearts sun.
  My blood drips empty.
  My son quiets me.
  My son departs.
  Act about. Act about. Act about.

I search.
My son goes into the blood.
Flowers. Earth.
Children sing in battle.
Men fall.
Sons.
Lower. Lower.
World howls.
Before me, my son is silent.
My son caresses his sick animal.
Earth quakes.
Corpses rest in my heart.
Faraway, my son visits me.
My child suffers the death of hunger.
The death of thirst.
My son.
My son lies naked on stones.
Heart-wound burns in light.
My son is silent.

THE MISTRESS:
  Men scream.
  Men go into battle.
  I dance. I sacrifice.
  Virgin kneels her knee in the dream.
  Earth blooms in my womb.
  Storm blows me in ravines.
  Scatters.
  Bloom. Break.
  Pain destroys under thigh and hands and mouth.
  I temper you homesickness.
  I close your eyes.
  I untie your human clothes.
  Men grope about me.
  Men ravish me.
  The dead men irradiate.
  Children.
  Lover.
  Virgin.

THE MAN:
  Man's birth.
  Women beat us with sin.
  Innocent children die with us.
  The rotting spirit blows poison.
  Noon devours the world.

The dark birds peck at our heart.
We prepare for the Last Supper.
Wake up. Wake up.
THE MISTRESS:
  Female sex.
  Male sex.
  I shatter.
THE MOTHER:
  I carry boys.
  I carry girls.
  Ripped apart.
THE MISTRESS:
  Stars circle.
  Stars don't come down here.
THE MOTHER:
  Lights fall.
  My womb circles bloody.
THE MISTRESS: Mother Earth.
THE MOTHER: Home sickness.
THE MISTRESS:
  Pushed out.
  Plague whips my flesh.
THE MOTHER:
  Murdered flowers.
  Cracked stone.
  Slaughtered animals.
  I chew the End.
  Gestures.
THE MISTRESS:
  Pierced through the heart.
  Abandoned.
  Rejected.
  Nameless.
  Remorseless.
  Empty.

| THE MISTRESS: | THE MOTHER: |
| Crucify . . . | . . . me. |

THE MOTHER AND THE MISTRESS:
  Preserve the earth.
  Nail in blinded glaze.

THE MISTRESS:	THE MOTHER:
Heart.	Spear in heart.
Skin.	Sword in skin.

THE MOTHER AND THE MISTRESS:
  Destroy.
  Annihilate.
  Strike.
  Nothing.
  In your arms.
  Purify.
  Take.
  Extinguish.
  Fire.
  Fire.
  Give away.
  Nothing.
THE MAN: The crucifix is empty.
THE MOTHER AND THE MISTRESS: God is dead.
THE MAN: The crucifix is empty.
THE MOTHER: Child. (*The Mother cries.*)
THE MISTRESS:
  Mother.
  Mother.
  Mother.
  Mother.
  Mother.
  Mother.
  Mother.
  Mother.
  Mother.
  Mother.
  Mother.

(*The Mother cries. The Mistress's judgment. Mankind's overthrow.*)

THE MOTHER, THE MISTRESS, AND THE MAN:
  Savior.
  Savior.
  Savior.
THE MAN:
  Confusion.
  Illumination.
  Change.
  Earth-heart bends to kiss.
  World collapsing.
  Peace in form.

Seeing.
Home.
THE MOTHER: Mother.
THE MISTRESS: Child.
THE MAN:
  To know.
  To have.
  Star seize around.
  Heaven-heart radiates all.
  Dancer.
  Revealer.
  Singer.
  Giver.
  Womb.
THE MISTRESS: Dead.
THE MOTHER: Love.
THE MAN:
  Light.
  To be.
  All light.
  All being.
  All we.
  All nothing.
  Allness.
THE MOTHER, THE MISTRESS, AND THE MAN:
  Savior.
  Savior.
  Savior.

(*Characters dance.*)

MOTHER AND MISTRESS:
  Doors open.
  Men open.
  Prepare the bed.
  High time.
  Holy time.
  The dove sings.
  The lamp jumps.
  Eat the bread.
  Drink the blood.
  Tongues blaze world-word.
  Worldless.
  Holy.

Holy.

THE MAN:

   Born on the cross.

   Wandered through sorrow.

   Died in world-womb.

   We separate from men.

   Life-sacred.

   Risen up.

   Man's overwounding.

   World embrace.

   Consciousness of doom.

   Mindless illumination.

   Sink in self.

   We carry you.

   Make yourself glow.

   Beam.

   Poor world.

THE MISTRESS:

   You take me.

   You give me.

   Body, my flesh vessel.

   Clear fire pour the star.

   My hand strokes tired men.

   My lips kiss mute mouths.

   My foot goes to you.

   Tears wash the dust.

   My heart dries your blood wounds.

   For you I am a maid.

   Around our sin. Sin.

   Disclose you.

   Raise you.

   Torture body.

   Heart cross.

   Beat in me.

   Vomit.

   Life the stone.

   Mankind sacrifice.

THE MOTHER:

   Earth-sperm cast into me.

   The people go.

   The people tread on.

   Night falls on brother and sister.

   Seize your hands. Cold.

   Feel your lips.

Kneel before your flesh modest.
Heart destroys man.
Earth spills on the small light.
Child-mother burns up.
Storm over.
Sun under.
Wilderness longs.
Mother world.
Wonder.
Death dies.
Love dies.
Love over us.
Death over us.
Come little child.
Let go, man.
You, child.

THE MAN:
Sinful sinner.
Dear mistress.
I receive you, mother.
Endure the sorrow.
We are fallen.
We are lost.
The stone is rolled away.
Light lights.
The voice is silent.
Wander into us.
Alone.

THE MISTRESS: Cross crucifies us.

THE MOTHER: I suffer.

THE MOTHER, THE MISTRESS, AND THE MAN:
We wander. Dream-wander. Wide-awake wander, far.
Savior strange.
Through mankind.
Scorn blood.
Mock blood.
Hate blood.
Love damned.
Pain in the poor world.
Far in the poor world.
Awake.
World.
Awake.   (*Characters exit.*)

END

MEL GORDON is Associate Professor in Theatre at the Tisch School of the Arts, New York University, and the author of *Lazzi: The Comic Routines of the Commedia dell'Arte*, a PAJ Publications title.